Gateway

Student's Book

2nd Edition

David Spencer

B2

macmillan education

Contents B2

1 Study helpline

Vocabulary

Studying at university

1a SPEAKING **Work with a partner. How many of these subjects do you know?**

> architecture • business studies • dentistry
> engineering • geology • law • medicine
> nursing • philosophy • politics
> psychology • sociology
> veterinary medicine

1b What other university subjects can you think of? Make a list.

1c Which of the subjects in 1a and 1b interest you?

2 SPEAKING **Work with a partner. Read part of an email and decide if the words in red are nouns or verbs. What do you think they mean?**

> Most of the students I've met so far are **undergraduates**. But there are others who've already **graduated** and are studying to get a second **degree** or a **master's**. On my **course** I have about 12 hours of **lectures** a week and I attend a couple of **tutorials**, too. Throughout the **term**, there's **continuous assessment** of our **coursework** and **assignments** – my **tutor** gives me a **grade** or **mark** for each piece of work. There are usually exams too, so, of course, I need to keep my **notes** up-to-date and **revise**. In some cases, if you **fail** an exam, you can **resit** it. But don't worry, that won't happen to me – I'm sure I'll pass!! What about you? How is life going at your university?

3 Now use a dictionary to check any words in 2 that you are not sure about. When using a dictionary, remember that many English words have more than one meaning and can have more than one form (e.g. they can be a noun *and* a verb).

4 LISTENING 01 **Listen to the vocabulary quiz. Answer the eight questions with words from 1 and 2.**

Life at university

5 Complete the sentences with words a–g.

1 Some people don't want to study in their country. They want to study …
2 At university it's usually easy to make new …
3 When you live away from home, you become more …
4 Students who don't live at home often live in a hall of …
5 If you haven't got enough money to pay for your studies you can apply for a student …
6 At university, there are lots of clubs that organise extracurricular …
7 Universities have gyms, libraries, language centres and other …

a abroad
b activities
c residence
d loan
e independent
f friends
g facilities

6a Complete the questions with the words a–g in 5.

1 Do you do any extracurricular ……………?
2 What special …………… for students are there in your school?
3 Do you find it easy to make new ……………?
4 Have you become more …………… in the way you study? How?
5 Would you like to study ……………, in the UK or the US, for example?
6 Would you prefer to live at home or in a hall of ……………?
7 Is it easy to get a student …………… in your country if you don't have enough money to study?

6b SPEAKING **Use the questions to interview your partner.**

1

2

3

4

5

1 SPEAKING **Work with a partner. Do you think you can study the things above at university? Why/ Why not?**

2 READING **Read the comments (a–e) from an Internet forum and match them to pictures 1–5.**

a .... b .... c .... d .... e ....

✓ EXAM SUCCESS

In reading activities where you match questions with texts, remember that the words in the question may not be exactly the same in the text.

➤ EXAM SUCCESS page 144

3 Match the people (a–e) with the questions below.

Which person …

- is excited about going to a particular place for their course? 1 ....
- is confident about their future thanks to their course? 2 ....
- thinks it's as valid to study modern culture as older culture? 3 ....
- believes that people think their subject is all practice and no theory? 4 ....
- thinks other people would like to study their course? 5 ....
- clearly prefers the practical side of their course? 6 ....

4 CRITICAL THINKING

Think! Then compare ideas with your class.

- Are these subjects too specialised, in your opinion?

5 What do the underlined words in the text mean? Guess and then check in your dictionary.

6 SPEAKING **What about *you*?**

Which of these subjects would you most like to study? Why?

Student
CHAT ROOM
The best place for help with university life

Home News Chat Profile Log in Register Search

You are here: Home > Forums > **Uni courses**

UNUSUAL DEGREES

28th October

a

Kat 19.10 reply Like

I'm having a brilliant time at uni at the moment. The only problem is that I'm not studying a typical subject like engineering or business studies. I'm doing baking technology management. Some people think that all I do is bake bread and cakes. But there is a lot more to it than that. It's true that on Wednesdays and Fridays we always do practical assignments, but on the other days we do essays and exam preparation like everybody else. There's another thing that drives me mad. People are forever asking me to make them their favourite cake!

b

Jsm95 19.25 reply Like

My first degree course wasn't very unusual. I did sociology. But now I'm in the middle of a master's course entitled 'The Beatles, Popular music and Society'. When I tell people, usually they'll start singing an old Beatles tune. Then they'll ask me why I'm wasting my time studying pop music. I don't see why they think it's OK to study classical music or literature but not the music and words of a group that changed the modern world. Anyway, what somebody studies is always a very personal choice.

c

Brad 19.40 reply Like

I'm doing a degree that's relatively new, Digital and Social Media. People think that I spend all day on social media networks. Of course, I enjoy using social media, but the degree goes into the whole area in great depth. We even study things like the philosophical and ethical implications of social media. But for me the best thing about the course is that it's very hands-on. For example, we get 12 weeks of work experience in a digital agency. Maybe that's why 91% of students who study this course find a job as soon as they graduate.

d

MikeyS 19.50 reply Like

You guys have it easy! People never stop asking me where my helmet is when I tell them that I'm doing Viking studies. I suppose that it does seem a strange thing to study, but I've always been fascinated by the Vikings. That's why I decided to specialise. People usually think that, because it's so specialised, there isn't much to do. It's just the opposite! We study Scandinavian languages, and learn about contemporary Danish and Icelandic culture. Undergraduates spend their third year in a Scandinavian university, which I'm looking forward to. And no, we don't need to wear Viking helmets when we're there.

e

Kooks 20.10 reply Like

People are usually really jealous when I tell them that I'm studying surf science and technology. It's only a two-year course, but we do a whole variety of subjects, including the history of surfing, sports psychology, and practical work creating a dynamic surfboard. What I really like about the course are the other students. We all share the same passion for surfing, so it means we all get on really well and work together as a team.

Present simple, present continuous and present habits

1a Look at the verbs in these sentences and name the tenses.

1 On Wednesdays and Fridays we always **do** practical assignments.
2 I**'m having** a brilliant time at the moment.
3 People **study** better when they're interested in the subject.
4 People **are** forever **asking** me to make them a cake.
5 They **think** that there isn't much to do.

1b Read the explanations and match them with the sentences in 1a.

a We use the **present simple** for routines and habits. ....
b We use the **present simple** for things that are generally or always true. ....
c We use the **present simple**, not the present continuous, for verbs that describe states and situations, not actions. ....
d We use the **present continuous** for actions that are happening at or around the moment of speaking. ....
e We can use the **present continuous** with *always*, *constantly*, *continually* or *forever* for habits that annoy or irritate us. ....

GRAMMAR REFERENCE ➤ PAGE 16

2 Choose the correct alternative.

1 Thanks to you, I *understand/am understanding* now.
2 The Moon *goes/is going* round the Earth.
3 Listen! Somebody *comes/is coming*.
4 Temperatures *get/are getting* higher each year.
5 My brother *usually walks/is usually walking* to the university, but this week he *goes/is going* by bus.
6 *Do you wear/Are you wearing* a uniform at your school?
7 I *don't agree/am not agreeing* that it's better to study at home.
8 That course *sounds/is sounding* really interesting.

3a PRONUNCIATION 02 Listen to the sentences and mark the word which the speaker stresses most.

1 They're constantly arriving late.
2 You're always saying that.
3 She's forever complaining.
4 He's continually talking about football.

3b Practise saying the sentences with the stress on the correct words.

4a Complete the dialogues with the present simple or present continuous form of these verbs.

coach • leave • play • say • study

1 **A:** What's the matter?
B: It's my brother. He .... music loud.
2 **A:** Why isn't your sister here?
B: She's at the Language Academy. She .... Italian on Wednesdays.
3 **A:** You're angry with me, aren't you?
B: Yes, I am. You .... your dirty plates on the table.
4 **A:** Why don't you like this TV presenter?
B: He .... the same things.
5 **A:** Are you coming on the trip on Saturday?
B: I can't. I .... the junior basketball team and there are matches every Saturday.

4b SPEAKING Work with a partner. Practise saying the dialogues using the correct word stress.

5 SPEAKING Talk about things people do that annoy you.

Present perfect simple and present perfect continuous

6a Match sentences 1–4 with the explanations of their uses a–d.

1 We**'ve been** here for four weeks.
2 I**'ve met** lots of interesting people.
3 I**'ve just realised** something.
4 I**'ve made** a timetable. It's on my wall.

a An action which started in the past and continues in the present
b An action that happened at an unspecified moment in the past
c A past action which has a result in the present
d An action which finished very recently

6b Look at these sentences. Which is present perfect simple and which is present perfect continuous? How do we form these tenses?

1 I**'ve been studying** here for a month.
2 I**'ve joined** three clubs.

6c Which tense gives more importance to …

1 the completion and result of an action?
2 the process and duration of an action?
3 how many times an action happens?
4 an action that is incomplete or has finished recently?

GRAMMAR REFERENCE ➤ PAGE 16

7 SPEAKING **Work with a partner. These words often go with the present perfect simple or present perfect continuous. Talk about why and how we use the words.**

1 for
2 since
3 ever
4 never
5 just
6 already
7 yet

8 Rewrite the sentences using the correct tense. Correct the words in bold.

1 She**'s been failing** six exams.
2 I've lived here **for** 2012.
3 We**'ve been** to that city in 2008.
4 **I've done** this assignment for two weeks, but I haven't finished yet.
5 My friend **has been** having an accident.
6 That artist **has been painting** more than a hundred paintings.
7 They've been revising for that exam **since** five hours.
8 Oh no! My keys and my wallet! **I lost** them.
9 **I haven't been doing** this exercise yet.
10 **I've waited here** for a bus for 20 minutes.

9a Complete the questions with the present perfect simple or present perfect continuous.

1 How long have you …?
2 How long have you been …?
3 Have you ever …?
4 How many times have you …?
5 What have you been …?
6 Have you just …?

9b SPEAKING **Interview your partner with the completed questions. Tell the class one interesting thing you found out about your partner.**

Developing vocabulary

do and *make*

1 Look at these words. Do they usually go with *do* or with *make*? Make two lists.

a cake • a course • a decision • an assignment
an exam • a noise • chores • friends • homework
the dinner • the shopping • the washing • well

2 Complete the rules with *do* or *make*.

1 We usually use .... with work at school or university.
2 We usually use .... with work around the house.
3 We usually use .... with things we produce, create or construct.
4 We usually use .... when we talk about activities in general.
5 We use .... with these words: *a mistake, a decision, a noise, friends, an appointment, an effort, an excuse, money, progress, a phone call, a plan, a promise, an offer, a suggestion.*
6 We use .... with these words: *your best, a favour, business, sport, your hair.*

3 Complete the text with the correct form of *do* or *make*.

Last year a good university (a) .... my brother an offer to study electronic engineering there. He (b) .... the decision to accept their offer. He has to (c) .... a lot of work, but his tutors say that he (d) .... very well at the moment and that he (e) .... a lot of progress. He has to (f) .... a lot of theoretical exercises, but he also has to (g) .... practical assignments. Right now, for example, they (h) .... a simple computer from old parts. The only problem is that my brother is becoming unhealthy because he never has time to (i) .... sports and he always eats out because he doesn't have time to (j) .... the shopping or (k) .... lunch or dinner. My mum says he needs to (l) .... an effort to (m) .... those simple chores, but I understand that it's hard. There isn't time to (n) .... everything!

4a Choose three expressions with *do* and three with *make*. Use the expressions to write questions to ask other people in your class.

What do you think is the best way to make new friends?
How do you feel when you make mistakes speaking English?
What course would you like to do at university?

4b SPEAKING **Interview as many people as possible with your questions.**

Managing study time

ACADEMIC SKILLS OBJECTIVES

- To think about how you manage your study time.
- To learn some tips for saving time when you're studying.
- To plan your study time for the next few weeks.

KEY CONCEPTS

distract [v]/distraction [n]: *The television can distract you/be a distraction while you're studying.* **put off [v phr]:** *Do it today, don't put it off until tomorrow!* **disturb [v]:** *Please don't come to my room and disturb me. I need to concentrate.* **deadline [n]:** *The deadline for the assignment is Friday. That's the last day you can hand it in.* **prioritise [v]:** *We need to learn to prioritise, and do everything in order of importance.*

1a Read the statements in the quiz. Decide how true each one is for you – very true (VT), quite true (QT) or not true (NT).

ARE YOU A GOOD TIME MANAGER?

	VT	QT	NT
1 I sometimes arrive late to class.			
2 I'm not very sure what lessons I have each day.			
3 I often have to finish assignments quickly at the last minute.			
4 I sometimes hand in work late.			
5 I sometimes forget to hand in homework or assignments.			
6 I take a long time to get myself ready to do homework or assignments.			
7 I'm quite easily distracted when I'm studying or doing homework.			
8 I don't have much time to relax from schoolwork.			

1b SPEAKING **Work with a partner. Are your answers similar? Read the key below and then discuss.**

- If you replied 'not true' to most answers, you seem to have very good time management. What techniques do you currently use and are there ways you could still improve?
- If you replied 'very true' or 'quite true' to most answers, you need to work on your time management. Do you have any ideas about what you could do to improve?

2 SPEAKING **Work with a partner. Look at these headings from a study guide about effective time management. What advice will each section give?**

A Don't keep putting things off until later
B Start small and easy
C Enjoy more free time!
D Use a timetable, study planner or diary
E Work backwards from deadlines
F Watch out for distractions
G Expect the unexpected

3 READING **Read the text and match each heading with the correct section.**

Effective time management

1 ……

This is essential. Students are busy people. There are always lessons to go to, homework and assignments to do, and exams and tests to prepare for. The only way you can remember all that is by having it written down somewhere. Write down everything you need to do as soon as you find out about it and make sure you check it at the start and end of each day.

2 ……

Many people find that the most difficult part of doing an assignment, homework or revision is getting started. And so they suddenly find excuses for not beginning. They need to check their emails, see if they have any text messages, prepare a hot drink … Decide on a specific time to start and finish the work you need to do, and stick to these times. Remember, the sooner you start, the earlier you finish.

3 ……

Sometimes a piece of work seems so long and difficult that we don't know where to begin. But remember the Chinese saying: 'The longest journey begins with just one step.' So start small. Break a big task into smaller pieces. Another trick can be to do the easiest part of the task first. This can encourage you to continue.

4 .... Don't let yourself get distracted and be particularly careful with technology. It may be OK to check your phone for urgent messages once or twice. But using social media networks is bound to keep you from your work. No excuses – there's a time to study, and another time to check out your friends' latest posts or a new viral video. Also, ask your family politely not to disturb you between specific times.

5 .... If you go to school by bus, remember that the bus can sometimes be late. If you need to use a computer or printer for an assignment, have a plan B if the technology breaks down. What you can't do is blame the bus five times a week, or spend a week making the excuse that you couldn't print out your homework.

6 .... When you know the deadline for handing in a piece of work, calculate how long you need to do it. Remember to include any reading or research. Decide if you need to do a draft version first. Finally, decide how long you need to write up your final version. Calculate the total time you need and, with your diary, check when you think you can fit the work in. With all of that information, decide when you need to start in order to finish before the deadline.

7 .... The good news is that when you use efficient time management strategies, you should finish work earlier and have more time to relax!

Saturday 26th September
- finish history essay
- review science notes
- learn English vocabulary
- take a break!

4 Read the text again and answer these questions.

1 Why does the author recommend using a diary, timetable or study planner?
2 What is the advantage of starting work on time?
3 Why is it useful to 'start small'?
4 What things does the author mention that can distract you from your work?
5 Is it fair to blame the bus or broken technology for not handing work in on time?
6 How do you 'work backwards from deadlines'?

5 LISTENING 03 **Watch or listen to four students talking about their time management. What issues do they ask for advice about?**

6 03 **Watch or listen again. Make notes of Deana's tips to the students about their time management.**

Student	Deana's tips
Sam	
Vanessa	
Bea	
Chris	

7 SPEAKING **Work with a partner. Which of the ideas in the video/listening do you …**

1 do already?
2 think are a good idea to try out?

LIFE TASK

You want to manage your time better.

Follow this plan:

1 *Make a list of all the schoolwork that you know you have to do in the next few weeks, plus the deadline for each piece of work.*
2 *Work backwards from the deadline dates and decide when you should start each piece of work.*
3 *Write a plan for the next few weeks. Mark the work which is most urgent in one colour, and the work that can wait in another.*
4 *Now make signs with the five most useful tips for you to manage your study time better. Keep them with you or in your room and make sure you follow the advice.*

1 SPEAKING **Work with a partner. Look at these statements made by students about revising for exams. Which ones do you think are a good idea?**

1 Reading your notes again and again is useful.
2 It's good to revise with other students.
3 I always go to the library to revise.
4 I revise by reading my notes and then asking somebody to test me.
5 I can't stand revising so I leave all my revision to the last week before the exams.
6 I feel stressed when I revise so I go running or swimming regularly to help me relax.
7 My revision strategy involves drinking lots of coffee and going to bed late.
8 I always need to take a break after 45 or 50 minutes of study.
9 The last thing I do before the real exam is do a practice exam.
10 I avoid revising everything. I just revise some of the topics and hope they come up in the exam.

2 LISTENING 04 **Listen to two teenagers talking about revision. Which three ideas in 1 does Scott mention? Has he prepared well for the exam or not?**

3 04 **Listen again and choose the best answer.**

1 Last night Scott …
a didn't sleep at all.
b didn't sleep much.
c slept badly because of nerves.

2 The students found out about the exam …
a four weeks ago.
b yesterday.
c four days ago.

3 On Fridays Scott …
a goes out.
b does sport.
c revises.

4 Scott …
a doesn't understand all the exam topics.
b doesn't like some of the exam topics.
c hasn't got notes for all the topics.

5 Scott thinks he isn't going to pass the exam as …
a he needs to answer all the questions.
b he's studied the wrong topics.
c he's studied last year's exam.

4 SPEAKING **What about *you*?**

1 Have you ever had a bad experience in a test or exam? What happened? Was it because you didn't prepare?
2 What is your top tip for doing well in exams? Why?

Grammar in context

Gerunds and infinitives – 1

1 **Match statements 1–10 in Listening exercise 1 with these rules.**

We use the **gerund**

a as the subject/object of a sentence. *1*
b with *go* to talk about physical activities.
c after prepositions.
d after verbs of liking or disliking (except when the verb goes with *would*, e.g. *would like, would prefer*).
e after certain verbs like *admit, avoid, consider, involve, risk, suggest*.

We use the **infinitive**

f to explain why somebody does something.
g immediately after adjectives.
h after *too, enough, the first, the last*.
i after certain verbs like *agree, appear, arrange, ask, decide, expect, forget, help, learn, manage, need, promise, try, want*.

GRAMMAR REFERENCE ➤ PAGE 16

2a Choose the correct alternative.

TWO UNUSUAL REVISION TECHNIQUES

It's amazing **(a)** *thinking/to think* how much revision we do while we're at school or university. The problem is that **(b)** *revising/to revise* can quickly become boring and repetitive. It's important **(c)** *using/to use* a variety of different revision techniques for **(d)** *keeping/keep* revision as effective as possible. Instead of **(e)** *doing/to do* the same old things, here are two unusual techniques that might work for you.

1 **(f)** *Leaving/To leave* revision cards all around your house can help **(g)** *checking/to check* what you've learnt. Put cards in the bathroom, kitchen, living room … everywhere. The idea is that you can revise and learn something even when you go to the kitchen cupboard **(h)** *getting/to get* a biscuit! But remember that it's essential **(i)** *having/to have* a real break from time to time.

2 Most people enjoy **(j)** *singing/to sing*, even if they don't actually sing very well. Some experts suggest **(k)** *singing/sing* your revision notes to the tune of a song that you like.

You can sing your notes all day long, even when you walk to school, go **(l)** *cycling/to cycle*, or do sport. Basically, music appears **(m)** *helping/to help* us to remember more. But don't forget **(n)** *keeping/to keep* your voice down in the exam when you're singing your notes to yourself! And check that people in your family don't mind **(o)** *listening/to listen* to you revising at home all weekend!

2b SPEAKING **Work with a partner. Would you use either of these techniques? Why/Why not?**

3 Is the gerund or infinitive used correctly in each sentence? If not, rewrite it.

1 I've been studying hard so I expect passing the exam.
2 She suggested to study together that evening.
3 We arranged to meet in the library.
4 My friends appeared finding the exam easy.
5 I was happy because I managed passing the exam with 90%.
6 Please promise not to cheat again!
7 You risk to fail if you don't start studying soon.
8 Have you ever considered to study another language?

4 Complete this exam advice with the gerund or infinitive form of the verbs given.

1 Plan your time at the start to make sure that you have enough time .... (finish) the exam.
2 .... (Start) the exam before you have read all the questions can be a bad idea.
3 We suggest .... (take) more than one pen or pencil to the exam.
4 Don't write too fast or carelessly to avoid .... (create) a bad impression.
5 Think about .... (leave) yourself time .... (check) your work at the end.
6 Check that you know how many questions you need .... (complete) because sometimes not all questions are obligatory.
7 Try .... (answer) all the questions that are obligatory.

5a Work with a partner. Complete these questions with the gerund or infinitive form of an appropriate verb.

1 Do you enjoy .... in the evening?
2 When you sleep, do you ever dream of ....?
3 Have you ever thought of ....?
4 Do you find it difficult ....?
5 Have you ever considered ....?
6 Do you think that you are brave enough ....?
7 Would you like to be the first person ....?
8 Are you interested in ....?
9 At the weekend, do you ever go ....?
10 Next year do you want ....?

5b SPEAKING **Interview other students using your questions. Tell the class some of the things you discovered.**

Giving personal information – preferences

1 Read questions 1–6 and match each one with one of the categories a–d.

1 What do you like about the place where you live?
2 What would you like to do when you finish studying at school?
3 Are you happier studying alone or with other people?
4 What things do you enjoy doing with your friends?
5 Do you like reading?
6 Are you happier doing mental or physical work?

a your home and family
b your interests
c your studies/work
d your plans for the future

2 LISTENING 05 Listen to six students answering the questions in 1. Match each student to one of the questions.

Student A .... Student D ....
Student B .... Student E ....
Student C .... Student F ....

3 05 Listen again. Does each student give a reason or any personal details to support their answer? Is it a good idea to give reasons and/or personal details? Why/Why not?

4 SPEAKING Work with a partner. Take it in turns to ask and answer the questions in 1. Remember to give reasons and personal details.

5 Look at the different ways of expressing preferences in the Speaking bank and then do exercise 6.

SPEAKING BANK

Expressing preferences

prefer
- I prefer to work alone.
- I prefer revising alone.
- I prefer studying alone to studying with other people.

would prefer
- I'd prefer to be a translator (than a musician).
- I'd prefer not to study music.

would rather
- I'd rather live in a big city.
- I'd rather not live in a small town.
- I'd rather study than work.

6 Put the verbs in the correct form.

1 I prefer .... (play) football to .... (do) homework.
2 I'd rather .... (go) by bus than .... (walk).
3 She'd prefer .... (not stay) in at the weekend.
4 She prefers .... (write) essays by hand.
5 He'd rather .... (write) a project than .... (do) an exam.
6 I'd prefer .... (go) by train than .... (fly).

PRACTICE MAKES PERFECT

7a SPEAKING Work with a partner. Ask and answer the questions. Remember to give reasons and personal details and to use expressions from the Speaking bank.

Student A: Ask these questions.
1 Which subject(s) do you prefer studying?
2 Would you rather study at home or in a library?
3 Would you like to have an end-of-year school trip this year or would you prefer to go somewhere with your family?

Student B: Ask these questions.
1 Would you prefer to study in your country or abroad?
2 Do you prefer studying with books or using a computer?
3 Would you rather have a school uniform or wear what you like?

7b Change partners and repeat.

An informal email replying to a request for information

1 Read this email from a British girl called Amy to a friend who lives in Italy. Underline the four main pieces of information that Amy asks for.

> Hi!
>
> Sorry I haven't written for a long time, but I've been revising hard for exams. I've finished them all now ☺ I hope I've passed! What about you? What have you been doing recently?
>
> I've got some great news! I spoke to my parents about your invitation to take part in an exchange programme this summer, and they say that I can! Which month do you think is better, July or August?
>
> By the way, I'd really like to learn more of your language when I'm there. What do you think is the best way for me to do that?
>
> Then after I've spent some time with you in Italy, you'll come back with me and visit my family here in England. Please let me know what type of things you'd like to do here.
>
> Anyway, I'm going out with my friends now to celebrate the end of our exams. I'll tell you all about it in my next email. Write back soon!
>
> Best wishes,
>
> Amy

2 Look at the style of the email in 1. What things in it are typical of informal emails?

exclamation marks

3 Look at the Writing bank. Match these topics with the groups of expressions. Can you add any other expressions?

1 Changing topic
2 Signing off
3 Greetings
4 Opening remarks
5 Asking about someone's health and activities

WRITING BANK

Useful expressions in informal emails

- *Hi, Dear …* (a) 3
- *Thanks for your last email, It was great to hear from you, Sorry I haven't written for a long time, I'm writing to tell you about …* (b) ......
- *What about you? How are you? How are things? Are you doing exams/on holiday at the moment? What have you been doing?* (c) ......
- *By the way, Anyway,* (d) ......
- *Write back soon, That's all for now, Bye for now, Best wishes, All the best,* (e) ......

4 Work with a partner. Imagine that you have received Amy's email. Make notes about the information she wants.

What have you been doing recently? – assignments at school, went away with family last weekend, started going to the gym …

5 You are going to write a reply to Amy. With your partner, make a paragraph plan. Decide what information to include in each paragraph.

Paragraph 1 – Thank Amy for her letter. Tell her what you've been doing.

6 PRACTICE MAKES PERFECT Write your reply to Amy. Use your notes and paragraph plan to help you. Make sure that you include all of the information she needs. Write between 120 and 150 words.

WRITING BANK ➤ PAGE 150

✓ EXAM SUCCESS

In this type of writing exercise, follow the instructions carefully. You lose marks if your reply does not include all the necessary information or if it is not in the correct style.

➤ EXAM SUCCESS page 144

Grammar reference

Present habits

- We use the present simple to talk about current routines and habits.
  I often listen to music.
- We use the present continuous with *always, constantly, forever, continually* for habits that annoy or irritate us.
  My brother and sister are always fighting.

Present perfect simple

We use the **present perfect simple** to talk about:

1 an action that happened at an unspecified moment in the past. What is significant is the actual experience, not when it happened.
I've seen Beyoncé in concert.

2 recent events which have a result in the present.
She's lost her bag. (= She hasn't got it now.)

3 actions that finished very recently.
They've just had an accident.

4 actions or situations which started in the past and continue in the present.
Mark's lived here for ten years. (= Mark started to live here ten years ago and he still lives here now.)

If we want to emphasise the completion and result of an action, or how many times an action happened, we can use the **present perfect simple**.
I've painted my bedroom. (It's finished).
I've seen that film three times. ~~*I've been seeing that film three times.*~~

Present perfect continuous

The **present perfect continuous** has a similar meaning to the present perfect simple. However, we use the continuous when we want to emphasise the process and duration of an action.
I've been studying in this school for five months.

For that reason, if an action is very short, we don't use the continuous form. ~~*I've been breaking the window.*~~
We also use the continuous to emphasise that an action finished very recently or is incomplete.
I've been washing the dishes … and my hands are wet.

Gerunds and infinitives – 1

We use the gerund:
as the **subject/object** of a sentence. *Study**ing** is hard but interesting.*
after **prepositions**. *I'm interested in study**ing** history.*
after **verbs of liking or disliking**, e.g. *like, love, enjoy, can't stand, don't mind, hate*. *I enjoy watch**ing** TV.*
with **go** to talk about physical activities. *go runn**ing**, swimm**ing**, cycl**ing**, shopp**ing**, swimming*
after **certain verbs** like *admit, avoid, consider, risk, suggest*. *I suggest **reading** this book.*

We use the infinitive:
to explain **why** somebody does something. *Why did he go to university? **To study** languages.*
immediately after **adjectives**. *It's good **to revise** with other people.*
after **expressions** with *too, enough, the first, the last*. *It's too cold **to go** out.*
after **certain verbs** like *want, learn, agree, decide, expect, forget, hope, seem, try, would like, appear, arrange, ask, try, manage, help, need, promise*. *I want **to work** for a newspaper.*

Vocabulary

Studying at university **Subjects** architecture • business studies • dentistry • engineering • geology • law medicine • nursing • philosophy • politics • psychology • sociology • veterinary medicine **Other** assignment continuous assessment • course • coursework • degree • fail • grade/mark • graduate • lecture • master's notes • pass • resit • revise • term • tutor • tutorial • undergraduate

Life at university become independent • extracurricular activities • hall of residence • make new friends student facilities • student loan • study abroad

do* and *make **do** a course, a favour, an assignment, an exam, business, chores, homework, sport, the shopping, the washing, well, your best, your hair **make** a cake, a decision, a mistake, an appointment, an effort, an excuse, an offer, a noise, a phone call, a plan, a promise, a suggestion, friends, money, progress, the dinner

Other words and phrases ➤ page 136

Grammar revision

Present simple, present continuous and present habits   / 6 points

1 Complete the sentences with an appropriate word.

1 Normally I .... like classical music, but this song is beautiful.
2 This year my best friend and his brother .... studying abroad.
3 In most universities they .... the first term with special activities for new students.
4 My parents are .... telling me to get my hair cut. It's so annoying.
5 My little brother is .... shouting! Day after day! It drives me mad.
6 Why are you always .... me for help with your homework?

Present perfect simple and continuous   / 7 points

2 Choose the correct alternative.

1 Have you _switched/been switching_ the TV off?
2 We've been here _for/since_ two hours.
3 My feet ache. I've _stood/been standing_ here for ages.
4 I love this film! I've _seen/been seeing_ it six times.
5 This is my American friend. She's _stayed/been staying_ in my house, but she's leaving tomorrow.
6 My eyes are tired. I've _read/been reading_ without the light on.
7 That's it! I've _finished/been finishing_ my work.

Gerunds and infinitives   / 7 points

3 Complete the second sentence so that it has a similar meaning to the first sentence, using the word given. Do not change the word given. Use between two and five words.

1 Don't do that as there's a chance you'll fail. **RISK**
Don't do that because you ....
2 He loves to ride his bike at the weekend. **GO**
He loves to .... at the weekend.
3 I think it's terrible to get up early. **STAND**
I .... early.
4 Please think about joining our club. **CONSIDER**
Please .... our club.
5 I think it's essential to have a valid passport. **PASSPORT**
I think .... is essential.
6 Nobody finished the exam before Sarah. **FIRST**
Sarah was .... the exam.
7 It would be great to see him in concert next week. **LOVE**
I .... him in concert next week.

Vocabulary revision

STUDYING AT UNIVERSITY   / 7 points

1 Complete the sentences with these words. There are two extra words.

degree • grades • lecture • notes • pass
resit • tutor • tutorial • undergraduate

1 I hope I don't fail. I don't want to .... the exam next month.
2 I got an A+ and a B for my last two pieces of work. What .... did you get?
3 Can I borrow the .... you took in yesterday's history class, when I was ill?
4 I need to speak to my .... because I'm having some problems with my studies.
5 My brother graduated last year. His .... was in economics.
6 This course is only for .... students, people studying at university for the first time.
7 The professor gave a really interesting .... There were 200 people there.

LIFE AT UNIVERSITY   / 6 points

2 Complete the sentences.

1 Some people study .... instead of studying in their own country.
2 I need to apply for a student ....
3 This university has got great .... , such as the science laboratories.
4 It's good to be .... and to do things for yourself.
5 I live with other students in a .... of residence.
6 .... activities can help to take your mind off your studies.

DO AND MAKE   / 7 points

3 Choose the correct alternative.

1 _do/make_ a course
2 _do/make_ a decision
3 _do/make_ a favour
4 _do/make_ a suggestion
5 _do/make_ progress
6 _do/make_ the lunch
7 _do/make_ the shopping

Total: / 40 points

2 Nine to five

Vocabulary

Work conditions and responsibilities

1 SPEAKING **Work with a partner. Try to think of one job for each letter of the alphabet.**

A – architect   B – builder   C – chef

2 **Read the job descriptions. What are the jobs?**

a You don't need special **qualifications** to do my job, except for a driving licence. I **deal with** the public. I'**m responsible for** getting them where they want to go. It's quite a **stressful** job because of the traffic and because my passengers are often in a hurry. I work **outdoors**, but because I'm inside my car I work in quite **good conditions**. I'm **self-employed**, not an **employee** in a company. I don't **earn** an enormous **salary**.

b I work in **dangerous conditions**. One day I'd just like to work **indoors** in an office and **do paperwork**, or maybe even **manual work**. I'm not very **well paid** considering the amount of work I do. It's a **skilled** job because you need special **training** to do it. For example, you need to learn to control a big crowd of people. But really, it's **experience** that teaches you to deal with criminals.

3 **Look again at the expressions in red. Check that you understand what they mean. Use a dictionary if necessary.**

4 LISTENING 06 **Listen to four people describing their jobs. Match each person to one of these jobs.**

architect • bank manager • construction worker
head teacher • office worker
personal assistant (PA) • physiotherapist
school caretaker • software engineer • vet

1 ....   3 ....
2 ....   4 ....

5 SPEAKING **Work with a partner. Describe a job using the expressions in red in 2. Can your partner guess the job?**

Working life

6 **Match the definitions 1–5 with the expressions a–g. There are two extra expressions.**

1 You have flexible working hours.
2 You sometimes work during the day and sometimes at night.
3 You work extra hours.
4 You spend a long time working.
5 You don't work all day.

a work long hours
b do shift work
c work from nine to five
d work full-time
e be on flexitime
f work part-time
g work overtime

7 SPEAKING **Work with a partner. In which jobs or situations do you think it is common to work …**

1 from nine to five?   2 long hours?   3 overtime?

8a **Put these different events in a logical order.**

apply for a job • be offered a job
get a promotion • look for a job • sign a contract

1 – look for a job

8b LISTENING 07 **Listen and check.**

9 **Match the expressions 1–5 with their meanings a–e. Use a dictionary if necessary.**

1 become unemployed
2 be made redundant
3 be sacked/fired/dismissed
4 retire
5 resign

a general expression for when you lose your job
b state formally that you are leaving a job permanently
c stop working, usually because you are officially too old to work
d lose your job, usually for doing something wrong
e lose your job because it is no longer necessary

10 SPEAKING **Work with a partner. Talk about your work plans.**

I'd like to find a job as a software engineer, designing games. I'd prefer …

1 SPEAKING **Work with a partner. Look at the photos of two people with unusual jobs. Where do you think they work?**

2 **Read the articles and check your answer in 1.**

WORKING LIFE

Sliding into a dream job

While 22-year-old student Sebastian Smith was doing his final university assignment, he heard an advert on the radio asking people to apply for 'the best job in the world'.

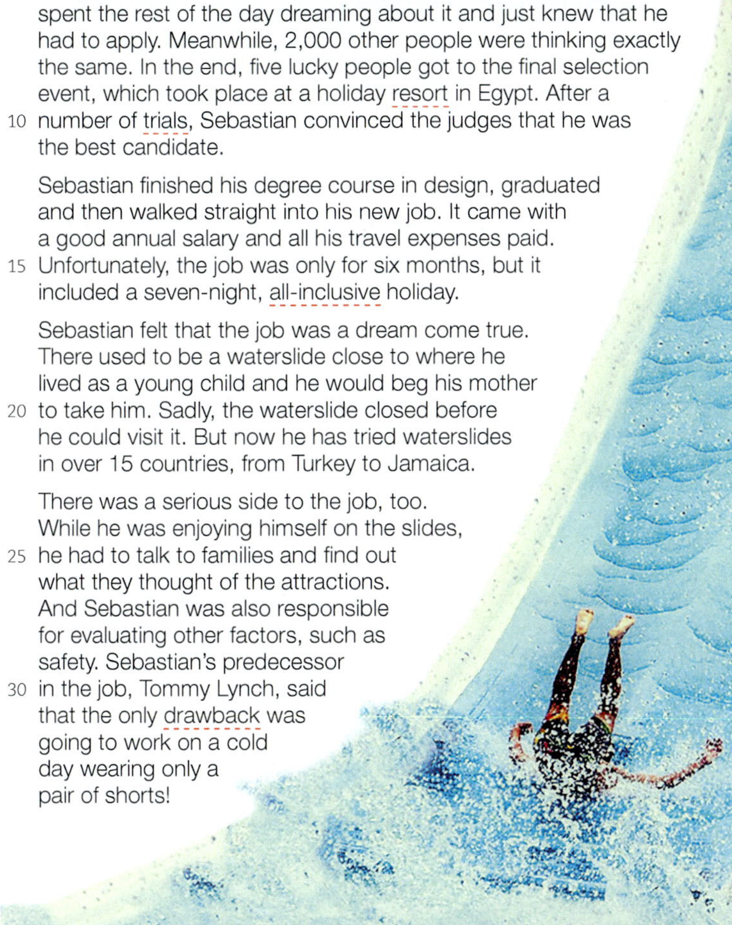

The job was to evaluate waterslides around the world. Sebastian spent the rest of the day dreaming about it and just knew that he had to apply. Meanwhile, 2,000 other people were thinking exactly the same. In the end, five lucky people got to the final selection event, which took place at a holiday resort in Egypt. After a number of trials, Sebastian convinced the judges that he was the best candidate.

Sebastian finished his degree course in design, graduated and then walked straight into his new job. It came with a good annual salary and all his travel expenses paid. Unfortunately, the job was only for six months, but it included a seven-night, all-inclusive holiday.

Sebastian felt that the job was a dream come true. There used to be a waterslide close to where he lived as a young child and he would beg his mother to take him. Sadly, the waterslide closed before he could visit it. But now he has tried waterslides in over 15 countries, from Turkey to Jamaica.

There was a serious side to the job, too. While he was enjoying himself on the slides, he had to talk to families and find out what they thought of the attractions. And Sebastian was also responsible for evaluating other factors, such as safety. Sebastian's predecessor in the job, Tommy Lynch, said that the only drawback was going to work on a cold day wearing only a pair of shorts!

This job is a nightmare!

When you see them on the street, you really don't think of it as a full-time job. But for eight hours a day, five days a week, Paul Edmeades works as a living statue.

Living statues have to stand still for hours

Some time ago, Paul made a special metal structure and attached it to a heavy base. He hid the structure in his gold-painted suit and learnt to sit back with just one foot on the ground and make it look as if he was defying gravity. Paul became one of the thousands of living statues working in the UK.

These statues have to put up with children and adults coming up to them and touching them to see if they are real. And standing still for hours can bring serious health problems. Matt Walters has been a living statue for over 30 years. He used to be able to stand completely still for three hours at a time. But the pain became too much. The cold certainly doesn't help. Paul wears four pairs of trousers and three pairs of socks. And there are other, even worse dangers. Members of the public sometimes hit Paul, insult him, or even steal the money he makes. Once when he was working in Trafalgar Square, a gang suddenly appeared and started kicking him. Luckily he escaped, but that was all because he was working in somebody else's spot.

So, what about promotion or a pay rise? Is it possible to get ahead in this profession? Paul says that living statues are currently very popular in the United Arab Emirates and the pay there is good. But the problem is the heat, which, for a living statue, is even worse than the cold!

3 **Read the articles again. Are these statements True (T), False (F) or is the information Not Mentioned (NM)?**

1. Sebastian was an undergraduate when he first heard about this special job. T/F/NM
2. At first, Sebastian wasn't very interested in the job. T/F/NM
3. Sebastian's mother thought waterslides were too dangerous for children. T/F/NM
4. Part of Sebastian's job was to see if any waterslides were dangerous. T/F/NM
5. It's important that people can't see the mechanism that Paul built. T/F/NM
6. One problem that living statues have is that people are not sure if they are real statues. T/F/NM
7. The worst problem for a living statue is the cold. T/F/NM
8. The psychological pressure of being a living statue is difficult to bear. T/F/NM

4 CRITICAL THINKING

Think! Then compare ideas with your class.

- Do you think 'dream jobs' really exist? Why/Why not?
- What factors do you think could make a job a dream job?

5 **What do the underlined words in the texts mean? Guess and then check in your dictionary.**

6 SPEAKING **What about *you*?**

Would either of the jobs in the articles be your idea of a dream job? Why/Why not?

Flipped classroom: watch the grammar presentation video.

Past simple and past continuous

1a Look at these sentences. Which verbs are past simple and which are past continuous?

1 Paul became one of the thousands of living statues in the UK.
2 He was working in somebody else's spot.
3 Sebastian finished his degree course, graduated and then walked into his new job.
4 While he was doing his assignment, he heard an advert.
5 Once when he was working in Trafalgar Square, a gang suddenly appeared.

1b Look at the rules. Is each rule for the past simple (PS) or the past continuous (PC)?

1 We use it to say that one thing happened after another. PS/PC
2 We use it to talk about an activity in progress at a moment in the past. PS/PC
3 We use it to describe scenes in a story or description. PS/PC
4 We use it to talk about finished actions or situations in the past. PS/PC
5 We use it to talk about an activity in progress in the past that was interrupted by another action. PS/PC

1c Is it more common to use the words *while* and *as* with the past simple or the past continuous?

GRAMMAR REFERENCE ➤ PAGE 28

2a How do we spell the *-ed* form of these verbs?

cry • develop • happen • hate • mention
occur • plan • prefer • step • stop • study
travel • try • visit

2b PRONUNCIATION 08 How do we pronounce the *-ed* form of the verbs in 2a: /d/, /t/, /id/? Listen and check your answers.

3 Are the underlined verbs in the correct tense? If not, rewrite them correctly.

1 When I got home, I was making the dinner.
2 As we were walking home, we helped an old lady to cross the road.
3 When I looked out of the window, I saw that it rained.
4 Last year, I was spending my holidays in the US.
5 When the phone rang, I stopped what I did and answered it immediately.
6 I was unlucky because I walked in the park when it started to rain.
7 I asked her why she cried.

4a Make the correct questions for these answers.

1 ....
I had a snack when I got home after school yesterday.
2 ....
No, I wasn't watching TV at 9 o'clock last night.
3 ....
My parents were working yesterday at 10 am.
4 ....
I went to Ireland last summer.
5 ....
Yes, I was listening to music while I was doing my homework yesterday.
6 ....
I ate out last Saturday.
7 ....
I was sleeping at 6 o'clock this morning.

4b SPEAKING Now interview your partner using the questions in 4a.

Past habits

5a Look at these sentences and answer the questions.

a There used to be a waterslide close to his home.
b He didn't use to go on waterslides.
c He would beg his mother to take him.
d The final took place at a holiday resort in Egypt.

1 Which events in a–d are things that happened regularly?
2 What happened just once?

5b Read rules 1–5 and complete 1–3 with *used to, would* or *the past simple*.

1 We use .... and .... to talk about past habits.
2 We use .... to talk about single events in the past.
3 We use .... with past actions but not past states.
He would arrive late, NOT ~~He would be late~~.
He used to like his job, NOT ~~He would like his job.~~
4 We do not usually use *wouldn't* to talk about past habits.
He didn't use to go to bed early. NOT ~~He wouldn't go to bed early.~~
5 When we give a period of time, we use the past simple, not *used to*.
He used to live on an island. He lived on the island for six months, NOT ~~He used to live on the island for six months.~~

GRAMMAR REFERENCE ➤ PAGE 28

6 **Choose the best alternative. If you think both alternatives are correct, choose both.**

1 When I was small, I _used to/would_ have a skateboard.
2 My brother _lived/used to live_ in France for a month.
3 We _didn't use to/wouldn't_ walk to school, but now we do.
4 When I was ten, I _used to/would_ play computer games for hours.
5 Once my friend _met/would meet_ a famous actor.
6 At primary school, I _used to/would_ go home for lunch.
7 In the past, everything _used to/would_ be cheaper.

7 **Complete this text with *used to*, *would* or the past simple. When both *used to* or *would* are possible, use *would*.**

A few years ago, Ben Southall had a dream job. He (a) .... (live) in a luxurious house on a tropical island, to promote tourism in Australia. He (b) .... (not have) much time for just relaxing because he (c) .... (work) up to 19 hours, seven days a week. Each day he (d) .... (do) lots of promotional events and press conferences. At the end of the day, he (e) .... (write) his blog before going to sleep. Above all, he (f) .... (love) the excitement of surfing, sailing and flying. There was one dangerous moment though. In the last week of the job, he (g) .... (jump) into the sea and he nearly (h) .... (die) because of a jellyfish sting! Luckily, a local doctor (i) .... (save) his life.

8a **Complete these sentences. Make some of them true for you and some false.**

1 I used to .... in the evenings.
2 I didn't use to .... at the weekends, but now I do.
3 When I was at primary school, I would ....
4 Once when I was at primary school, I ....

8b SPEAKING **Work with a partner. Read out your sentences. Can your partner say which ones are true and which are false?**

Phrasal verbs connected with work

1 **Match the phrasal verbs in red with their meanings (a–h).**

1 If you want to **get ahead**, you need to work hard.
2 He applied for a job in an international company, but they **turned** him **down**.
3 She **took over** the project last year. It's hers now.
4 They're going to **set up** a new office in Tokyo.
5 This new job is really hard, but I'm going to **keep at** it.
6 We're **working on** a new product to get it just right.
7 To apply for the job, you need to **fill in** this form.
8 I'm so busy at work that I can't **keep up with** it all.

a spend time producing or improving something
b start (a business, an organisation, etc.)
c continue doing something even if you want to stop
d be more successful, or progress faster
e go at the same speed as something or someone
f add information to a document, e.g. your name/address
g not accept an offer, request or application
h take control of something

2 **Complete the sentences with the correct form of the phrasal verbs in 1.**

1 Don't stop trying! .... it!
2 I'm ambitious. I want to .... and get to the top of the company.
3 Don't forget to .... this section of the questionnaire with your email address.
4 They offered me a promotion, but I .... it .... because it wasn't well paid.
5 You need a lot of money and original ideas to .... a new business.
6 We need to work faster if we want to .... our competitors.
7 Let's .... this project first and when we finish we can look at something else.
8 We used to be independent, but a big company .... us .... last year.

3a **Complete the questions with the correct preposition or adverb.**

1 Are you working .... any school assignments?
2 Do you find it easy or difficult to keep .... all of your homework?
3 What qualities do you think you must possess to get .... in a job?
4 Would you like to set .... your own business one day? What type of business?

3b SPEAKING **Work with a partner. Take it in turns to ask and answer the questions in 3a.**

Evaluating jobs

LIFE SKILLS OBJECTIVES

- To think about what you want from work.
- To decide what factors in a job you value the most.
- To consider what different jobs can offer and decide if they are attractive to you.

KEY CONCEPTS

job satisfaction [n]: *Job satisfaction is so important because if your job doesn't make you feel good, it can affect your general happiness.* **rewarding [adj]:** *When you see that your work helps others, it's very rewarding.* **in-service training [n]:** *Our company offers in-service training so that you can continue developing your skills while you work here.* **prospects [n]:** *Once you join the company, your prospects for promotion are good, you have a good chance of success.*

1 SPEAKING **Work with a partner. Make a list of important factors when choosing a job.**

salary, indoors or outdoors, interesting or repetitive

2 READING **Read the careers advice leaflet. Does it mention any of your ideas in 1?**

What do you want from work?

Most people work because they need money to live. But, apart from that, there are factors that might make one job more attractive than another. We spend hours working each day, so if you're unhappy with your job, this will affect your personal life, too. That's why it's essential to think about what you want from work and decide on your priorities.

Look at what these people say about the factors they think are important in a job.

1 *'I really want to get a job where I can help others, maybe look after them. Job satisfaction is important to me, more important than just money. For me, making people happy and helping them is more rewarding than a massive salary.'*

4 *'I'd like to do a job where they offer in-service training. It's great to have the chance to keep on learning new things. When a job is interesting and there are always new opportunities, it's easier to stay motivated in your job.'*

2 *'The most important thing for me is the salary. I don't mind doing a repetitive or boring job or working long hours, but it has to be well paid.'*

5 *'A really important factor for me is working with others, in a team. I think it would be really boring to work on your own all the time. I'd also prefer a job where you deal with people, not just paperwork.'*

3 *'Above all, I'd like to find a job that I enjoy. The salary isn't so important to me. I'd prefer to do a job that doesn't pay well but that I like, rather than do a job with a great salary that I hate.'*

6 *'I want a job where you get good, long holidays or flexibility to work from home or choose your hours. I have lots of other hobbies that I enjoy. I'd prefer to work fewer hours and get paid less, but have the freedom to do the things that I like.'*

3 **Read the text again. Find the key factor in each speech bubble (1–9).**

1 – help others

4a **Give each factor (1–9) a mark from 0 (you completely disagree) to 5 (you completely agree).**

4b **Use your marks in 4a to help you to create a 'factors diamond'. At the top of the diamond put the factor that is most important. Then move down until at the bottom of the diamond you have the factor that is least important. Look at this example. What does this person think is most and least important in a job?**

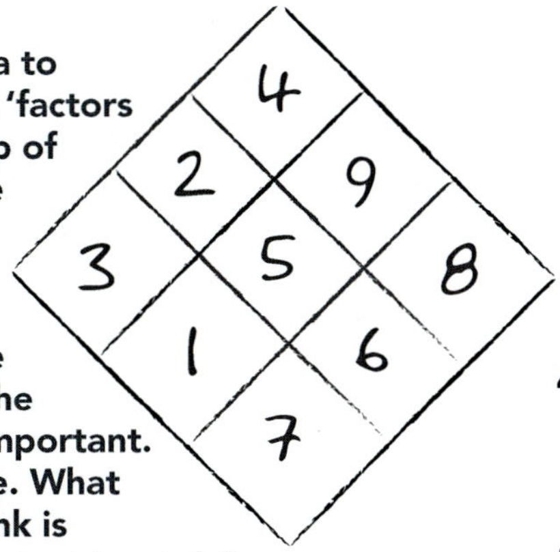

7 *'I want an outdoor job. I hate the idea of being trapped inside an office all day long. Actually, I'd really like to do something connected with the environment or nature because I think those are the most important things in life.'*

8 *'For me, perhaps the most important thing is travel. I think some jobs can give you the chance to go to different countries and see the world. That's what I want from a job.'*

9 *'I'd like a job with prospects. The idea of getting ahead, taking on more responsibility and getting a promotion is important to me. I want my job to be challenging and to offer me goals.'*

4c SPEAKING **Work with a partner. Compare your diamonds and justify your answers. Are they similar or different?**

5 LISTENING 09 **Watch or listen to Deana, James and Tope talking about their jobs. Who works with young people?**

Deana: .... James: .... Tope: ....

6 09 **Watch or listen again. Which speaker or speakers say …**

1. they wouldn't change their career if they could? D / J / T
2. they wanted flexibility in their job role? D / J / T
3. they had a clear idea of what they wanted to do when they were at school? D / J / T
4. their love of films inspired their job choice? D / J / T
5. that patience is an important quality in their job? D / J / T
6. they have a passion for language? D / J / T
7. they keep developing skills in their job? D / J / T
8. their job requires a good eye for detail? D / J / T

LIFE TASK

You want to find the right job for you.

Follow this plan:

1. *Choose a job that you think you might possibly be interested in doing in the future. Research the job and find out which factors from the leaflet in 2 it involves. For example, does it involve travel, helping others, a big salary …?*
2. *Write up a fact file about the job. Put the title:* ***So you want to be a (software engineer)?*** *Then write:* ***This job is good for people who …*** *and a list based on your research.*
3. *Share job fact files with other members of the class. Which jobs can you find that fit with your 'factors diamond' in 4b?*

Listening

1 SPEAKING **Work with a partner. Read this definition of a gap year. Do you think gap years sound interesting? Why/Why not?**

gap year (n) /gæp jɪə(r)/
A year, usually between finishing school and starting university, when you travel or work.

✔ EXAM SUCCESS

Before listening tasks, it's a good idea to read the questions and underline any important information. When you listen, remember that different speakers may use words that are in other questions, but you are listening for the ideas, not just the words that express them.

➤ EXAM SUCCESS page 144

2 LISTENING ▶ 10 **Listen to five people talking about their gap year experiences. Match each statement (A–F) with the correct speaker. Use the letters only once. There is one extra letter.**

A I didn't work at any moment during my gap year.
B I learnt two languages during my gap year.
C My gap year prepared me to study hard.
D I was fired from my gap year job because I didn't enjoy it.
E I enjoyed being close to nature during my gap year.
F Although my gap year experience was difficult, it is going to influence my choice of a career.

Speaker 1: ....
Speaker 2: ....
Speaker 3: ....
Speaker 4: ....
Speaker 5: ....

3 SPEAKING **What about *you*?**

1 Which of these gap years do you like the most? Why?
2 What would be your perfect plan for a gap year?

Grammar in context

Past perfect simple

1a Look at the sentence and then decide which action happened first.

When I had finished school, I bought a ticket to travel round the world.

a I finished school.
b I bought a ticket.

1b Choose the correct alternative.

We use the past perfect simple to talk about actions that happened _after/before_ another action in the past.

1c How do we form the past perfect simple?

GRAMMAR REFERENCE ➤ PAGE 28

2 **Complete the sentences with the past simple or past perfect simple form of the verbs given.**

1 When she .... (write) her letter of application, she sent it.
2 The teacher didn't let her do the exam because when she arrived, the exam .... (start).
3 He unlocked the door and .... (step) inside.
4 Before today's conversation, I .... (not speak) to the boss.
5 When the wind .... (blow), the leaves on the trees shook.
6 They didn't want to see the film again because they .... (see) it twice already.
7 They weren't hungry because they .... (eat).

3 **Complete the sentences in a logical way using a verb in the past perfect simple and the words in bold.**

1 We couldn't get into the room because … **lock**
2 They gave her the job because … **questions**
3 I couldn't go out last Saturday because … **homework**
4 She arrived late for work because … **bus**
5 My little brother was crying because … **ice cream**
6 People on the beach were frightened because … **shark**
7 He didn't feel well because … **pizza**
8 They got wet because … **umbrella**

Past perfect continuous

4a Do these sentences contain verbs in the past perfect simple or the past perfect continuous?

1 I'd been working for almost 12 months when I had an idea.
2 When I'd earned enough money, I decided to go skiing in France.
3 I'd been organising my gap year for a long time.
4 When I'd finished that job, I worked as a volunteer in Madagascar.

4b Which sentences give more importance to the duration of the action? Which give more importance to the completion of the action?

4c How do we form the past perfect continuous?

GRAMMAR REFERENCE ➤ PAGE 28

5 Choose the best alternative.

1 We had _waited/been waiting_ for an hour when finally the director arrived.
2 They were tired because they _have/had_ been running for more than an hour.
3 By the time we got there, they had _eaten/been eating_ all the food.
4 He had _written/been writing_ three novels by the time he was 25.
5 She couldn't open the door because she had _lost/been losing_ the key.
6 When I saw her face, I knew she had _cried/been crying_ for a long time.
7 The teacher was angry because the boys had _talked/been talking_ all through the lesson.

6 Make sentences in the past perfect simple or continuous to explain the situations.

1 Why was the little girl upset?
somebody steal sweets
Somebody had stolen her sweets.

2 Why were his parents angry with him?
not study hard enough
....

3 Why were her hands dirty?
work all morning in the garden
....

4 Why did she feel really sleepy?
study for hours
....

5 Why didn't he want to read the book?
read it twice before
....

6 Why did he fail his final exam?
not pay attention to his teacher all year
....

7a Read the story of Yu Youzhen. What did she do and why? Ignore the gaps at the moment.

A few years ago, a Chinese woman called Yu Youzhen became a millionaire. Before becoming a millionaire, she had (a) .... working hard for nearly 40 years. She (b) .... been a farmer, cook and even a lorry driver. Then she applied (c) .... the job of street cleaner. One day the government gave her money for her land. She used the money to set (d) .... her own business. After a few years, she had made about £1 million by buying apartments. But she decided she (e) .... want to stay at home doing nothing. So she (f) .... the decision to continue keeping the streets clean. She wanted to be a good example to her children. She wasn't happy with them because they (g) .... just sitting at home all day. They hadn't been (h) .... anything for years. And even though she had already (i) .... enough money to live well without doing anything at all, she put on her orange jacket and went to work six days a week. It worked! Now her children (j) .... started working!

7b Read the text again and think of the word which best fits each gap. Use only one word in each gap.

7c SPEAKING Work with a partner. What do you think of the story of Yu Youzhen?

Negotiating and collaborating – 1

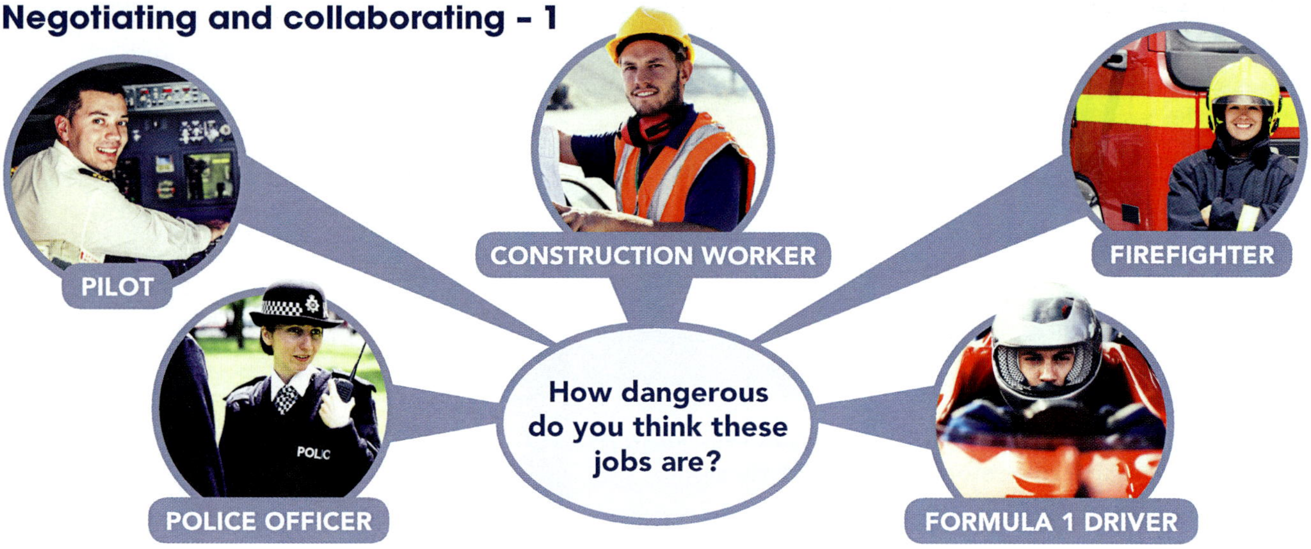

1 SPEAKING **Work with a partner. Look at the jobs in the diagram. Would you like to do any of these jobs? Why/Why not?**

2 LISTENING ▶ 11 **Listen to two students doing a listening task and answer these questions.**

1. What does the examiner ask them to talk about?
2. What second question does the examiner ask them?
3. What is the students' final answer to that question?
4. Do you agree with their answer? Why/ Why not?

3 ▶ 11 **Listen again and answer these questions.**

1. Do the two students talk about all of the jobs?
2. Do they listen to each other and respond to each other's comments?
3. Does one student speak much more than the other?
4. Do they ask each other's opinions?
5. Do they fail to come to a decision at the end of the conversation?

✔ EXAM SUCCESS

In the second part of the listening task, the best strategy is to agree with your partner's first idea, but then suggest alternative ideas. It is better not to agree completely straight away because the conversation will end too quickly.

➤ EXAM SUCCESS page 144

4 **Look at the expressions in the Speaking bank. What are the three different categories?**

SPEAKING BANK

Negotiating and collaborating – 1

1 ....

What do you think? ▪ What do you think about (architects)? What about you? ▪ What about (bank managers)? Do you agree? ▪ Don't you think so?

2 ....

Yes, I agree. ▪ Yes, you're right. ▪ Sure. ▪ OK. I think you're right. ▪ That's true. ▪ I agree with you. I see what you mean. ▪ That's a good idea.

3 ....

I see what you mean, but … ▪ I suppose so, but … I'm not sure. ▪ Maybe, but … ▪ I agree up to a point, but …

5 SPEAKING **Work with a partner. Practise doing the task in 2 giving your own opinions.**

PRACTICE MAKES PERFECT

6 SPEAKING **Work with a partner and do this task. Use expressions from the Speaking bank.**

1. Here are some different jobs. Talk to each other about how these jobs help to improve society.
2. You have a minute to decide which job you think helps society the most.

An opinion essay – 1

1 SPEAKING **Work with a partner. Read this writing task. Do you agree or disagree with the statement? Write notes with your main ideas.**

> *It's a bad idea for teenagers to do part-time work while they are still studying.*

2 **With your partner, copy and complete this plan with your ideas.**

Paragraph 1:
Introduction with general statement on the topic and your opinion

Paragraph 2:
First and most important reason for your opinion

Paragraph 3:
One or two other reasons for your opinion OR other people's arguments against your opinion and why you don't agree with them

Paragraph 4:
Summary and conclusion restating your opinion

3 **Read this essay, ignoring the gaps. Does it follow the paragraph plan in 2? Is the opinion of the writer similar to your opinion?**

In some countries, the US for instance, many teenagers work while they are still studying at school or at university. (a) ...., this is a bad idea.

(b) ...., studying at school or university is a full-time occupation. Students need time to take notes, revise, do assignments and research topics. In my opinion, students who work in the evenings or at the weekends do not have time to do these things properly.

(c) ...., young people often work in bad conditions or late at night. This means that after work they find it difficult to pay attention and concentrate.

(d) ...., some people say that work experience can help to make you more independent and responsible. (e) .... up to a point. However, there is time for students to gain this experience when they finish their studies.

(f) ...., I believe that a student's real responsibility is to learn as much as possible. They can only do this if they study full-time, with no other distractions.

4 **Complete the essay with these phrases.**

As far as I'm concerned • Furthermore
I agree with this • On the other hand
To begin with • To sum up

5 **Put the expressions in 4 in the correct place in the Writing bank.**

WRITING BANK

Useful words and expressions in opinion essays

- Expressing opinions
  Personally, I think ...
  ....
  In my opinion,
  ....
  I believe that ...
- Adding opinions and putting them in order
  Firstly, ...
  Secondly, In addition, ..., *What is more,*
  Finally, Lastly,
- Contrasting opinions
  However, Nevertheless, ...
- Concluding
  In conclusion, ..., *All things considered,*

PRACTICE MAKES PERFECT

6a **Work with a partner. Look at this task. Write notes with your ideas and then complete the plan in 2 for this topic.**

'School does not prepare students for the world of work.' Do you agree?

6b **Use the plan in 6a and words and expressions from the Writing bank to write your essay.**

WRITING BANK ➤ PAGE 151

Grammar reference

Past simple

We use the **past simple** to:

1 describe finished actions or situations in the past.
I went to Ireland last year.

2 say that one thing happened after another.
When the teacher came in, we took out our books.

Past continuous

We use the **past continuous** to:

1 talk about activities in progress at a moment in the past.
At 4 o'clock this afternoon I was watching TV.

2 describe scenes in a story or description.
They were all wearing coats because it was bitterly cold.

3 talk about an activity in progress in the past that was interrupted by another activity.
I was listening to music when my father suddenly ran into the room.

Past habits

FORM

Used to

My grandfather used to work as a postman.
He didn't use to have much free time.
Did your grandmother use to work?
Yes, she did./No, she didn't.

Would

They would work eight hours a day.

USE

- We use **used to** and **would** to talk about past habits, things we did regularly in the past but don't do now. We cannot use **used to** and **would** to talk about single events in the past. In this case, we use the past simple.
- We use **would** with past actions but not past states.
*He **would** come and visit us on Sundays.* NOT ~~*He would have a bike.*~~
- We do not usually use **wouldn't** to talk about past habits.
*He **didn't use to** give us presents.* NOT ~~*He wouldn't give us presents.*~~
- When we give a period of time, we use the past simple, not **used to**.
*She **used to** work in a factory. She **worked** there for five years.*
NOT ~~*She used to work in a factory for five years.*~~

Past perfect simple

FORM

To make the **past perfect simple**, we use *had* + past participle.

USE

We use the **past perfect simple** to talk about actions that happened before another action or actions in the past. It gives importance to the completion of an activity.
When the interview had finished, I left.

Past perfect continuous

FORM

To make the **past perfect continuous**, we use *had* + *been* + verb-*ing*

USE

We use the **past perfect continuous** to talk about actions that happened before another action or actions in the past. It gives importance to the duration of an activity.
I was tired because I had been studying all night.

Vocabulary

Work conditions and responsibilities be responsible for • deal with • do paperwork • earn • employee experience • good/bad/dangerous conditions • indoors • manual work • outdoors • qualifications • salary self-employed • skilled • stressful • training • well paid

Working life apply for a job • become unemployed • be made redundant • be on flexitime • be offered a job be sacked/fired/dismissed • do shift work • from nine to five • full-time • get a promotion • long hours look for a job • overtime • part-time • resign • retire • sign a contract

Phrasal verbs connected with work fill in • get ahead • keep at • keep up with • set up • take over turn down • work on

Other words and phrases ➤ page 137

Grammar revision

Past simple and past continuous — / 6 points

1 Put the verbs in the correct form of the past simple or past continuous.

She (a) .... (get) up and (b) .... (look) out of the window. The sun (c) .... (shine) and there wasn't a cloud in the sky. While she (d) .... (look) out of the window, she (e) .... (see) something strange. Two boys (f) .... (play) football in her garden.

Past habits — / 7 points

2 Choose the correct alternative. In one sentence, both alternatives are correct. Which one?

1 When he was small, he *used to/would* be really shy.
2 I *used to study/studied* in Ireland for two months.
3 I *use to/usually* go to the cinema at the weekend.
4 Last year my brother *had/used to have* a big party to welcome his American friend.
5 Did you *use/used* to have a pet?
6 Children *used to/would* work in factories in Britain in the 19th century.
7 They *didn't use to/wouldn't* go out on Friday evenings, but now they do.

Past perfect simple and past perfect continuous — / 7 points

3 Is the underlined part of the sentence correct? If not, rewrite it.

1 I have been waiting for an hour when the film finally started.
2 He was tired because he had painted all day.
3 She had been writing seven emails.
4 Everything was white because it had been snowing.
5 When they ate their dinner, they washed the dishes.
6 They heard a loud noise and thought that somebody had fallen over.
7 When they had been finishing their homework, they turned the TV on.

Vocabulary revision

WORK CONDITIONS AND RESPONSIBILITIES — / 8 points

1 Complete the sentences with these words.

dealing • earn • employee • for • overtime qualifications • shift • skilled

1 I'm responsible .... helping customers.
2 My job involves .... with all the paperwork.
3 This company isn't mine. I'm just an ....
4 I .... quite a good salary.
5 This is a .... job. It requires a lot of training.
6 I do .... work. Sometimes I work at night.
7 He often arrives home late as he works ....
8 Have you got any ....? A university degree, for example?

PHRASAL VERBS CONNECTED WITH WORK — / 6 points

2 Match the parts of the phrasal verbs with their definitions.

Verb	Particle	Definition
1 set	ahead	not accept an offer, request or application
2 get	on	start a new business, office, etc.
3 turn	up	progress faster than other people
4 work	in	add information on a document
5 fill	over	spend time working or improving something
6 take	down	take control of something

WORKING LIFE — / 6 points

3 Complete the text.

When Rose finished her degree she started to (a) .... for a job. She found an interesting post in a multinational company and so she (b) .... for it. She got the job, but soon after the company told Rose that they didn't need her anymore. She was made (c) .... and became (d) .... Luckily, another company contacted her soon afterwards. An employee at the company had just been (e) .... because he was always late. Rose went for an interview. They really liked her and she was (f) .... the job. She accepted, of course!

Total: / 40 points

Reading

➤ TIP FOR READING EXAMS

In matching activities, remember …

Read the text quickly for a general understanding. Then read the questions and work out what piece(s) of information you need to find. Are there any key words that help you to find the text or part of the text which contains the information?

➤ EXAM SUCCESS page 144

1 **Read the first paragraph of the text. What is the Erasmus programme? What do you think are the advantages of doing an Erasmus exchange?**

2 **Read the text and answer the questions.**

1 Do the students mention any of the advantages that you thought of in 1?

2 What subject does each student study?

STUDYING AROUND EUROPE

The Erasmus programme is a popular student exchange programme involving university students in the European Union. Students spend at least three months studying abroad in one of over 30 countries involved in the programme. Here is what some Erasmus students say about their experiences.

Nelly Samuels, The Netherlands

A

The decision to study abroad has changed my life in so many ways. Academically, I immediately fell in love with the style of the lessons we received. Before, I wouldn't express my opinions much in tutorials. But thanks to the stimulating, open atmosphere I became much more confident about constructing my own arguments and defending them. It helped that all my classmates, mostly Dutch, felt very passionate about modern history, my area of study. Socially, things couldn't have been better either. Before, I found it difficult to make new friends, but in this situation I felt happy and relaxed being with all the students I got to know.

John Vaughan, Poland

B

I'd never really studied languages before. But, being a business student, I knew languages would give me an advantage later in the world of work. It was so frustrating at first, knowing I probably spoke the language worse than a five year old, but my Polish classmates were very patient with me and after a month or two I'd made sufficient progress to be able to follow the tutors' explanations. I shared a house with students from five different countries. Often we could only communicate using sign language. What really opened my eyes during my six months abroad was the shock of seeing my subject from a totally different cultural perspective. That really added something to my understanding when I went back to the UK.

Teresa Lopez, UK

C

I studied in a new, relatively small uni in the UK. The fact that it was small turned out to be a good thing because in no time at all I got to know lots and lots of people. There were a lot of international students like me. I have invitations from people in about 20 different countries round the world to go and visit them one day. This could be really useful later on if I move around. Campus life was really stimulating. For example, I got the chance to work as a presenter for a weekly news programme shown on the university website. That was something that I'd always wanted to do and it related well to my degree in media studies. In terms of studying, it took me a bit longer to get used to a different style of teaching and learning from what I'd known in Spain. But in the end I came to prefer UK style education!

Keith Johnson, Slovakia

D

The one thing that affected me the most during my time studying abroad was realising that, at the end, I didn't consider myself British. I was now European. I suppose that feeling is natural after spending every day with young people from so many different European countries. Despite our differences, we all had so much in common. As a student of politics, I think this was so important. It helped me to see that even when people have different opinions and backgrounds, we can work together constructively if we really want to. Now I know that, when I finish my degree, I want to study a master's degree. But only on the condition that I can do at least part of it abroad.

3 **Match students A–D with the questions below.**

Which student says …

1 they took a while to get over linguistic difficulties? ....

2 the Erasmus experience will be a practical help when they travel internationally? ....

3 they didn't use to socialise much? ....

4 they managed to fulfil an old ambition? ....

5 they want to repeat their Erasmus experience? ....

6 they immediately preferred the different teaching style? ....

7 the Erasmus experience made a difference to the way they see themselves? ....

8 their attitude to the teaching method changed completely? ....

4 SPEAKING **What about *you*?**

Would you like to study in another country? Why/Why not?

Writing

➤ TIP FOR WRITING EXAMS

In transactional tasks, remember …

Do not simply reply to questions in the email or letter with 'Yes' or 'No'. Add extra information, context and questions.

➤ EXAM SUCCESS page 144

5 You have received this email from a friend. Underline the information that you should include in your reply.

Hi!

How are you? It was great to see you on Friday. I really enjoyed going to that new pizza place. I'm attaching a photo I took on my phone! We should go again soon.

When I saw you, I forgot to tell you that Rachel is coming back on Wednesday. She's been away on a school exchange in Germany for three whole months! I thought I might arrange a special 'Welcome home' party for her on Thursday evening. What do you think?

I don't mind having the party at my house. But I'd need help preparing food and stuff. Could you come and give me a hand getting things ready on Thursday afternoon?

Apart from food, is there anything that you can think of that would make the party really special? You know that Rachel has really missed us all so I'd really like to make the party memorable for her.

Write back soon so that I can start organising things.

Bye for now

JT

1 attachment

6 Make a plan of your reply to the email. Decide how many paragraphs to have and what to include in each one.

7 Write your reply. Include all the necessary information. Write between 120 and 150 words.

Listening

➤ TIP FOR LISTENING EXAMS

In matching activities, remember …

Read the opinions before you listen. This can help you to know what the people may say and helps you to concentrate more while you listen. But don't forget that speakers may express the same opinion using different words or expressions.

➤ EXAM SUCCESS page 144

8 SPEAKING **Work with a partner. Look at this extract from a newspaper article. Do you think 'helicopter' or 'lawnmower' parents are a good thing or a bad thing? Why?**

Nowadays, more and more university professors and employers complain about 'helicopter' parents (parents who pay very close attention to their children and are always hovering over them, even when they are at university or start work). They also complain about 'lawnmower' parents (parents who try to solve all their children's problems and remove any obstacles in their path). These parents insist on helping their children, whether they need them to help or not.

9 LISTENING 12 **You are going to hear five people talking about helicopter and lawnmower parents. Choose the opinion each speaker expresses (A–F) from the list below. Use the letters only once. There is one extra letter.**

A I turned somebody down because of their helicopter parent.

B I think a parent's job is to help their children when they can.

C I know I probably make mistakes, but I need to be independent.

D I don't think you can make decisions for your children.

E I think everybody needs a lawnmower parent.

F I've started to see a change in the way people behave where I work.

Speaker 1: .... Speaker 3: .... Speaker 5: ....

Speaker 2: .... Speaker 4: ....

10 SPEAKING **What about *you*?**

In what ways do you show your parents that you are responsible and ready for independence?

Speaking

➤ TIP FOR SPEAKING EXAMS

In negotiating activities, remember …

Listen to what your partner is saying and respond to it. You can agree, disagree, make suggestions or ask questions.

➤ EXAM SUCCESS page 144

11 Look at the task and the diagram on page 158 and think about what you are going to say.

12 SPEAKING **Work with a partner and do the task.**

3 On the move

Vocabulary

Words connected with transport and travel

1 SPEAKING **Work with a partner. Talk about the photos using these words.**

astronaut • board (v) • crew • flight • gate
get in/off/on/out • high-speed train • land (v) • launch (n, v)
motorway • orbit (n, v) • passenger • platform • rocket
spacecraft • space station • take off
the Underground/subway/tube • traffic jam

2 Match the words in 1 with these definitions.

1 the people who work on a ship, plane, etc.
2 a line of cars waiting to move
3 a public transport system where trains travel in tunnels
4 a general word for something that travels in space
5 what a plane does when it begins its journey
6 what a plane does when it finishes its journey
7 the place at an airport where people board a plane

3 LISTENING 13 **Listen to six short travel announcements. Choose the correct alternative.**

1 Passengers on Platform 3 should *get on the next train/stand away from the edge of the platform*.
2 Passengers for Newbury *should/shouldn't* get on this train.
3 Passengers *should/shouldn't* get on the train as soon as the doors open.
4 There is *a/no* problem for passengers who want to get off at *East/West* Kensington station.
5 If you are on flight Jet 325 to Manchester, you *need/don't need* to go to gate D34 quickly.
6 Passengers shouldn't leave their *tickets/bags* unattended.

journey, travel, trip, voyage

4 Read the dictionary entries. Then choose the correct alternative.

journey (n)
an occasion when you travel from one place to another, especially when there is a long distance between the places: *We had a long journey ahead of us.*

travel (n)
the activity of travelling: *Foreign travel never really appealed to him until he retired. Our agency deals mostly with business travel.*

trip (n)
an occasion when you go somewhere and come back again: *a fishing/camping/sightseeing trip*

voyage (n)
a long journey, especially by boat or into space: *the long voyage home*

1 Last year we went on a school *journey/trip* to York.
2 It was a long and difficult *trip/voyage* for Columbus and his crew.
3 *Journey/Travel* teaches you a lot about the world.
4 Marco Polo's *journey/travel* took many years.
5 My parents sometimes have to go away on business *journeys/trips*.
6 One day spacecraft will go on incredible *trips/voyages* that will take years and years.
7 We spend a lot of money on foreign *journey/travel*.
8 The *trip/voyage* to my village takes just 20 minutes.

5 SPEAKING **Work with a partner. Ask and answer these questions.**

1 Do you ever travel abroad in the holidays? What are your favourite destinations?
2 How important is travel for you? Why?
3 Where is a good place to go on a day trip from your town or city? Give reasons.
4 Do you like going on sightseeing trips? Why/Why not?
5 What type of transport do you prefer for short trips? And for long journeys? Give reasons.
6 What is the longest journey you've been on? Give details.

1 SPEAKING **Work with a partner. What do you think the photo in the article shows?**

2 **Read the article quickly and answer the questions.**

1 What is the name for this type of transport?
2 Which other types of transport are mentioned?

A JOURNEY INTO THE FUTURE

Our world is on the move. (1) .... But there is also more and more pollution, there are more and more accidents, and transport seems to be going slower than before, not faster. So shouldn't we be thinking of ways to revolutionise the world of transport?

American millionaire Elon Musk is quite clearly a man who wants to help bring about this revolution. With his Tesla Motors company he has managed to reinvent the electric car, producing a popular all-electric sports car. (2) .... But his boldest plan for future transport is the Hyperloop, a plan which looks and sounds like pure science fiction.

If everything goes according to plan, the Hyperloop will be a system of long tubes set on top of towers which will run next to motorways. Inside the tubes people will travel inside capsules: about six passengers plus their luggage per capsule. (3) .... With no friction, Musk believes they will be able to travel at speeds of up to 1,220kph, nearly the speed of sound! It will take just half an hour to travel from Los Angeles to San Francisco. Currently the journey takes seven hours. The attraction of the Hyperloop is that it is much faster than a high-speed train, and, unlike planes, there will be no time wasted in taking off and landing.

Nevertheless, for journeys over 1,600 kilometres, Elon Musk believes that supersonic air travel will be preferable. In the last 50 years, there has been a sharp increase in the number of people travelling by air. (4) .... With this in mind, the company Airbus has already made plans for how they are going to make flying more attractive.

The engineers at Airbus think that in 2050, with new construction techniques and materials, planes will have transparent sections allowing you panoramic views from your seat. Seats will change size and shape to give you a more comfortable flight. And passengers will be able to choose between different zones in the plane such as an Interactive zone, where you'll be able to meet people and play electronic games, and a Relaxation zone, where special seats will give you a massage!

For shorter journeys, experts predict that cars will probably remain the most common means of transport. Of course, soon the self-driving car will be the norm, hopefully limiting the number of road accidents. But it probably won't be too long before we start seeing flying cars in our skies. (5) .... Soon, when you look up, you'll see hundreds of drones carrying everything from pizzas to heavy packages. A group of experts is meeting again next month to talk about the impact of drones on air traffic. But imagine when cars take to the skies, too. A major challenge will be how to produce flying cars that do not create terrible air and noise pollution, or serious collisions.

(6) .... Maybe that's one of the reasons why Japanese engineers are drawing up plans to put tourists into space using a massive elevator that will travel more than 35,000 kilometres into orbit. Thirty passengers and their small crew will spend a week travelling a quarter of the way to the Moon at speeds of up to 190kph. At the end of the journey, they'll reach a space station where they'll be able to get an astronaut's view of the Earth, with little or no training beforehand. The only problems at the moment are the cost of the elevator's construction (roughly estimated at $6 billion), and the fact that it could take 40 years to build!

3 **Read the text again. Complete the gaps with sentences a–f.**

a All the evidence suggests that this trend is going to continue.
b Meanwhile, another of his companies, SpaceX, produces and launches various spacecraft and rockets.
c There are more and more people using public transport, driving their own cars, and flying around the world.
d Talking of accidents, it is often said that the safest form of transport is the elevator.
e Indeed, one of the biggest changes in the future will be the number of vehicles in the sky.
f The capsules will create a cushion of air underneath them.

✓ EXAM SUCCESS

In tasks where sentences are missing from a text, read the text carefully looking at the information before and after each gap. Then read the sentences and look for words and phrases which connect with information in the text.

➤ EXAM SUCCESS page 144

4 **CRITICAL THINKING**

Think! Then compare ideas with your class.

- Are these future transport projects useful? Why/Why not?

5 **What do the underlined words in the text mean? Guess and then check in your dictionary.**

6 SPEAKING **What about *you*?**

Which of the different types of transport mentioned in the article would you most like to try? Why?

Future forms

1a Look at the sentences. What tense is the verb in blue?

a All the evidence suggests that that trend is going to continue.
b A group of experts is meeting again next month to talk about that question.
c Airbus has already made plans for how they are going to make flying more attractive.
d The engineers think that planes will have transparent sections.
e When you look up, you'll see hundreds of drones.

1b Complete the rules with *will*, *be going to*, *the present simple* or *the present continuous*.

We use:

1 .... for predictions based on evidence.
2 .... for plans and intentions.
3 .... for predictions based on thoughts, opinions and expectations.
4 .... for confirmed plans and arrangements.
5 .... after time expressions like *when, before, after, by the time, until, as soon as*.

1c Look at sentences a–c below and complete the rules with *will* or *the present simple*.

a This year it will be the 120th anniversary of the first transatlantic flight.
b I've just missed the bus. I know! I'll get a taxi.
c Their flight leaves tomorrow morning.

We use:

1 .... for decisions made at the moment of speaking.
2 .... for future facts.
3 .... for events that are part of a timetable or routine.

GRAMMAR REFERENCE ➤ PAGE 42

2 SPEAKING Look at these sentences. Work with a partner. Explain why *will* is used in each sentence.

1 Tomorrow will be the last day of the holidays.
2 That looks heavy. I'll carry it for you.
3 Scientists believe that the Hyperloop won't be easy to build.
4 Who do you think will win the competition?
5 My friend will be 18 next week.
6 Are you leaving now? I'll come with you.

3 Is the underlined part of the sentence correct? If not, rewrite it.

1 As soon as the class will start, I'll take my books out.
2 Don't worry. I'm going to answer the door.
3 The weather forecast says it's raining next weekend.
4 Some scientists predict that there will be a new ice age.
5 The concert takes place next July.
6 That's it! I've got my tickets. My friends and I will go to the cinema tonight.
7 What are your plans? What do you do next weekend?
8 I've already decided that next year I'm eating healthier food.
9 Next year February will have 29 days.
10 Look at that waiter! He'll drop all those plates.

4a Complete the sentences with an appropriate future form of the verbs given.

1 I think humans .... (land) on Mars before I .... (be) 50.
2 Next Sunday it .... (be) my birthday.
3 Kate and I .... (meet) at 9 o'clock tonight.
4 What .... you .... (do) next summer?
5 Do you think it .... (snow) next week?
6 Alice is pregnant. She .... (have) a baby.
7 **A:** It's too hot in here. **B:** Don't worry. I .... (open) the window for you.
8 As soon as I .... (get) home tonight, I .... (switch) the TV on.
9 I .... (see) the doctor tomorrow. The appointment is for half past ten.
10 Take an umbrella. It .... (rain).

4b SPEAKING Work with a partner. Compare your answers in 4a. Be ready to explain your choice.

I think number one is 'will land'.

Why?

Because it's a prediction based on a thought or belief.

I agree.

The Paravelo

5 Read the text and choose the correct alternative.

Two British inventors (a) are/have created a flying bicycle, called the Paravelo. It seems clear to everybody that traffic problems (b) become/are going to become worse in the future. John Foden and Yannick Read believe that their bike could be a solution. When you (c) are/will be in a traffic jam, you (d) are/will be able to start up the bike's fan and simply take (e) off/up! They calculate that the cost of the flying bike (f) is being/will be £10,000. That isn't expensive when you compare it with the price of a helicopter. Another advantage is that you (g) will/won't need a pilot's licence to fly it – anyone can do it! In the next few weeks, the two inventors (h) are talking/talk to different companies to see how they can get their plans off the ground.

6a Complete the *Yes/No* questions about the future with your own ideas.

1 .... before you go home?
2 .... tonight?
3 .... next weekend?
4 .... when the summer comes?
5 .... when you finish school?
6 .... in 2030?
7 .... when you're 70 years old?

Are you going to do your homework before you go home?

6b Predict your partner's answers. Write down your predictions.

6c SPEAKING Ask your partner your questions. How many predictions did you get right?

Prefixes

1 Each of these words contains a prefix. Find the prefixes and match them with the meanings below.

cooperate • discomfort • interactive • miscalculate • overpopulated • postgraduate • reinvent • subway • supersonic • underestimate

1 wrong, incorrect ....
2 after ....
3 not enough ....
4 too much ....
5 between ....
6 the opposite, not ....
7 again ....
8 with, together ....
9 below ....
10 more, bigger, better ....

2 Complete the sentences by adding the correct prefix to the words.

dis • mis • over • re • sub- • super • under

appeared • booked • human • paid • understood • write • zero

1 She saw a strange object in the sky, but it suddenly .... and she couldn't see it anymore.
2 Most people think they're .... They think they should get more money.
3 Sorry. I .... you. I thought you said 'no'.
4 It's so cold there in the winter. They have .... temperatures!
5 This essay has got a lot of mistakes. I'd like you to .... it.
6 The flight was .... There were too many passengers.
7 It took .... strength to lift the wheel.

3a Make the negative form of these words. Use the prefixes *dis-, il-, im-, in-, ir-* or *un-*.

advantage • agree • believable • capable • complete • expected • likely • logical • necessary • obey • patient • possible • regular • responsible • successful • visible

3b 14 Listen and check your answers.

3c PRONUNCIATION 14 Underline the stress in the negative form of the words in 3a. Listen, check and repeat.

disadvantage disagree

4a Make three sentences using negative words from 3a.

'Go' is a common irregular verb.

4b SPEAKING Read out your sentences without saying the negative word. Can anybody guess the word?

'Go' is a common .... verb.

Investigating FOOD MILES

21ST CENTURY SKILLS OBJECTIVES

- To learn about food miles and their impact on the environment.
- To think about what we can do to reduce the impact of food miles.
- To investigate and evaluate our own food buying habits.

KEY CONCEPTS

environmentally friendly [adj]: *Cars cause a lot of pollution so they aren't very environmentally friendly.* **carbon dioxide [n]:** *Carbon dioxide is a gas which is harmful to the atmosphere.* **carbon emissions [n]:** *Vehicles and factories are producing carbon emissions which affect the environment.* **transport [n, v]/transportation [n]:** *Lorries transport products to supermarkets.* **in season [phr]:** *Strawberries are usually in season from May to August or September in the UK.* **label [n]:** *Read the label on that bottle to see what the ingredients are.*

1a SPEAKING **Work with a partner. Look at the food label. It shows a product sold in the US. How far did it travel before getting to the US?**

1b Look at the title of the article. What do you think 'food miles' are?

2 READING **Read the introduction. Were your ideas in 1 correct? How serious a problem do you think food miles are? Why?**

FOOD MILES | THE GREAT DEBATE

When you sit down for dinner tonight, just think of the long journey your food has taken to get to your table. The average item of food in a British supermarket has travelled 1,600 kilometres to get there. We use the expression 'food miles' to describe how far food travels from the place it's produced until it gets to our table. Some people say that food miles will have a catastrophic effect on the environment in the coming years, but others say that they aren't that important. Let's see what both sides have to say.

A FOOD MILES: An environmental time bomb

There used to be a time when apples would only appear in shops in the autumn in the UK, and strawberries in the summer. Now, however, we can eat just about everything at any time of the year. But, at what price for our planet? Just look at these facts:

- 95% of fruit in the UK comes from abroad, and 50% of vegetables. Some apples travel nearly 18,000 km from New Zealand to reach the UK!
- 30% of all products transported by lorry around the UK are food products. These lorry journeys produce 25% of all CO_2 emissions.
- Environmentally unfriendly planes carrying food are already responsible for 11% of all carbon emissions.
- Some food products like potatoes are often grown in one place, then travel somewhere else to be packaged, and then travel back to near where they were grown to be sold!
- Experts have calculated that if we all bought food produced within a 20 kilometre radius from where we live, the country would save over two billion pounds in environmental costs.

The message is clear. We need to produce food locally, and we need to buy locally produced food. It's cheap, it's environmentally friendly and it's natural.

Jonah Williams, farmer

3 READING **Work with a partner. Student A, read Text A and answer the questions below. Student B, read Text B and answer the questions below. Make a note of your answers.**

QUESTIONS FOR TEXT A

1. Why wasn't it possible to eat apples in the summer in the UK in the past?
2. How do lorries carrying food affect the environment?
3. What impact do planes carrying food have on the environment?
4. Why does the writer mention the transportation of potatoes?
5. What does the writer recommend us to do and why?

QUESTIONS FOR TEXT B

1. What two options exist if we want to eat apples in the summer in the UK?
2. Which of the two options does the writer think is preferable and why?
3. Why is it a good idea to buy Spanish, not British, tomatoes in the UK in the winter?
4. Apart from environmental reasons, why does the writer suggest that buying fruit from countries like Africa is a good idea?
5. What is the writer's conclusion about food miles?

B FOOD MILES: Exploding the myth

Mary Barfield, scientist

"A while ago everybody started saying that food miles showed how the world was going mad. Producing apples in New Zealand or green beans in Africa and then flying them to the UK? Think of all the carbon emissions from flying all that distance! Scandalous!

But let's think again. OK if we want UK apples in the summer we have to keep them cool for nearly a whole year. But the energy that you need to keep them fresh for ten months will be worse for the environment than the carbon emissions created by air transportation.

Remember that we buy food from other countries because their weather provides the ideal natural conditions for producing that food. You can produce tomatoes in the UK in the winter, but you need energy to heat the greenhouses to recreate the warm, sunny weather of Spain. That means that in the UK it makes sense to buy Spanish tomatoes in the winter, even taking into account the food miles.

And let's not forget about the one million African workers, for example, who depend on selling fruit and vegetables to the UK and other markets. If we stop buying food from other parts of the world, it might have a catastrophic impact on their economies, and then our own.

So, food miles are not ideal. But sometimes they're better than the alternative!"

4 SPEAKING **Work with your partner. Student A, explain why food miles are a serious problem. Student B, explain why the alternative to food miles can be worse. Use your notes in 3 to help you.**

5 With your partner, talk about how serious you think the question of food miles is. What do you think is good advice when you go to buy food? Use the information in texts A and B to help you.

6a LISTENING ▶ 15 **Watch or listen to Ben from Sourced Market. Does he mention any of your ideas in 4 and 5?**

6b ▶ 15 **Complete the sentences with one or two words. Watch or listen again to check your answers.**

1. My responsibility is .... the business.
2. I learnt what it takes to get food from field ....
3. To sell apples in June means keeping them in a .... facility all year.
4. The best thing would be if people ate more ...., (that is depending on the time of year).
5. How many miles it takes to get a product from A to B is known as ....
6. The best place to start would be your local farmer's ....

6c Work with a partner. What does Ben say about these things?

a. locally sourced food
b. agribusiness
c. product labelling

21ST CENTURY TASK

You want to find out more about food miles in your area.

Work in a group and follow this plan:

1. *Collect different food labels or packaging and bring them to class.*
2. *Using a world map, create a display to show each item and where it came from and/or where it was packaged.*
3. *Find out which of the products could be produced or packaged closer to where you live, and what the benefits could be.*
4. *Present your findings to the class. What are your conclusions?*

Listening

1 SPEAKING **Work with a partner. Look at the photo of a drone. What could it be used for? Make a list.**

You could use it to deliver parcels.

2 LISTENING 16 **Listen to a radio programme about drones. Tick (✓) any of the ideas in your list that they mention.**

3 16 **Listen again and choose the correct alternative.**

1 UAV means Unmanned *Aerial/Automatic* Vehicle.

2 Many people prefer the name UAV because the word 'drone' has a *scientifically imprecise/negative* meaning.

3 In a park in Namibia they use UAVs to *observe/stop* rhino hunters.

4 Film directors will be able to use UAVs to film *aerial images/action movies*.

5 Filming sports events with UAVs *is too expensive/offers us new reporting possibilities*.

6 Scott thinks it will be *quite possible/too difficult* for the general public to buy a UAV in 2025.

7 Scott *thinks/doesn't think* there should be limits on the use of UAVs.

4 **What are some of the positive points of UAVs according to Scott and Kim? Do they mention any possible negative points? If so, what?**

5 SPEAKING **What about *you*?**

Do you think UAVs will change the world in a good or bad way? Explain your opinion.

Grammar in context

Future continuous, future perfect simple and future perfect continuous

1a **Look at these sentences. What tense are the verbs in blue? Explain how we form the tenses.**

1 Soon we'll be seeing UAVs flying over the heads of football players.

2 In 2025 thousands of normal people will be using them.

3 By 2025 UAVs will have become incredibly big business.

4 In five or ten years the price will have dropped.

5 By February next year, the US Army will have been using drones for 42 years already.

1b **Complete the rules with *future continuous, future perfect simple* or *future perfect continuous*.**

1 We use the .... to talk about activities that will be finished by a certain time in the future.

2 We use the .... to talk about activities in progress at a particular moment in the future.

3 We use the .... to talk about how long an activity has been in progress before a particular moment in the future.

4 We often use *by* with the .... and the ....

GRAMMAR REFERENCE ➤ PAGE 42

2 **Explain the difference between the sentences in each pair.**

1a At 7 o'clock I'll be seeing the doctor.
1b At 7 o'clock I'll have seen the doctor.
2a She's giving the talk in half an hour.
2b She'll have given the talk in half an hour.
3a In 2050 humans will have gone to the Moon again.
3b In 2050 humans will go to the Moon again.
4a I'm going to have lunch with my friends at 1 pm tomorrow.
4b I'll be having lunch with my friends at 1 pm tomorrow.

Flipped classroom: watch the grammar presentation video.

3a Read Sarah's schedule for tomorrow and complete the sentences with the future continuous, future perfect simple or future perfect continuous form of the verbs given.

LAUNCH DAY SPECIAL – SCHEDULE

9 am	Breakfast in hotel
10 am	Bus ride to the Space Centre
10.30 am	Visit the Rocket Garden
11.30 am	See the Astronaut Hall of Fame
12.15 pm	Lunch with an astronaut, with the chance to ask questions
1.30 pm	Special film showing previous space launches
3 pm	See the launch of a Delta IV rocket live!
5 pm	Visit our full-size model of the International Spaceship
6 pm	Bus back to hotel
7.30 pm	Dinner at hotel

1 At 9.30 she .... (have) breakfast at the hotel.
2 At 10 she .... (eat) breakfast.
3 At 10.35 she .... (arrive) at the Space Centre.
4 By 11.25 she .... (go) round the Rocket Garden for nearly an hour.
5 At 1.00 she .... (have) lunch with an astronaut.
6 By 3.00 she .... (see) a film about space launches.
7 At 3.10, she .... (watch) the rocket launch.
8 By 4.30 pm, she .... (watch) the rocket launch for one and a half hours.

3b Write four questions about the schedule, two using the future continuous and two using the future perfect.

What will she be doing at quarter past five?

3c SPEAKING **Ask your partner your questions.**

4 Put the verbs in the correct form of the future continuous or future perfect simple.

'The future is a mystery. What (a) .... I .... (do) when I'm 30? Will I be unemployed or (b) .... I .... (work)? I know that I (c) .... (finish) school, and I imagine I (d) .... (leave) university because not many people continue studying at the age of 30. One thing I do know is that I (e) .... (not live) in this town because I want to leave here when I go to university. I'm sure I (f) .... (learn) to drive by the time I'm 30 because that's one of the first things I want to do when I'm 18. I don't think I (g) .... (buy) a car because they're really expensive, but I imagine I (h) .... (save) up my money each month to buy one. The future's a mystery, but I know it's going to be interesting.'

5a Write predictions about yourself in the year 2040. Use the future continuous, future perfect simple or future perfect continuous.

The future me!

1 live in this city
2 live with my parents
3 stop playing computer games
4 become famous
5 get married
6 speak English
7 work in an office
8 learn Chinese
9 appear on TV
10 do exercise regularly

I won't be living in this city./I will have been living in this city for 30 years.

5b SPEAKING **Work in small groups. Compare your sentences and ask questions to find out what your partners have written. Are any answers particularly common?**

Will you be living in this city?

Yes, I think so. That means I'll have been living here for 30 years. What about you, Eva?

No, I won't. I think I'll be living in another country, maybe England or Ireland. And you, Ana?

5c Tell the class any common answers.

Most of us don't think we'll be living in this city in 2040.

Talking about photos – 1

1 SPEAKING **Work with a partner. Look at the photos. Think of similarities and differences between them.**

Similarities	Differences

2 LISTENING 17 **Read the task below. Listen to a student doing this task and answer the questions.**

Compare the photos and say what problems you think people have travelling around the city in these ways.

1 Does the student mention any of your ideas?
2 Does she describe each photo in detail?
3 Does she do both parts of the task?

3 17 **Complete what the student said with phrases from the Speaking bank. Listen again if necessary.**

(a) .... people travelling in a city. **(b)** .... the people are using the Underground, **(c)** .... in the second photo the woman is cycling in the road. **(d)** .... the first photo shows a big crowd of people waiting on the platform **(e)** .... in the second one the woman seems to be alone and is on the move. **(f)** .... the cyclist the people in the station seem unhappy – maybe they're impatient to get home. **(g)** .... is that in the Underground there can't be much fresh air, while the cyclist is outdoors and so the air is probably better.

(h) .... is that there are problems with both ways of travelling around the city. In the Underground you don't have much space and it's probably quite difficult to sit down when it's busy. But I think it can be very dangerous cycling in a big city. At least the woman in the photo is wearing a helmet though. Also, when it rains it isn't nice to be cycling.

SPEAKING BANK

Useful expressions to compare and contrast photos

- Both photos show …
- In both photos,
- One similarity is that …
- In the first/second photo,
- One big difference between the photos is that …
- Another important difference …
- Compared with …
- The first photo shows … whereas/while the second photo shows …

4 SPEAKING **Work with a partner. Use the phrases in the Speaking bank to talk about the similarities and differences between the photos in 1.**

PRACTICE MAKES PERFECT

5a SPEAKING **Work with a partner. Student A, look at the photos below. Student B, look at the photos on page 158. Think about the similarities and differences between your two photos.**

5b Student A, do the task below. Student B, listen to your partner.

Compare the photos and say how you think the people feel in these situations.

5c Now change roles. Student B, your task is on page 158.

A story

1 SPEAKING **Work with a partner. Read the task and think of some ideas for a story.**

We want stories for our new international magazine for teenagers. Your story must begin with this sentence:

I was both excited and nervous as I stood there waiting at the airport.

Your story must include:
- **a surprise**
- **a journey**

2 **Read this story. Are there any similarities with your ideas?**

I was both excited and nervous as I stood there waiting at the airport. It wasn't the first time that I had flown, but it was the first time I was travelling on my own. I had been waiting for this trip for a long time.

Four months ago, I had applied for a place at an astronomy summer camp near Florence, Italy. Astronomy became my main hobby at the age of eight after receiving a small telescope as a present from my parents. So it was a brilliant surprise when I learnt that they had given me a place at the camp!

Luckily, my plane took off on time. It was a short flight and we were soon preparing for landing. Having collected my luggage, I immediately saw a sign with my name on it. A small group of students from the camp were there waiting for me.

The camp was an amazing experience. There were students from all over the world, all with the same interest in astronomy. Every night we would observe the stars using different telescopes, helped by expert teachers. The camp was away from the city and the skies were clear so visibility was perfect. But, apart from learning more about astronomy, I also made some great friends.

It was a trip that I'll never forget.

3 **Would this type of trip interest you? Why/ Why not?**

4 **Put the events of the story (a–g) in order.**

1 .... 2 .... 3 ....
4 .... 5 .... 6 ....
7 ....

a The narrator applied for a place at an astronomy camp.
b The narrator had an amazing time at the camp.
c The narrator went to the airport.
d The narrator became interested in astronomy.
e Some people from the astronomy camp went to meet the narrator.
f The narrator got a telescope.
g The narrator had a brilliant surprise.

5 **Look at the advice in the Writing bank. Find examples in the story in 2 for each one.**

Variety of past tenses – past continuous: we were soon preparing for landing.

WRITING BANK

Useful language for writing stories

- Use a variety of past tenses: the past simple, past continuous, past perfect simple and continuous, and *used to/would*.
- Use participle clauses:
  Looking up, she saw …
  After looking up, she saw …
  Having looked up, she saw …
- Use linkers of time and sequence:
  Last weekend, Three years ago, On Friday …
  At first, Next, Then, After that, Finally, In the end …
- Use adjectives and adverbs to make the story more descriptive.

EXAM SUCCESS

When you write a narrative, make sure that the main events of the story are clear. Before you begin writing, plan the beginning, the middle and the end. Don't forget to describe scenes and give background information, too.

➤ EXAM SUCCESS page 145

PRACTICE MAKES PERFECT

6a **Look again at the task in 1 and plan your own story. Think about the main events, the background and any important scenes.**

6b **Write your story. Remember to follow the advice in the Writing bank and Exam success.**

WRITING BANK ➤ PAGE 152

Grammar reference

be going to, will, present continuous and present simple for future

1 We use **be going to** to talk about plans and arrangements for the future, i.e. things that we have already decided to do in the future.

They've decided that they're going to fly to Dublin.

2 We can also use **be going to** to make predictions about the future, particularly when we have evidence for the prediction.

The sun is up already. I think it's going to be hot today.

3 We use **will** and **won't** to make general predictions about the future. We often use *think*, *hope*, *expect*, *imagine*, etc. with **will** and **won't** to show that our prediction is based on thoughts, opinions and expectations.

I think humans will land on Mars one day.

4 We also use **will** and **won't** for decisions made at the moment of speaking, for example when we suddenly offer to do something for someone.

A: *I can't answer the phone. My hands are wet.*
B: *I'll get it for you.*

5 We use **will** and **won't** to talk about the future when we consider it to be a future fact.

Next week it will be my birthday.

6 We use the **present continuous** to talk about plans and arrangements that have been confirmed.

Tomorrow I'm having my first job interview. They called me for the interview last week.

7 We use the **present simple** with time expressions like *when*, *as soon as*, *by the time*, *until*, *after* and *before*. We cannot use *will* with these time expressions.

When I go to university, I'll study chemistry.

8 We can also use the **present simple** to talk about the future when the action is part of a timetable or routine.

Tomorrow I have my English class at 2 o'clock.

Future continuous

FORM

- We form the **future continuous** with *will/won't* + *be* + verb-*ing*.

USE

- We use the **future continuous** to talk about activities in progress at a particular moment in the future. The activities are in progress and so they are unfinished.

At this time tomorrow, he'll be flying to the US.

Future perfect simple

FORM

- We form the **future perfect simple** with *will/won't* + *have* + the past participle.

USE

- We use the **future perfect simple** to talk about activities that will be finished by a certain time in the future. We often use the preposition *by* with the future perfect simple. It means 'some time before'.

I will have gone to bed by midnight.

Future perfect continuous

FORM

- We form the **future perfect continuous** with *will/won't* + *have been* + verb-*ing*.

USE

- We use the **future perfect continuous** to talk about how long an activity has been in progress before a particular moment in the future. We often use the preposition *by* with the future perfect continuous. It means 'at that point'.

By 8 pm I'll have been revising history for five hours!

Vocabulary

Words connected with transport and travel astronaut • board (v) • crew • flight • gate • get in/off/on/out • high-speed train • journey • land (v) • launch (n, v) • motorway • orbit (n, v) • passenger • platform • rocket • spacecraft • space station • take off (v) • the Underground/subway/tube • traffic jam • travel • trip • voyage

Prefixes cooperate • disadvantage • disagree • disappear • discomfort • disobey • illogical • impatient • impossible • incapable • incomplete • interactive • invisible • irregular • irresponsible • miscalculate • misunderstand • overbook • overpopulated • postgraduate • reinvent • rewrite • subway • sub-zero • superhuman • supersonic • unbelievable • underestimate • underpaid • unexpected • unlikely • unnecessary • unsuccessful

Other words and phrases ➤ page 138

Grammar revision

Future forms — / 6 points

1 Make the correct future form of the verbs. Use *will*, *be going to* or the present simple/continuous.

1 Get your books ready before the teacher .... (come).
2 **A:** I can't do this! **B:** I .... (help) you.
3 Last week I took a decision. Next year I .... (do) more exercise.
4 Mark and Jenny .... (get) married next Saturday.
5 I think computers .... (take) over the world one day.
6 The coach .... (leave) at 8.10 tonight.

/ 6 points

2 Which sentence in 1 ...

a is a confirmed plan or arrangement? ....
b is a prediction based on an opinion? ....
c is an event that is part of a timetable or routine? ....
d is a plan or intention? ....
e is a decision taken at the moment of speaking? ....
f has a special tense after a time expression? ....

Future continuous, future perfect simple, future perfect continuous — / 8 points

3 Tick (✓) the correct sentences and rewrite the incorrect ones.

1 I can't go out at 7 o'clock because I'll have done my homework then.
2 She started driving home at 3 pm. By 6 pm she'll have been driving for three hours.
3 Don't call me at 9 o'clock as I'll be watching a film.
4 I can write a summary of the book tomorrow because I'll be reading it by then.
5 At 5 o'clock next Saturday I'll have been playing basketball.
6 I can't give you my assignment tomorrow because I won't be finishing it.
7 I'll be wearing my new jacket when I go to Paul's party tomorrow.
8 When I'm 20, I'll have finished school.

Vocabulary revision

WORDS CONNECTED WITH TRAVEL AND TRANSPORT — / 8 points

1 Complete the sentences with the correct word.

1 Which p .... does our train leave from?
2 I work on this ship. I'm part of the c ....
3 The plane l .... on time despite the storm.
4 You rarely find a t .... j .... on the motorway.
5 We need to get to the g .... Our plane's about to leave.
6 Let's take the h ....-s .... train. If not, we'll be late.
7 I think six astronauts live in the s .... s ....
8 They're going to l .... the rocket tomorrow.

JOURNEY, TRAVEL, TRIP, VOYAGE — / 5 points

2 Complete the sentences with *journey*, *travel*, *trip* or *voyage*.

1 We went on a school .... to London.
2 I think .... is a great way to learn more.
3 Will astronauts make the long .... to Mars one day?
4 We were tired because the .... by plane and coach had lasted 18 hours!
5 Last year we went on a day .... to Brighton.

PREFIXES — / 7 points

3 Complete the sentences with prefixes added to the words in capitals.

1 Please don't .... me. I wasn't being serious, it was just a joke. UNDERSTAND
2 It was such a lovely surprise! Totally ...., thank you. EXPECT
3 I can't do it. I'm totally .... CAPABLE
4 I'm sorry, but there's no space on this flight. It's already .... BOOKED
5 I don't know why you did that. In my opinion, it was .... NECESSARY
6 Do what she says. Don't .... her. OBEY
7 She already has a degree in architecture. Now she's doing a .... course. GRADUATE

Total: / 40 points

4 Extraordinary talents

Vocabulary

Personality adjectives

1 SPEAKING **Work with a partner. Think of possible opposites for these words. Do you know any synonyms for the words?**

clever • friendly • hard-working • patient polite • quiet • reliable • serious • tidy

clever – opposites: slow, silly
synonyms: bright, intelligent

2 **Read this description of a teenager called Luke. Do you think you would like him? Why/Why not?**

Luke is one of my best friends, but we're very different. He's usually quite **shy** and **reserved**. When you go out with him to a party, he doesn't usually talk to many people, especially if he's never met them before. He's a very **sensitive** and **tactful** person. He does his best not to hurt anyone's feelings. In that sense, he's quite **mature**. He's really **gifted** and **talented**, too. He can play three instruments really well. But because he's so **modest** and **down-to-earth**, only his good friends know just how talented he is. His favourite type of music is classical, but he's quite **broad-minded**, musically speaking. He'll listen to any type of music as long as it's good. I don't want to give the idea that Luke is perfect though. He can be very **insecure** at times, especially when he starts worrying about how he's going to do in exams. And he can also be a bit **bad-tempered**, getting angry for no good reason. He's still a great friend though.

3 **Match the words in red in the text with their opposites. Which two words in the text do not have an opposite in the box? What do they mean?**

big-headed (2 words) • good-natured/easygoing immature • narrow-minded • outgoing (2 words) self-confident • tactless (2 words)

4 **From each pair of adjectives, choose the one that describes you the best. You can qualify the adjective with *very*, *quite* or *a little bit*.**

insecure/self-confident – I'm a little bit insecure.

5 SPEAKING **Work with a partner. Talk about the adjectives you chose in 4 and why.**

6 **Decide which adjective in each pair has a positive meaning and which has a negative meaning. Use a dictionary if necessary.**

1 ambitious/pushy
2 self-confident/arrogant
3 bossy/assertive
4 frank/brusque
5 stubborn/determined

7 LISTENING ▶ 18 **Listen to descriptions of three people. Write down two adjectives from this page to describe each one.**

1 ..../..........................
2 ..../..........................
3 ..../..........................

8a SPEAKING **Work with a partner. Decide what type of personality you need to do these jobs. Give reasons for your answers.**

1 a professional musician
2 the director of an international bank
3 the President
4 a Formula 1 driver
5 a TV presenter

8b **Discuss your ideas with the rest of the class.**

1 SPEAKING **Work with a partner. Look at the photos in the article and describe what you can see.**

2 **Read the article. Did the person in the photo have an easy childhood? Why/Why not?**

THE INCREDIBLE RISE OF DYNAMO

He's the British illusionist who walks on water and has hundreds of celebrity fans and friends. But he started doing tricks to stop his bullies at school.

Steven 'Dynamo' Frayne is no ordinary illusionist. During our interview a pack of cards appears to levitate from the table and land in his hand before disappearing. He continues talking, stops for a second, then takes the cards from his mouth.

As he explains to me, it's his job and his life's mission to amaze people. He believes that, as we get older, we all want to feel young again and that tricks and illusions can give us that feeling. Dynamo's shows certainly do that.

Steven grew up in one of the most dangerous areas in Bradford. Since his childhood, he has had a serious stomach illness. That meant that as a child he wasn't as strong as his classmates. Weak and shy, he was a target for bullies. When he was 11, his mum used to send him to school with two older kids, but they didn't look after him. One day he told his great-grandfather about it, who taught him a few tricks. From then on, Dynamo's life changed.

He demonstrates to me one of the tricks he learnt to stop the bullying. He asks me to pick him up, which I do easily. Then he looks at me for less than a second and tells me to do it again. Impossible! I try harder but can no longer lift him! Once he started doing tricks like this on the bullies, they left him alone. But their fear of him meant that nobody wanted to be near him. So he spent his time in his bedroom practising. The longer you practise, the better you get!

Thanks to that dedication and hard work, Dynamo is one of the most famous illusionists in the world today, but he's possibly the most modest, down-to-earth person you'll ever meet. He remembers how his career really started. When he had to spend six months in hospital because of his stomach illness, it was one of the worst times in his life. He started wondering how people would remember him if he died. This motivated him to make something of his life. He started doing tricks in the street. He talked his way backstage at concerts and did tricks for famous artists such as Snoop Dogg, One Direction and Coldplay. Soon he had a massive following on social media networks, with tens of millions of people worldwide watching his videos. Then came his own TV series which he has since sold to more than 190 countries, attracting 250 million viewers.

His ability to get attention was evident in 2011 when he amazed people by walking on the River Thames in London. At first, there were just 50 people watching, but soon there were thousands. He had walked halfway across the river when the police stopped him. So, how did he do it? Was there transparent plastic under the surface of the water? Even when you look more closely at the images, it's impossible to know.

> ***"The best distraction is an audience."***

'I can honestly say that if I started explaining it all,' Dynamo says, 'you'd be so bored you'd be begging me to stop after a minute.' After all, as he says, intrigue is the most powerful part of it.

Dynamo's illness has never gone away. But he finds that when he's working his stomach hurts him the least. 'The best distraction is an audience. My stomach hurts the least when I'm performing. Adrenaline stops me feeling any pain.' There can't be many people in the world who are so calm and easygoing about walking through windows or levitating above the tallest building in London. But Dynamo is no ordinary person.

3 **Read the text again and choose the best answers.**

1 Dynamo thinks that …
   - a doing tricks and illusions keeps him young.
   - b illusions can remind us of when we were young.
   - c people are less happy when they get older.

2 Other children used to bully Steven because …
   - a of his personality and build.
   - b he had a strange appearance.
   - c he had more money than them.

3 Dynamo got better at illusionism because …
   - a he needed new tricks to beat the bullies.
   - b he wanted people to be frightened of him.
   - c he had a lot of free time alone.

4 At the start of his career …
   - a famous people asked to see his tricks.
   - b he made his own TV series.
   - c he did his tricks outside on strangers.

5 Dynamo thinks people …
   - a wouldn't understand if he explained his illusions.
   - b are more impressed as they can't explain his tricks.
   - c don't like it when he explains his tricks.

4 **CRITICAL THINKING**

Think! Then compare ideas with your class.

- Why do you think Dynamo is so successful?

5 **What do the underlined words in the text mean? Guess and then check in your dictionary.**

6 SPEAKING **What about *you*?**

Do you like watching illusionists? Why/Why not?

Grammar in context

Flipped classroom: watch the video on the Resource Centre or Online Workbook.

Comparative and superlative adjectives and adverbs

1a Look at the sentences. Which contain comparative forms and which contain superlative forms?

1 I try **harder** but can no longer lift him.
2 He grew up in one of the **most dangerous** areas in Bradford.
3 Even when you look **more closely**, it's impossible to know.
4 He is **better** than the rest.
5 My stomach hurts the **least** when I'm performing.
6 He practises the **longest**.
7 It's **easier** for him to do a trick than explain it.

1b Look at the sentences again. Which contain adjectives and which contain adverbs?

GRAMMAR REFERENCE ➤ PAGE 54

2 SPEAKING **Work with a partner. Complete the table below and then explain the rules for the different groups of adjectives.**

Adjective	Comparative	Superlative
long slow		
big thin		
friendly tidy		
ambitious hard-working		
good bad far little (determiner)	 *less*	 *the farthest/the furthest*

For one-syllable adjectives, add -er to make the comparative.

3a Match the rules and examples for comparative and superlative adverbs.

1 We usually make comparative and superlative adverbs with *more* and *the most*.
2 With some irregular adverbs we add *-er* and *the -est*.
3 Some comparative and superlative adverbs are irregular.

a *well, bad, little*
b *carefully, quietly, easily, beautifully, often*
c *fast, hard, early, late, long, soon, near*

3b Make the comparative form of the adverbs in 3a (a–c).

4 Rewrite the sentences using the correct comparative and superlative form.

1 In my opinion, Caleb is the friendlier person in this class.
2 I think Emma is slightly taller that Claire.
3 That is definitely the most silly thing I've heard today!
4 You can write much quicklier on a computer than by hand.
5 Sorry I couldn't come more soon.
6 Is it much more further to your house?
7 You need to try more hardly if you want to be a professional illusionist.
8 Houdini was one of the more famous illusionists in the world.
9 That film was terrible! It's the less interesting film I've ever seen.
10 She did more well than me in the test.

5a SPEAKING **Work with a partner. Decide who in your class ...**

1 talks the fastest.
2 shouts the loudest.
3 speaks the most quietly.
4 draws the best.
5 runs the furthest.
6 arrives the earliest.
7 writes the most neatly.
8 laughs the most often.

5b Say one of the names you chose in 5a. Can your classmates guess the description?

Other ways of making comparisons

6 Look at the sentences and answer the questions a–c.

1 I tried **as** hard **as** the others.
2 He was **not as/so** big **as** his classmates.
3 When he works, his stomach is **less** painful **than** when he rests.
4 We get **older and older**.
5 **The longer** you practise, **the better** you get.
6 **The earlier** you start, **the easier** it is.

a When do we use *as ... as*?
b When do we use *not as ... as, not so ... as*, or *less ... than*?
c How do you say 4–6 in your language?

GRAMMAR REFERENCE ➤ PAGE 54

7 **Complete the second sentence so that it has a similar meaning to the first sentence, using the word given. Do not change the word given. You must use between two and five words, including the word given.**

1 Liam enjoys surfing the Net as much as playing computer games.
ENJOYABLE
For Liam, surfing the Net .... computer games.

2 Eating fruit and vegetables is healthier than eating fast food.
LESS
Eating fast food .... eating fruit and vegetables.

3 When you walk at a higher speed, you get more tired.
FASTER
The .... more tired you get.

4 Dylan thinks judo is better than karate.
NOT
For Dylan, karate .... judo.

5 Olivia is quick when she writes, and so is Amy.
AS
Amy writes .... Olivia.

6 Chinese is much harder to write than English.
DIFFICULT
English is .... than Chinese.

7 Basketball becomes easier depending on your height.
TALLER
The .... basketball becomes.

8 She's getting increasingly good at maths.
AND
She's getting .... at maths.

8 SPEAKING **Work with a partner. Match the halves of these common expressions. Check that you understand what they mean and then think of a situation when you might use them.**

1	The sooner	a	than done.
2	Better late	b	to worse.
3	Easier said	c	than never.
4	Better to be safe	d	the harder they fall.
5	The more	e	the merrier.
6	This is going from bad	f	the better.
7	The bigger they are	g	than sorry.

The sooner the better. You use it when you want something to happen as soon as possible, for example the start of the holidays.

Noun suffixes

1 **Look at these words. Each one contains a noun suffix. Which of the nouns are for a person?**

abil**ity** • act**or** • art**ist** • differ**ence** • direct**ion**
enjoy**ment** • ill**ness** • perform**ance**
politic**ian** • writ**er**

2 **Make nouns from these words using the suffixes in 1. You may need to change the spelling. Sometimes you can make more than one noun from each word.**

act • appear • confident • create • different
educate • electric • employ • happy • improve
invent • investigate • mad • music
relevant • science

3 **Complete the text below with the correct form of the words given.**

EXAM SUCCESS

In this type of exercise, you may need to add a prefix or a suffix or both. Sometimes the word needs to be plural. Look at the context carefully to decide.

➤ EXAM SUCCESS page 145

Sometimes you can get the impression that (a) .... (science) today spend all their time just improving high tech toys and phones. But just think of the (b) .... (important) of some of the biggest inventions of the past. Take (c) .... (electric), for example, or, more specifically, the electric light bulb. The (d) .... (create) of the light bulb is one of the key moments in human progress. Its (e) .... (invent) was the extraordinarily talented Thomas Edison. Edison's biggest skill was to take another person's idea and make (f) .... (improve) to it. Electric light bulbs meant the (g) .... (appear) of unsafe gas lighting. Before electric lights, people couldn't do much when it got dark at night. Edison gave people the (h) .... (able) to see at night. What a (i) .... (different) that made!

Learning about INTELLIGENCE

ACADEMIC SKILLS OBJECTIVES

- To find out about Gardner's Theory of Multiple Intelligences.
- To learn some study tips and think about the type of learner they can help.
- To find out which type of learner you are.

KEY CONCEPTS

general knowledge [n phr]: *In a general knowledge quiz, they ask things like 'What is the capital of France?'* **measure [v]:** *Many tests are used to try to measure intelligence.* **strength [n]:** *One of her strengths is her attention to detail.* **grasp [n, v]:** *I didn't grasp what you said. Can you explain it again?*

1 SPEAKING **Work with a partner. When we call somebody 'intelligent', what do we mean? Give examples of people you think are intelligent.**

2a Choose what you think is the best alternative. Think about why.

1 Intelligence *means/doesn't mean* knowing lots of facts.
2 There *is/isn't* just one type of intelligence.
3 You *can/can't* easily measure intelligence.
4 Your intelligence *stays/doesn't stay* the same throughout your life.
5 Your circumstances in life *affect/don't affect* your intelligence.

2b SPEAKING **Compare your answers with a partner.**

3 READING **Read a text about one theory of human intelligence. Which alternatives in 2a does the writer agree with? What arguments do they give to justify their answers?**

THE THEORY OF MULTIPLE INTELLIGENCES

When we talk about intelligence, some people have the idea that intelligence is what we need to answer general knowledge questions, such as *What is the capital of Venezuela?* or *How many legs does a spider have?* And when somebody knows the answers to all those questions, we say they're really clever or that they know a lot. The idea is that you're clever if you know a lot of facts and data. However, most experts would say that this is only one part or type of intelligence. There are other ways that we can think of intelligence, for example the creativity that you need in order to find answers to questions that you've never seen before, or to grasp new concepts.

This brings us to the American psychologist Howard Gardner. Gardner says that there isn't just one type of intelligence. There are what he calls 'multiple intelligences'. He talks about seven different types of intelligence, shown in the table opposite. Of course, each of us may be naturally strong in more than just one of these intelligence types.

When you look at the table, you can see that Gardner's multiple intelligences cover everything we do in our lives and is a much more complete and realistic way of thinking about intelligence. For example, we all know people who aren't so good linguistically, but who are very strong in logic or mathematics. We would probably all agree that this doesn't mean one person is more intelligent than another. They're both intelligent, but in different ways, with different strengths. One important reason for it not being very easy to measure intelligence is because it all depends on what type of intelligence we're talking about.

The good news is that most of Gardner's intelligences can be developed. With practice, you can learn to see things in a more scientific or logical way, or you can learn to appreciate literature or music. It is possible for children to become great musicians if they start early, and there are many bilingual or multilingual children in the world. The interesting thing here is that your life opportunities can make a big difference to your intelligence. If a child lives in an environment where they speak two languages they'll learn to understand and speak them. If somebody has access to a musical instrument and has lessons, we naturally expect them to learn more than somebody who doesn't. So intelligence is not just a question of being born intelligent. The environment you live in can make a huge difference.

4 Read the text again and answer these questions.

1. What does the writer say about knowing facts and data?
2. Why does the writer say that Gardner's theory is more realistic than the traditional view of intelligence?
3. According to the writer, why is it difficult to measure intelligence?
4. What examples does the writer give to show that intelligence is not just a question of being born intelligent?

GARDNER'S MULTIPLE INTELLIGENCES

1 LINGUISTIC
Includes reading, writing, talking, listening, poetry …

2 LOGICAL AND MATHEMATICAL
Includes ability with numbers, legal thinking …

3 SPATIAL
Includes driving, navigating a boat or plane …

4 MUSICAL
Includes playing an instrument, composing music …

5 BODILY-KINAESTHETIC
Includes sports, drama, making things …

6 INTERPERSONAL
Includes understanding other people, communicating with them, helping them …

7 INTRAPERSONAL
Includes understanding yourself, reflection …

5 Look at the table of Gardner's Multiple Intelligences. Where do you think these go?

a dance
b singing
c literature
d architecture
e being in control of yourself
f scientific thinking
g teaching people

6 SPEAKING **Work with a partner. What do you think of Gardner's Theory of Multiple Intelligences? Do you agree with it? Why/Why not?**

7 LISTENING 19 **Watch or listen to Deana talking about study tips. Make notes about her study tips for each intelligence 1–7.**

Intelligence 1: ....
Intelligence 2: ....
Intelligence 3: ....
Intelligence 4: ....
Intelligence 5: ....
Intelligence 6: ....
Intelligence 7: ....

8 SPEAKING **Work with a partner. Talk about each tip. Which of these things do you already do? Which would you like to try? Why?**

ACADEMIC TASK

Find out what type of learner you are.

Follow this plan:

1. *Do the Multiple Intelligence Test on page 159.*
2. *Work with a partner. Talk about your results in the test. Do you agree with the results? How might the results help you in your studies?*
3. *Do some research to find a study tip or activity that can help learners with your natural strengths. When you are ready, work in groups and share your tips and activities.*

Listening

Free climbing in the mountains

1 SPEAKING **Work with a partner. Look at the photo and answer these questions.**

1 Would you like to be in this situation? Why/Why not?
2 What type of people do you think normally do this type of activity?
3 How much training do you think you need to do this?

2 LISTENING 20 **Listen to two people talking about a new TV series. Are these statements True (T), False (F) or is the information Not Mentioned (NM)?**

1 For Sue Wilson, there wasn't much competition for best programme of the week. T/F/NM
2 She had the wrong idea about the programme *Hidden Talent* at first. T/F/NM
3 To make this programme, they invited people with special talents to do tests. T/F/NM
4 Maggie Reenan had always wanted to try rock climbing. T/F/NM
5 Being a nurse was possibly an advantage for Maggie when rock climbing. T/F/NM
6 Being able to detect lies is quite a common ability. T/F/NM
7 With the FBI, Brenda Chamberlain watched videos of suspects again and again. T/F/NM
8 Sue thinks that Maggie never knew about her talent before because she never had time for herself. T/F/NM

3 20 **Listen again and answer the questions.**

1 How many people did the tests for *Hidden Talent*?
2 How many tests did they do?
3 What do you know about Maggie's family situation?
4 How high was the rock she climbed?
5 What often makes the rock more difficult to climb?
6 How many people do they say have a strong ability for detecting lies?
7 What two things did the FBI teach Brenda?
8 What did the programme make Sue think?

4 SPEAKING **What about *you*?**

1 Would you like to watch this TV series? Why/Why not?
2 Would you like to do tests to see if you have a hidden talent? Why/Why not?

Grammar in context

Articles

1 **Read these sentences.**

1 There was **a** programme that stood out.
2 **The** programme was **the** first in **the** series.
3 **[–]** Nurses treat **[–]** patients in **[–]** emergencies.
4 You could be **the** best diver in **the** world.

2 **Match the sentence halves to make rules. Find an example of each rule in a sentence in 1.**

1 We use *a/an* …
2 We use *the* …
3 We use *the* …
4 We use *the* …
5 We use no article …

a to talk about a singular countable person or thing for the first time, or to say that the person or thing is one of a number of people or things.
b to talk about a specific person or thing or a person or thing mentioned before.
c to talk about things in general in the plural.
d to talk about someone or something that is unique.
e with superlative adjectives, adverbs, *first* and *last*.

GRAMMAR REFERENCE ➤ PAGE 54

3 **Choose the correct alternative.**

1 In general, I think *the/[–]* teachers can help *the/[–]* young people to develop their talents.
2 Last night I saw *a/[–]* programme about *a/the* young girl who has *a/the* really good voice.
3 Did you read *a/the* book I gave you yesterday about *the/[–]* science?
4 I reckon she's *the/[–]* better than most TV presenters.
5 *A/The* biggest problem with *a/the* world today is that we are all too busy.
6 I've got *a/the* friend who trains *the/[–]* animals to appear in *the/[–]* films.
7 Last week I read *an/the* article about *the/[–]* first episode in *a/the* new comedy series.
8 I think *the/[–]* rock climbers do *the/[–]* most amazing things.

4 **Complete the text with *a, an, the* or *[–]*.**

I've got (a) ………… friend who has (b) ………… amazing talent. She has (c) ………… incredible memory. She's really good at remembering (d) ………… faces. She once met (e) ………… man for just a few seconds. When she saw (f) ………… man again six months later, she recognised him immediately, even though (g) ………… clothes he was wearing were completely different and now he had (h) ………… beard. I'm exactly the opposite. I think I have (i) ………… worst memory in (j) ………… world!

5 Read the text and correct seven mistakes in the use of articles.

One of the most interesting episodes of *Hidden Talent* was about a boy called James Whinnery. He was only 19. They discovered that the boy had a special talent for the languages. He learnt the Arabic in just 19 weeks. He did a test working in Turkish restaurant for a day, talking to the waiters in Arabic. Then, for his training, they say he learnt the new words – one hundred words each day! At the end of the episode, he travelled to Jordan and they interviewed him in Arabic on a special programme. Of course, nobody can really learn new language in just 19 weeks. But James learnt a lot of things in that time. It seems that sometimes the TV programmes can have positive effect on people and their lives.

so, such, too, enough

6 Look at these sentences and complete the rules below with *so, such, too* or *enough*.

- a The weather is usually **so** bad that it can be a scary experience.
- b She did it **so** well.
- c It's **such** a difficult climb that you usually need many years of experience.
- d It's **such** a pity.
- e She's always been **too** busy to find the time.
- f She was(n't) good **enough** to do it.

1. We use .... to say if something is or isn't excessive. It comes before an adjective or adverb.
2. We use .... to say if something is or isn't sufficient. It comes after an adjective or adverb.
3. We use .... to intensify a noun (with or without an adjective). If the noun is singular we use *a/an* before the noun.
4. We use .... to intensify an adjective or adverb.
5. We use *to* + infinitive after .... and ....
6. We use *that* after .... and ....

GRAMMAR REFERENCE ➤ PAGE 54

7 Complete the sentences with these words. You can use the words more than once. If no word is necessary, put [–].

a • enough • so • such • to • too

1. I'm 15, so I'm .... young to vote in a general election.
2. It's such .... beautiful day today.
3. She isn't tall .... to get the book off the top shelf.
4. It's too late .... say that you're sorry.
5. I have such .... good memories of living by the sea.
6. The film was .... exciting I watched it twice.
7. When you're 18, you're old .... to drive in most countries.
8. Rebecca and Christine are .... good friends that they seem like sisters.
9. I love that band. Their music is .... good!

8 Complete the second sentence so that it has a similar meaning to the first sentence, using the word given. Do not change the word given. You must use between two and five words, including the word given.

1. That artist does such good pictures that everyone copies her. **SO**
   That artist's pictures .... copies her.
2. The water was so cold we couldn't swim. **TOO**
   The water was .... swim.
3. Her paintings are so good you could sell them. **ENOUGH**
   Her paintings .... sell.
4. It was so cold that day that they stayed at home. **SUCH**
   It was .... they stayed at home.
5. He's so insecure that he'll never be a good leader. **SELF-CONFIDENT**
   He .... be a good leader.
6. Kate doesn't sing very well so she won't become a professional singer. **ENOUGH**
   Kate doesn't .... to become a professional singer.

9a Use your imagination to complete these sentences.

1. They've got such a big house that …
2. There was a woman who was so rich …
3. My friend is so quiet …
4. I knew somebody who was too lazy to …
5. We aren't fit enough to …
6. I'm such a good student that …
7. My friend is so clever …

9b SPEAKING **Work in small groups. Compare your sentences in 9a. Choose the best ones and tell them to the rest of the class.**

Presentations – 1

A

B

C

D

1 SPEAKING **Work with a partner. Talk about the people in the photos. Who are they and why are they famous?**

2 SPEAKING **How would you define a 'hero'? Would you call any of the people in 1 heroes? Why/Why not?**

3 SPEAKING **Work with a partner. Look at the presentation topic and discuss if you agree or disagree with the statement. Make notes of your ideas. Think of arguments to justify and explain your opinions.**

'There are no heroes in today's world, just celebrities.'
Do you agree? Why/Why not?

4 LISTENING 21 **Listen to a student giving a presentation on this topic. What is their opinion? Do they mention any of your ideas in 3?**

5 21 **Listen again and tick (✓) the expressions in the Speaking bank that you hear.**

SPEAKING BANK

Useful expressions to structure a presentation

Beginning your presentation

- I'd like to begin by saying …
- To start with …
- The first thing I'd like to say is …
- I'm going to talk about …

Ordering your arguments

- First of all,
- Firstly,
- Secondly,
- Another thing is that,
- Furthermore,
- What's more,
- It's important to remember that …
- It's also true that …

Concluding your presentation

- In conclusion,
- Finally,
- To sum up,
- Last but not least,
- The point I'm trying to make is …
- In short,

6 **Organise your notes from 3 in a logical order, with an introduction and a conclusion.**

7 SPEAKING **Work with a partner. Read the advice in Exam success. Take it in turns to give a presentation with your opinion. Remember to use expressions from the Speaking bank. When you finish, discuss how well you did your presentations.**

✓ EXAM SUCCESS

When you give a presentation remember that you can look at your notes, but don't just read them aloud. Don't forget to look at your audience to see if they understand you and are interested.

➤ EXAM SUCCESS page 145

PRACTICE MAKES PERFECT

8a SPEAKING **Prepare a presentation about somebody that you admire. Give reasons why you admire them. It can be a famous person or someone in your life, for example a friend or relative.**

8b **Give your presentation to the class.**

An article – 1

1 SPEAKING **Work with a partner. Read this announcement and talk about people that you could write about and what talents they have.**

Young journalist

Articles wanted

Extraordinary talents!

We want to know who you think are the most talented people in the 21st century!

Write about one famous person who you think has extraordinary talents. Describe them and what they do. It could be an actor, singer, musician, writer, artist ... anyone with an amazing talent!

Send us your articles ... now!

2 Read an article written about the singer Ed Sheeran. What talents does the writer of the article say that Ed Sheeran has? Make a list.

Ed Sheeran

A How many good singers are there today? Hundreds, maybe? But how many can write great songs? And how many can perform a whole concert on their own, without any other musicians? In my opinion, there's only one, and his name is Ed Sheeran.

B Apart from his red hair, Ed Sheeran doesn't look very special. Maybe that's also because he tends to wear normal clothes like jeans and T-shirts. But when he starts to sing, you can tell that he is in fact incredibly special. As for his personality, what I love about him is that he's modest, funny and friendly.

C One of Ed Sheeran's most important talents is that he can play and sing in lots of different styles. For example, he has some very romantic songs, but he also raps sometimes. Another of his great talents is being able to write lyrics. He usually writes about down-to-earth things that young people understand. He also makes brilliant videos. In one video, he shows that he's a talented dancer, too!

D Ed Sheeran is already a great singer and performer. But the most exciting thing is that he's still very young. Just watch how he gets better and better!

3 Match the paragraphs A–D to these topics.

- Brief conclusion ....
- The person's name/introductory information about them ....
- The person's main talent(s) ....
- The person's appearance and personality ....

4 Read the Writing bank and underline examples in the article in 2.

WRITING BANK

Useful language in descriptions

- He/She seems ...
- He/She looks ...
- He/She is very/really/extremely + 'normal' adjectives (*good, big* ...)
- He/She is completely/totally/absolutely/really + 'extreme' adjectives (*fantastic, huge* ...)
- He/She is quite/rather + 'normal' adjectives
- He/She can be ...
- He/She tends to ...
- He/She has a ... side.
- He/She shows that ...
- What I like (most) about him/her is ...

5 SPEAKING **Use expressions in the Writing bank to talk about the people you chose in 1.**

What I like most about Daniel Radcliffe is his sense of humour.

PRACTICE MAKES PERFECT

6a Choose one person and write your article. Follow the paragraph plan in 3 and use expressions from the Writing bank.

6b When you finish writing your article, check it carefully. Have you included the relevant information? Is it easy to understand the ideas and information? Are there any grammar or spelling mistakes?

WRITING BANK ➤ PAGE 153

Grammar reference

Making comparisons

- We usually make **comparative and superlative adverbs** with ***more*** and ***the most***.
  carefully → more carefully, the most carefully
- With these adverbs we add ***-er*** and ***the -est***:
  fast → faster, the fastest
  late, long, soon, near, hard, early
- These adverbs are irregular:
  well → better, the best
  badly → worse, the worst
  little (determiner) → *less, the least*
- ***Less*** is the opposite of ***more***.
  *Animals are **less** intelligent **than** humans.*
  (= Humans are more intelligent than animals.)
- We use ***as … as*** to say two things are the same.
  *Dogs are **as** clever **as** cats.*
- We use ***not as … as*** or ***not so … as*** to say that the second person or thing is more … than the first one.
  *Animals **aren't as** intelligent **as** humans.*
  (= Humans are more intelligent than animals.)
- We use ***The* + comparative, *the* + comparative** to talk about two things that happen together.
  ***The** faster I run, **the more** tired I feel.*
  ***The** harder you study, **the better** your results.*
- We use **comparative and comparative** to talk about situations that are increasing.
  *Things are getting **better and better**.*

Articles

a/an

- We use ***a/an*** with singular countable nouns. We use it when we mention something for the first time, or to say that the person or thing is one of a number of people or things.
  *I've got **a** computer. It's **a** laptop.*
- We use ***a/an*** to say what somebody's profession is.
  *He's **a** scientist.*

the

- We use ***the*** with countable (singular and plural) and uncountable nouns. We use it to refer to something or somebody previously mentioned.
  *I've got a computer. **The** computer's really fast.*
- We also use ***the*** to talk about specific things or people.
  ***The** computer I bought was quite cheap.*
- We use ***the*** to talk about something unique, that there is only one of.
  the Sun, the government, the floor, the world
- We use ***the*** with superlative adjectives and adverbs, and with *first* and *last*.

No article

- We do not use an article with plural countable nouns or uncountable nouns when we are talking about people or things in general.
  Scientists say that animals have complex brains.

so, such, too, enough

- We use ***so*** to intensify an adjective or adverb.
  *She's **so** hard-working. She works **so** hard.*
- We use ***such*** to intensify a noun, with or without an adjective. We use ***a/an*** after ***such*** with a singular countable noun, but not with uncountable or plural nouns.
  *It's **such** a pity. He asks **such** difficult questions.*
- In sentences with a ***so*** or ***such*** clause we can continue the sentence with ***that***.
  *His theory is **so** complicated **that** I don't understand it.*
  *She's **such** a good boss **that** everybody loves her.*
- We use ***too*** to say that something is excessive. It is not the same as *very* because it has a negative meaning. ***Too*** comes before the adjective/adverb.
  ***A:** He's very clever.* (= positive)
  ***B:** Yes, but sometimes he's too clever.* (= negative)
- We use ***enough*** to say that something is sufficient and ***not enough*** to say that something is insufficient. It comes after adjectives/adverbs. We use *to* + infinitive after ***too/enough***.
  *He's gifted **enough** to win a Nobel Prize. I'm **not** patient **enough** to wait.*

Vocabulary

Personality adjectives ambitious • arrogant • assertive • bad-tempered • big-headed • bossy • broad-minded brusque • determined • down-to-earth • easygoing • frank • gifted • good-natured • immature • insecure mature • modest • narrow-minded • outgoing • pushy • reserved • self-confident • sensitive • shy • stubborn tactful • tactless • talented

Noun suffixes ability • action • activity • actor • appearance • artist • confidence • creation • creativity creator • darkness • difference • direction • education • electrician • electricity • employer • employment enjoyment • happiness • illness • importance • improvement • invention • inventor • investigation investigator • madness • musician • performance • politician • relevance • scientist • writer

Other words and phrases ➤ page 138

Grammar revision

Making comparisons / 8 points

1 Choose the correct alternative.

1 She doesn't work as *hard/hardly* as me.
2 My classmates are a lot less hard-working *than/as* me.
3 The sunnier it is, *it gets hotter/the hotter it gets*.
4 She speaks *faster/more fast* than anybody else I know.
5 The Theory of Relativity is not *as/so* difficult as people imagine.
6 They're the *most/more* confident people I know.
7 The sooner she finishes her work, the *earlier/earliest* she can get home.
8 When you rewrite your essay, do it more *careful/carefully* this time.

Articles / 7 points

2 There are no articles in these sentences. Add seven articles in the correct places.

1 I met friend yesterday in city centre.
2 Most important thing in life are good friends.
3 Experts say government is having problems.
4 When I'm bored I pick up book and read.
5 I like listening to actors and things they say about life in Hollywood.
6 Programmes I watch are all on late at night.

so, such, too, enough / 8 points

3 Match the sentence halves and complete the sentences with *so, such, too* or *enough*.

1 The test was .... long
2 My uncle was .... serious
3 My friend wasn't patient ....
4 He arrived .... late
5 It was .... a long film
6 He was strong ....
7 His assignment was .... bad
8 We stayed in .... a beautiful hotel

a to see the start of the film.
b that we didn't stay to see the end.
c that we've decided to go there again next year.
d to carry all the dictionaries.
e to wait for me.
f that he never laughed.
g that the teacher gave it a 0.
h to finish in just one lesson.

Vocabulary revision

PERSONALITY / 9 points

1 Complete the sentences with an appropriate adjective of personality.

1 A .... person is someone who is not very careful in the way they speak and behave.
2 He's very famous, but he's still modest and ....
3 A .... person is someone who accepts many different types of behaviour and is not easily shocked.
4 Being .... is the opposite of being self-confident.
5 If someone is ambitious but in a negative way, they are ....
6 His friends say he's determined, but other people say he's ....
7 She's 25, but she's quite .... because she acts like she's still a child.
8 A .... student is one who has an impressive natural ability.
9 Please be .... and tell me what you think.

NOUN SUFFIXES / 8 points

2 Put the words in the correct noun form.

1 One day she'd like to become a professional .... (MUSIC).
2 What an .... (IMPROVE). Your work is much better now.
3 Playing a sport well is often a question of .... (CONFIDENT).
4 They're spending more and more money on health and .... (EDUCATE).
5 There was no light, just .... (DARK) everywhere.
6 Who was the .... (CREATE) of Facebook?
7 The lights aren't working. We need to call an .... (ELECTRIC).
8 Your .... (APPEAR) is important in creating a good impression.

Total: / 40 points

Reading

> **➤ TIP FOR READING EXAMS**
>
> In missing sentence activities, remember …
> If there are gaps which you cannot complete, continue with other, easier gaps first and then go back later to the difficult ones.
>
> ➤ EXAM SUCCESS page 144

1 You are going to read a text called 'What makes a genius?' Before you read the article, answer the questions.

1 In your opinion, what is a genius?
2 How do you think somebody can become a genius?

2 READING **Read the text. What is the main message?**

3 Read the text again. Complete the gaps with sentences A–H.

A It's almost impossible to reach that number all by yourself.
B It's no good if you're still at high school.
C His father probably wrote down all the earliest pieces, and perhaps improved them in the process.
D The good but not great students had totalled 8,000 hours.
E Gates went to a very exclusive school.
F In fact, researchers have agreed on what they believe is a special number to become a true expert.
G But around the age of eight, real differences began to appear.
H By the time Gates left Harvard, he'd been programming non-stop for seven years.

4 SPEAKING **What about *you*?**

The text suggests that to be a genius you need to work hard and have opportunities. Do you agree? How important is natural talent?

WHAT MAKES A GENIUS?

In the early 1990s, the psychologist K. Anders Ericsson and two colleagues did some investigation at Berlin's elite Academy of Music. With the help of the academy's professors, they divided the school's violinists into three groups. First were the stars – the students with the potential to become world-class soloists. Second were those who were very good, but not as good as the stars. In the third group were the students who would probably never play professionally. All the violinists were to answer the same question: 'Over the course of your career, ever since you first picked up the violin, how many hours have you practised?'

Everyone, from all three groups, started playing at around the same age – around five. In those first few years, everyone practised roughly the same – two or three hours a week. **(1)** .... The students who would become the best in their class began to practise more than everyone else. Six hours a week by age nine, eight by age 12, 16 a week by age 14, until by the age of 20 they were practising well over 30 hours a week. By then, the elite performers had all totalled 10,000 hours of practice over the course of their lives. **(2)** .... And the third group just 4,000 hours.

This idea – that excellence at a complex task needs a critical, minimum level of practice – appears again and again in studies. **(3)** .... It's 10,000 hours. 'In study after study, of composers, basketball players, fiction writers, ice-skaters, concert pianists, chess players,' writes the neurologist Daniel Levitin, 'this number comes up again and again.'

This is true even of people we think as prodigies. Mozart, for example, famously started writing music at six. But, compared to the standards of mature composers, Mozart's early works are not outstanding. **(4)** .... People generally agree that Mozart didn't write his first masterwork until he was 21. By that time Mozart had already been composing concertos for ten years.

Ten thousand hours is, of course, an enormous amount of time. **(5)** .... You need parents who are encouraging and supportive. You can't be poor, because if you have to do a part-time job to earn money, there won't be enough time in the day.

Let's turn to the history of Bill Gates. A gifted young mathematician discovers computer programming. He leaves Harvard. Then he starts a little computer company called Microsoft with his friends. Being brilliant, ambitious and hard-working, he builds it into the giant of the software world. Now let's look more closely. **(6)** .... One year the school spent $3,000 on a computer terminal. From that moment on, Gates lived in the computer room, learning how to use this strange new machine. In one seven-month period in 1971, Gates and his friends ran up 1,575 hours of computer time.

(7) .... So, he had spent a lot more than 10,000 hours on computers. Very few teenagers at that time had the kind of experience Gates had.

January 1975 was the start of the personal computer age. Who was in the best position to take advantage of it? You don't want to be too young. **(8)** .... The perfect age to be in 1975 is young enough to see the coming revolution but not so old as to have missed it. You want to be 20 or 21, born in 1954 or 1955. When was Bill Gates born? 28 October 1955.

Use of English

➤ TIP FOR USE OF ENGLISH

In word formation cloze activities, remember …
To change the type of word, you will usually need a suffix (e.g. *-ion* to make a noun, *-ly* to make an adverb). To change the meaning of the word, you will usually need a prefix (e.g. *im-*, *re-*).

➤ EXAM SUCCESS page 145

5 Work with a partner. Make a list of things that you think you know about Albert Einstein. Then read this short text and see if it mentions any of the things on your list.

One exceptional talent in the world of science was, of course, Albert Einstein. As we all know, Einstein's fame and **(a)** .... came from his Theory of Relativity, which changed the way that the **(b)** .... community understood space and time. However, it's interesting to note that Einstein took an **(c)** .... long time to begin to speak. He didn't start until after his second birthday. He was also rebellious towards authority when he was at school. These two facts may have been the origin of a popular myth that the **(d)** .... was a bad student and that he failed at school. This is simply not true. We should not **(e)** .... his amazing **(f)** .... in science subjects. Einstein was already an outstanding **(g)** .... and a very good **(h)** .... when he was young. At 16 he wrote a brilliant essay that had a direct **(i)** .... with his later work on relativity. But the myth may also come from the fact that when he was 16 he tried, **(j)** ...., to get into the prestigious Federal Polytechnic in Zurich, failing some of the non-science subjects. The normal entrance age was 18, so he was two years younger than usual. The next year, when he was just 17, he passed!

(a) IMPORTANT
(b) SCIENCE
(c) USUAL
(d) SCIENCE
(e) ESTIMATE
(f) ABLE
(g) PHYSICS
(h) MATHEMATICS
(i) CONNECT
(j) SUCCESSFUL

6 Read the text again. Complete the gaps with the correct form of the words at the end of the lines.

Speaking

➤ TIP FOR SPEAKING EXAMS

In presentations, remember …
Don't speak too fast. If you do, people will not be able to follow you.

➤ EXAM SUCCESS page 145

7 Look at this topic. Prepare a presentation: make notes, but do not write complete sentences.

You can choose three famous, talented people to go on an excursion with. Who are you going to choose and why?

8 SPEAKING **Work with a partner. Brainstorm any expressions you know for …**

1 beginning a presentation.
2 ordering your arguments.
3 concluding a presentation.

9 SPEAKING **Work in groups. Take it in turns to give your presentations. Use expressions from 8.**

Writing

➤ TIP FOR WRITING EXAMS

In stories, remember …
Use a variety of past tenses and linkers of time and sequence to make it clear when the different events in the story happened.

➤ EXAM SUCCESS page 145

10 Work with a partner. Read this task and plan your story. Think about the main events, the background and any important scenes.

Your English teacher has asked you to write a story for the school magazine. Your story must begin with this sentence:
Jack didn't usually enjoy travelling, but today was different.
Your story must include:

- a famous person
- a competition

11 Write your story. Follow the advice in the Writing bank on page 152.

5 Money matters

Vocabulary

Buying and selling

1 SPEAKING **Work with a partner. How many different types of shop can you name in two minutes?**

2 **Complete the text with these words. Use a dictionary if necessary.**

afford • bargain • cash • change • discount
receipt • refund • sale • value for money • waste

SOPHIE'S BLOG

About | Follow | Contact

Pop Shop, in the Westgate shopping centre, are having a big weekend sale. I don't often buy clothes there because I can't (a) .... it, it's just too expensive for me. But yesterday they had a special (b) .... there and everything was cheaper than usual. They had a (c) .... of between 20% and 50% on most of the things there. I found a real (d) .... – a jacket that cost just £35 instead of £120! That's great (e) .... because it's really cheap for a jacket made by a top designer. I paid with the (f) .... that my parents gave me for my birthday. I gave the shop assistant a £50 note and they gave me £15 (g) .... I asked for the (h) .... because if you have problems afterwards you need to have proof that you bought it in that particular shop. Once I bought a coat, but then I decided I didn't like it. I didn't want to (i) .... my money so I took it back and, luckily, they gave me a (j) ....
Anyway, all bargain-hunters go down to Pop Shop! The sale ends at 5 pm today.

3 SPEAKING **Work with a partner. Ask these questions.**

1 Do you usually carry some change in your pocket?
2 How do your parents usually pay in shops?
3 Do you or your family usually buy things in the sales? What types of things?
4 Do you usually keep the receipt when you buy something? Why/Why not?
5 Have you or your family ever asked for a refund?
6 Do students get special discounts in your country?
7 Have you ever wasted your money? When?
8 What have you bought recently that was good value for money?

Money and banking

4 **Match these words and phrases with the definitions. Use a dictionary if necessary.**

ATM/cashpoint • bank charges/fees • bill
current account • get into debt • interest
lend money/give somebody a loan • overdraft
savings account • withdraw money

1 an agreement with your bank that allows you to spend money when there is no money in your account
2 a bank account that you use to keep and save money
3 give money to somebody for a period of time, after which they give it back
4 amount of money you have to pay a bank for the services that they give you
5 a bank account that you can take money out of when you want
6 take money from a bank account
7 money you get from a bank for keeping your money there, or money that you pay to a bank when you borrow money from them
8 a written statement saying how much money you owe for goods or services you have received
9 machine that gives you money when you put a bank card in it
10 start to owe money

5 LISTENING ▶ 22 **Listen and answer the eight questions. You will hear each question twice.**

1 ....
2 ....
3 ....
4 ....
5 ....
6 ....
7 ....
8 ....

6a PRONUNCIATION **How do you say these words? What do they all have in common?**

answer • business • climb • debt • doubt
eight • half • honest • knowledge • listen • litre
psychological • receipt • talk • through • written

6b ▶ 23 **Listen to the words and correct your pronunciation if necessary.**

1 SPEAKING **Work with a partner. Look at the photos in the article and answer the questions.**

1 How are they connected with the title of the article?
2 Do you think all the objects could be used as money? Why/Why not?

2 READING **Read the article and check your answers in 1.**

Money: A brief history

Whether we like it or not, money plays a central role in society today. We all use it, more or less every day. Because of the importance of money, we probably all ought to have a clear idea of the history of money, and how money works.

A world without money ...

Perhaps the easiest way to think about the role of money is to consider a world without it. We would have to barter for everything. In a barter economy, we need to exchange every item we want for something that we can provide. For example, a person who specialises in fixing cars and needs to trade for food must find a farmer with a broken car. But what if the farmer doesn't need to have his car fixed? Or what if the farmer only has eggs, more eggs than the mechanic can possibly use? The difficulty with this system is finding the right person to barter with.

The advantage of money is that you don't have to find 'the right person'. You just need to go to a market to sell your goods or services. You exchange these for a common medium of exchange – that is, money. You can then use that money to buy what you need from others who also accept the same medium of exchange.

Chocolate money?

Many different things have been used as money over the years, including cocoa beans, salt and cows. At first, the value of money was fixed by its alternative uses. For example, you could use the cocoa beans to make chocolate, or the salt to make food taste better. These uses give them a basic value. On the other hand, many people may want strawberries and be happy to trade for them, but they make poor money because they last for such a short time. There is also the problem that not everything of value is easy to divide, and standardising each unit is also hard. For example, not every strawberry has the same size or quality. So it is not easy to establish the value of strawberries.

Properties of money

So, money should be something that maintains its value over time, can be easily translated into prices, and be widely accepted. Precious metals such as gold and silver seem to serve all three needs. They are hard to obtain. There is a finite supply of them in the world. It is easy to divide them into standardised coins and they do not lose value over time or when made into smaller units.

Until relatively recently, the coins that people used were mainly made of gold and silver. But gold and silver are heavy. People had to carry their precious metals around all the time to exchange them for goods. Over time, people realised they needn't carry their gold and silver around with them. They could leave them at a bank and buy and sell using a note from the bank. But when they wanted their gold or silver again, they could go to the bank with their note and withdraw it.

Worthless notes

Eventually, the paper note or receipt was separated from the actual metal. And they stopped making coins with precious metals. When those links were broken, 'fiat money' was born and that is the money we use today. Fiat money, the cash we carry around with us, is materially worthless. But it has value simply because a nation collectively agrees to give a value to it. In theory, governments could print as much money as they liked. But they mustn't do this because it leads to higher prices and money loses its value. To ensure that governments don't just print money when they like, most countries today have given the task of deciding how much money to print to independent central banks.

3 **Read the text again and answer the questions.**

1 What happens in a 'barter economy'?
2 What does the story of the mechanic and the farmer demonstrate?
3 What is the first advantage of a system that uses money, not bartering?
4 Why did some people use cocoa beans or salt as money in the past?
5 Why are strawberries unsuitable for use as money?
6 Why were precious metals used as money?
7 What was the disadvantage of silver and gold?
8 What was the first 'paper money' like?
9 What is 'fiat money'?
10 Why can't governments print money when they like?

4 CRITICAL THINKING

Think! Then compare ideas with your class.

- How do you think money will evolve over time?

5 **What do the underlined words in the text mean? Guess and then check in your dictionary.**

6 SPEAKING **What about *you*?**

Do you think our society gives too much importance to having money? Why/Why not?

Flipped classroom: watch the grammar presentation video.

Modal verbs of obligation, prohibition and advice – present

1a Look at the sentences and answer the questions below.

a We **ought to** have a clear idea about money.
b It **should** be something that maintains its value.
c You **don't have to** find 'the right person'.
d The mechanic **must** find a farmer to get food.
e We all **have to** use money.
f Governments **mustn't** do that.
g You**'d better** keep your money in your pocket.
h They **aren't allowed to** print money when they like.
i People **need to** trade for food.
j You **needn't** carry it all with you.
k He **doesn't need to** have his car fixed.
l They **can't** do what they like.

Which grammatical structure(s) do we use to …
1 express obligation or necessity?
2 say there is no obligation or necessity?
3 say something is prohibited or not possible?
4 give advice or recommendations?

1b Answer these questions.

1 Which structures need *to* + infinitive? Which need the infinitive without *to*?
2 How do you make sentence e into a question?
3 How do you make sentences b and g negative?
4 How do you make sentence j affirmative?
5 Is '*d* short for *had* or *would* in sentence g?

GRAMMAR REFERENCE ➤ PAGE 68

2 Correct these sentences.

1 You don't have to give false information when you open a bank account.
2 Have you to sign your name on your credit card?
3 You needn't to open a bank account if you don't want to.
4 She would better get a credit card because it isn't safe to take lots of cash everywhere.
5 We ought ask for advice because we don't know much about banking.
6 Students don't need have a bank account, but it's a good idea to have one.

3 Complete the sentences with some of these words.

are • aren't • had • has • have • must
mustn't • needn't • needs • ought

1 You .... better hurry or you'll miss the bus.
2 My dad .... to wear a uniform because he's a firefighter.
3 We've just eaten. I think we .... to have a rest before we swim again.
4 14-year-olds .... allowed to drive.
5 You .... buy me a present for my birthday. I don't really want anything.
6 Parents always tell their children that they .... lie to them.

4 SPEAKING **Work with a partner. A British student is coming to study for one month at your school. Think of useful information to give them. Write one sentence with each of these modal verbs.**

~~are allowed to~~ • can't • don't have to
had better not • must • mustn't • needn't
ought to

In some classes we are allowed to use our mobile phones.

Modal verbs of obligation, prohibition and advice – past

5a Look at the sentences and answer the questions below.

a People **had to** carry their precious metals everywhere.
b With banks, people **didn't have to** take their silver and gold with them.
c They **needn't have carried** their silver and gold for so many years.
d They **weren't allowed to** print more money.
e They **needed to** find more suitable money.
f They **should**/**ought to have** used something that lasted longer.
g They **shouldn't have taken** that decision.
h They **didn't need to** take all their coins.
i He **couldn't** find the right person.

Which grammatical structure(s) do we use to:
1 express obligation and necessity in the past?
2 say that something happened but it was not necessary?
3 say that something was not necessary and maybe it happened or maybe it didn't?
4 say something was prohibited or not possible?
5 criticise a past action or say that it was a mistake?

5b Complete the structure.

should/shouldn't/ought to/needn't +
.... + ...

GRAMMAR REFERENCE ➤ PAGE 68

6 Write these sentences in the past.

1 You should ask them for advice.
2 She must arrive on time every morning.
3 Do you have to go to the meeting?
4 We mustn't wear jeans and T-shirts.
5 I don't need to get up early. (but I did)
6 She doesn't need to wear a uniform. (so she didn't)
7 We ought to work as a team.

7 Rewrite these sentences. Use each of these expressions once.

didn't have to • had to • needed to • needn't have • ought to have • shouldn't have • wasn't/weren't allowed to

1 I did the exercises last night because they were obligatory.

I ....

2 Taking food to the party was optional for us, but we took some.

We ....

3 She didn't revise for the exam and that was a big mistake.

She ....

4 They didn't have permission to go into the office.

They ....

5 It was necessary for the plane to land.

The plane ....

6 It wasn't necessary to show my receipt to the shop assistant, so I didn't.

I ....

7 I got angry with you yesterday and that was a silly thing to do.

I ....

8a Think about when you were at primary school. Write sentences about things that were obligatory, not obligatory, prohibited, and that you should/shouldn't have done. Use the structures in 5a.

In some classes we had to sit on the floor.

8b SPEAKING **Compare sentences in small groups. Were your experiences similar?**

Phrasal verbs connected with money and shopping

1 Look at the phrasal verbs used in these sentences and match them with the definitions.

1 If you want to buy a tablet, you should **set** some money **aside** each week.
2 The government say that they aren't going to **cut back** on education.
3 She lent me some money last week, but next week I have to **pay** it **back**.
4 The bill **comes to** £43.50.
5 He doesn't earn much, but it's enough for him to **get by**.
6 I **picked up** some amazing bargains in the sales.
7 I couldn't buy that new game because they'd already **sold out**.
8 She's going to **splash out** and buy that designer jacket.

a give someone the same amount of money they lent you
b save money from a larger amount to use it later
c reduce the amount of money you spend
d buy
e buy something expensive
f have just enough money so that you can do what you need to
g reach a total when you add all the parts together
h stop selling a product because there are no more available

2 Rewrite each sentence using one of the phrasal verbs above.

1 Can you buy some milk on the way home?
2 That coat is expensive, but I'm going to buy it.
3 We need to reduce the amount we spend on luxury items.
4 We haven't got much money, but we're surviving.
5 I can't go to the concert because I need money for the summer holidays.
6 You should buy the game now because they're disappearing fast.
7 I'll give you the money you lent me tomorrow.
8 The book was £10 and the magazine was £2.50 so the total was £12.50.

3 Choose the correct alternative.

1 Do you set any money _apart/aside_ each week or month? What for?
2 Does anybody need to pay you _back/up_ at the moment? Why?
3 Have you or your family ever splashed _away/out_ on something? What was it?
4 Have you ever gone to buy something and found that they had already sold _out/up_? What was it?
5 Do you usually have enough money to get _across/by_ each week?
6 Have you ever picked _away/up_ a bargain in the sales? What was it?

4 SPEAKING **Ask your partner the questions in 3. If they answer 'yes', ask questions to find out more information.**

Avoiding DEBT

LIFE SKILLS OBJECTIVES

- To learn about student debt and its different causes.
- To learn some tips to avoid getting into debt.
- To practise planning a simple budget.

KEY CONCEPTS

budget [n, v]: *She plans a budget to see how much money she has to spend.* **run out of (money) [v phr]:** *When you buy expensive things, you soon run out of money.* **expense(s) [n]:** *Students have new expenses like buying food and electricity bills.* **live on (sth) [v phr]:** *We live on £70. That's all we can spend to survive.* **be in/go into the red [v phr]:** *I had £100 in my account and I spent £150, so I've gone £50 into the red.*

1 **Work with a partner. Match the expressions with their definitions. Use a dictionary if necessary.**

1	peer pressure	a	the influence of famous people on other people's behaviour
2	celebrity culture	b	the influence that other people of your age have on you
3	payday loans	c	a credit card that you can use in a particular shop
4	store card	d	small, short loans with very high interest

2 **How do you think the things in 1 could encourage young people to spend too much money?**

3 READING **Read the article. What do these numbers refer to?**

750 3,657 38 1,509

New research has shown

50%

of all undergraduates run out of money before the end of the month

nearly

33%

of students blame 'unexpected expenses' for their financial problems

38%

admit that they splash out more often than they should

THE DANGERS OF DEBT

The Money Charity has already warned that some students in England may need as much as £750 a month to pay for their accommodation. This could leave the average English student with just £400 to live on each month.

But expert Vivi Friedgut said the majority of students still do not use their money efficiently: 'The biggest cause of unnecessary debt is peer pressure. That, combined with the influence of celebrity culture and constant invitations to access credit, tempts many to spend money they don't have. Debt is the new normal for students.'

One charity called StepChange has revealed that students who called its helpline had average debts of £7,818. Seventy-five per cent of those callers had gone into the red on their overdrafts, owing an average of £1,509, while more than 50% needed help with credit-card debt, typically worth £3,657. And 21% of student inquiries to the charity's helpline last year related to payday-loan debt, at an average of £1,069 per person.

Jonathan Chesterman, advice manager at StepChange, said: 'Students must be aware of the risks of high-cost forms of credit, such as payday loans and store cards, which can quickly get out of control due to the high levels of interest and charges.'

Linda Isted, communications manager at the Debt Advice Foundation, said: 'The problem is that so many financial companies are throwing credit at students, with banks in particular throwing credit cards and overdrafts in their direction. There is not enough financial education at school or in the home to teach young people how to deal with those messages.'

“The biggest cause of unnecessary debt is peer pressure. ... Debt is the new normal for students.”

4 Read the article again and decide if the statements are True (T) or False (F).

1 Over a third of undergraduates say that they buy expensive things more often than they really should. T/F

2 Students generally spend less on accommodation than on other things. T/F

3 Students who called the StepChange helpline got into debt because of either overdrafts, credit cards or payday loans. T/F

4 Linda Isted thinks that the danger is that some companies are trying to make it easy for students to spend more than they have. T/F

5 She also thinks teachers and parents should help young people to know more about credit and debt. T/F

6 The only financial help that universities give students is on the phone. T/F

7 Vivi Friedgut recommends paying for things with cash to control your spending. T/F

8 She also says that the bigger the overdraft you get, the better. T/F

Both StepChange and the Debt Advice Foundation offer help in creating budgets and action plans to control spending and reduce debt. Most universities and colleges now offer some form of face-to-face debt advice service as well as an out-of-hours phoneline, thanks to the Association of Student Money Advisers. Many universities also provide small emergency loans for students in need.

"There is a massive danger with debit cards. ... Limiting yourself to cash really helps you to control your spending."

Ms Friedgut advises withdrawing a certain amount of cash from an ATM each week to spend in local shops or on the high street. 'There is a massive danger with debit cards. Companies like these methods because they encourage customers to spend money. Limiting yourself to cash really helps you to control your spending.'

If you run out of cash, you should resist the temptation to use your debit card so you can learn to live within your limits. For that reason, it may also be sensible to avoid accounts that offer large overdrafts so that you do not borrow without a very good reason. It's also important to get into the habit of checking your bank account regularly. This has now become easier with new online banking services and apps.

Finally, don't be afraid to discuss money with your friends. Suggest free or cheap things to do and search websites such as savethestudent.org for good deals. Using an NUS (National Union of Students) discount card and a Young Person's 16–25 Railcard will also help you to make valuable savings.

5 SPEAKING Work with a partner. Ask these questions.

1 Who does the writer say is responsible for many students being in debt – students themselves, banks and other financial institutions, or both? Why?

2 Does the writer say that anybody else is responsible? If so, who?

3 Who do *you* think is responsible and why?

4 In the last half of the text, what suggestions do they give for avoiding getting into debt?

5 Which of those suggestions in the last three paragraphs do you like and why?

6 LISTENING 24 Watch or listen and answer the questions.

1 Why should teenagers think about budgeting?

2 What are the top tips for avoiding debt?

3 What are the steps involved in planning a budget?

4 Why is it important to keep a record of what you spend each month?

5 How does modern technology affect the way we spend money?

7 24 Watch or listen again. Write down Tope's suggestions about how to manage your money. How many of the things do you do? Discuss your answers in pairs.

LIFE TASK

You want to plan a simple budget.

Follow this plan:

1 *Read the information about a student called Samara on page 159.*

2 *Use the information to plan a monthly budget for Samara using your answers in 6.*

3 *Work in a small group. Compare your budgets. Are they similar or not? Do you agree about what is essential and non-essential?*

Listening

1 SPEAKING **Work with a partner. Look at the photo. What do you think it represents?**

2 **Read the text, ignoring the gaps. Do you think Bitcoins are good or bad? Why?**

Bitcoins are completely **(a)** .... They only exist as **(b)** .... which you keep in your smartphone or computer. There are three ways to get Bitcoins. You can buy them with **(c)** .... money. You can sell things and let people pay for them with Bitcoins. Or you can actually create Bitcoins through a process called **(d)** .... To make your own Bitcoins, your computer has to solve a complicated mathematical problem. These problems are becoming increasingly more **(e)** ....

Bitcoins are not controlled by banks or **(f)** .... One consequence of this is that the value can change **(g)** .... Another consequence is that it appears that some **(h)** .... use them.

The creator of Bitcoins used the name Satoshi Nakamoto. Journalists found a man with this name in **(i)** ...., but he was **(j)** .... and suffering from an illness. The creator of Bitcoins obviously didn't want people to know details about his **(k)** .... His collection of Bitcoins might be worth more than a **(l)** .... dollars.

3 SPEAKING **Work with a partner. Predict what words or types of word could go in each gap.**

✔ EXAM SUCCESS

When you need to listen and complete notes, always read the incomplete notes *before* you listen. This helps you to know what to listen for. Look carefully at the words that come just before or after each gap and think about the meaning and *type* of word that is missing.

➤ EXAM SUCCESS page 145

4 LISTENING ▶ 25 **Listen to an interview with an expert on Bitcoins. Complete the text in 2 with one word or number in each gap.**

5 SPEAKING **What about *you*?**

Would you buy or use Bitcoins? Why/Why not?

Grammar in context

Modal verbs of speculation and deduction – present and future

1 **Look at these sentences and complete the rules below with the verbs in blue.**

- **a** A cyber-criminal **might** steal or destroy your money.
- **b** It **must** be easy to become a millionaire if you can make your own money!
- **c** This **may** or **may not** be true.
- **d** Bitcoins **might not** be such a good idea.
- **e** It **can't** be long before physical money disappears.
- **f** It **could** take years to get just one Bitcoin.

1. We use ...., ... and .... when there is a 50% possibility that something is or will be true. The negative forms are .... and .... We cannot use the negative form of .... when there is a 50% possibility that something isn't true.
2. We use .... when we are 90% certain that something is true.
3. We use .... when we are 90% certain that something isn't true.
4. When we are speculating and making deductions, the opposite of *must* is ....

GRAMMAR REFERENCE ➤ PAGE 68

2 **Look at these things. What do you think they may, must or can't be? Explain why.**

A
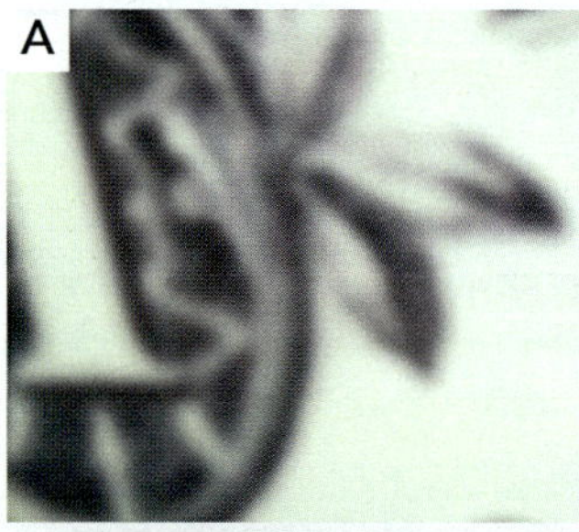
B
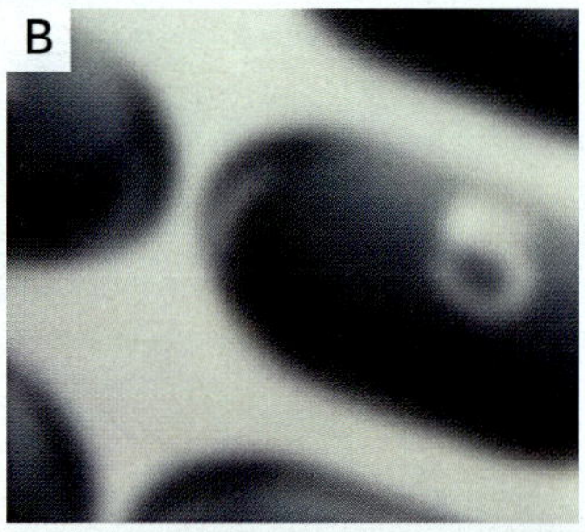
C

D
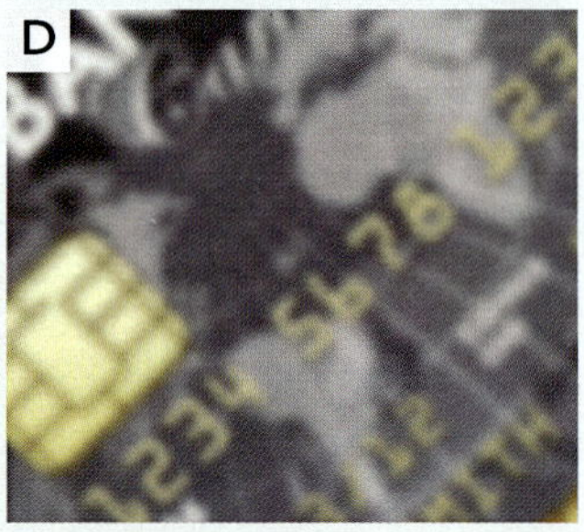
E

3 Complete the sentences with *must, can't, may* or *might (not).*

1 That .... be Jack's wallet because his is brown and this one's black.
2 He's seen that film ten times. He .... love it.
3 It's unusual that Beth hasn't come to school yet. She .... be well, or perhaps her bus is just late.
4 I .... go to the party tomorrow, but I'm not sure. I hope my parents let me.
5 She .... have a lot of money because she spends a fortune on clothes.
6 He .... play the guitar very well because nobody wants to listen to him.
7 It .... be hard to become a millionaire because not many people manage it.
8 My parents .... lend me some money or they .... I don't really know because I've never asked them before.

Modal verbs of speculation and deduction – past

4 Look at these sentences and complete the rules below with the verbs in blue.

a He **must have made** a lot of money from Bitcoins.
b It **can't have been** him because he didn't know what Bitcoins were!
c He **may**/**might**/**could have used** a Japanese pseudonym.
d He **mightn't**/**may not have been** the inventor.

1 We use .... , ... and .... when there is a 50% possibility that something was true, but we cannot use .... in the negative form with this meaning.
2 We use .... when we are 90% certain that something was true.
3 We use .... when we are 90% certain that something wasn't true.

GRAMMAR REFERENCE ➤ PAGE 68

5 Correct the mistakes in these sentences.

1 It's only lunchtime and you look terrible. You must have a bad morning.
2 Somebody's unlocked the door. It must have been Mike because he hasn't got a key.
3 I think Josh might sent me an email last night.
4 Emma hasn't replied to my email. She mightn't has received it.
5 William isn't here. He must have went already.
6 Let's not buy her that DVD. I'm not sure, but I think she might buy it already.
7 You can't be read that book already! It's 600 pages long and you only started yesterday!
8 It mustn't have rained last night because all the streets are dry.

6 Complete the text with past modal verbs of speculation and the verbs given.

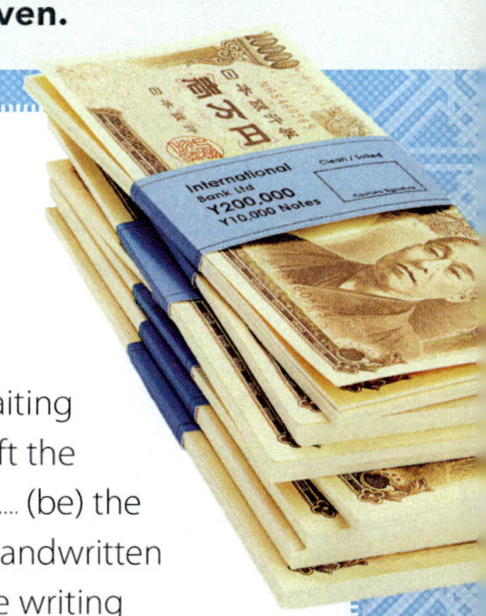

Something very mysterious happened in Tokyo a number of years ago. For a few weeks many civil servants who went to the toilet found a 10,000 yen note (around £50) waiting for them. Nobody knows who left the notes, but it **(a)** .... (be) the same person because they left handwritten messages with the notes and the writing was always the same. They are quite sure that a woman **(b)** .... (leave) the notes because they always appeared in the men's toilet. More than 425 people found notes, so the man **(c)** .... (have) a lot of money. He always left the message 'Please be happy' with the money. This suggests that the man **(d)** .... (be) happy himself, but, of course, we can't be sure. Again, nobody can be sure, but other people think that the man **(e)** .... (work) as a civil servant himself once and he gave the money away to make other civil servants happy. One thing is clear, he **(f)** .... (move) quickly because in one morning he left 18 ¥10,000 notes in 18 different toilets in Tokyo. The man's handwriting was getting worse and worse and so people think he **(g)** .... (have) a serious illness. That probably explains why he was giving away all his money.

7a SPEAKING **Work with a partner. Look at these situations and write at least two sentences with *must have, might have* and *can't have* to explain them.**

1 My uncle didn't use to be rich, but now he's a millionaire.
2 Susan always passes her exams, but last week she failed an exam.
3 Ben can usually go out with his friends at the weekend, but last weekend his parents didn't let him.
4 Justin is a very careful driver, but yesterday he had an accident.
5 Gemma usually beats everybody at tennis, but last weekend she lost.
6 Jamie loves watching football matches, but he was really angry the last time he saw a match.
7 Sarah used to be really unhealthy, but now she's really fit.
8 The last time I saw my cousin she couldn't speak a word of English, but now she's fluent.

7b Compare your ideas with the rest of the class.

Talking about photos – 2

1 SPEAKING **Work with a partner. What words and expressions can we use to talk about similarities and differences between photos? Make a list.**

Both photos show …, In this photo there is X whereas in the other photo there is Y …

2 **Use the words and expressions in 1 to talk about the two photos.**

3 LISTENING 26 **Listen to a student talking about the photos and answer the questions.**

1 Which of the things that you mentioned in 2 does the student talk about?
2 Does the student talk about each photo in detail?
3 Apart from comparing and contrasting the photos, what question do you think the examiner asked the student?

✓ EXAM SUCCESS

When you have to talk about two photos, you shouldn't describe each photo in great detail. Compare and contrast the two photos. Listen very carefully to the examiner's instructions because you may have to answer one or more questions related to the photos. You will lose marks if you don't complete the whole task.

➤ EXAM SUCCESS page 145

4 **Look at the lists of words and expressions in the Speaking bank. Match a title to each list. When is each list of expressions useful in a speaking exam?**

1 Describing
2 Speculating
3 Comparing
4 Giving opinions
5 Using fillers

SPEAKING BANK

Useful language to talk about photos

- ………………: *must (have), may (have), might (have), could (have), can't (have)*
- ………………: *more … than, (not) as … as, less … than*
- ………………: *I'm not sure but …, I imagine …, It looks/seems like/as if …, Let me think …, I mean …*
- ………………: *In the background, At the top, In the middle*
- ………………: *Personally, In my opinion, I think …*

5 SPEAKING **Work with a partner. Use each expression in 4 to talk about the photos in 2.**

PRACTICE MAKES PERFECT

6a SPEAKING **Work with a partner. Student A, look at the photos below and do the task. Student B, listen to your partner.**

Compare the photos and say why you think people enjoy meeting in these different ways.

6b **Now change roles. Student B, your task is on page 158.**

A formal letter/email of complaint

1 Read the instructions on how to use a cashpoint to withdraw money. Put the steps in the correct order.

a Select *Cash* and select or enter the amount to withdraw.
b Choose whether you want a receipt and select *Yes* or *No*.
c Don't wait more than 30 seconds to take your card out of the machine or it will swallow the card so that nobody can steal it.
d Insert your card into the machine.
e Enter your PIN (Personal Identification Number) and press *Enter*.
f Wait while the machine processes your transaction. When the machine bleeps, take your card and money (and receipt if you asked for one).

2 SPEAKING Work with a partner. Explain the different steps in 1 using *must*, *shouldn't*, etc.

3 Read this email and answer the questions.

1 Why is the person writing?
2 What solution do they want?
3 What will they do if there is no solution?

Dear Sir or Madam,

1 I am writing to complain about an incident that took place last week at your cashpoint on Anderson Street. The incident has left me without my debit card and has caused me a great deal of inconvenience.

2 On the evening of Sunday 21st December I inserted my debit card into your bank's cashpoint in order to withdraw £40. I selected the amount that I wished to withdraw, but the machine immediately told me that it had retained my card.

3 I contacted my bank the next day and they informed me that they could see no reason why the machine had swallowed the card as there was sufficient money in my account. They then informed me that they had to cancel my card and send me another one. This will take between 7 and 10 days.

4 I am very disappointed with the treatment I have received from your bank. I now have no easy access to cash, through no fault of my own. I expect you to send my new card urgently. I would also like assurance that you will charge me no bank fees for issuing me with a new card. If I do not hear from you in the next 14 days I shall be forced to consider moving my current account to another bank.

I look forward to hearing from you very soon.

Yours faithfully,

Jonathan Squire

4 Find the formal equivalents of these words and expressions in the email.

1 something happened *(Paragraph 1)*
an incident took place
2 made a lot of trouble for me *(Paragraph 1)*
3 chose *(Paragraph 2)*
4 wanted *(Paragraph 2)*
5 enough *(Paragraph 3)*
6 told *(Paragraph 3)*
7 I'll have to *(Paragraph 4)*

5 SPEAKING Work with a partner. Find examples of the characteristics in the Writing bank in the email in 3.

WRITING BANK

Characteristics of formal letters/emails

- If we don't know the name of the person we are writing to, we begin *Dear Sir or Madam*. We finish *Yours faithfully*.
- If we know the name of the person we are writing to, we begin *Dear Mr/Mrs/Ms* and their surname. We finish *Yours sincerely*.
- We do not use contractions.
- We use longer, more formal words and expressions.
- We do not use many phrasal verbs.
- We write complete sentences.
- We do not usually use abbreviations.
- We use formulaic expressions to begin and end the letter.

PRACTICE MAKES PERFECT

6a Look at this task. Write notes and add your own details.

Last week you were at a train station. In the station there was a vending machine selling books. You wanted a book to read on the train so you put money in, but it didn't give you the book or any change. Write a letter of complaint to the company that is responsible for the vending machine and demand a solution.

Plan

Paragraph 1: Why are you writing?
Paragraphs 2 and 3: What happened? What are the facts?
Paragraph 4: What solution do you demand? What will you do if there is no solution?

WRITING BANK ➤ PAGE 154

6b Write your letter. Use your notes and the information in the Writing bank.

Grammar reference

Modal verbs of obligation, prohibition and advice – present

USE

- We use **have to** to talk about things which are obligatory or necessary, often imposed on us by other people and authorities.
- We use **don't have to** to talk about things which are not obligatory or necessary.
- We use **must** to talk about rules, regulations and obligations, that often come from ourselves.
- We use **mustn't** to talk about prohibitions.
- We use **need to** to talk about things which are obligatory or necessary.
- We use **don't need to** or **needn't** to talk about things which are not obligatory or necessary. With **needn't** we do not use *to* before the infinitive.
- We use **are/aren't allowed to** to talk about things that are prohibited.
- We use **can't** to refuse permission.
- We use **should**, **shouldn't**, **ought to**, **had ('d) better** to give and ask for advice and recommendations. **Had better** is especially for when we think we should do something because it's a good idea. **Ought to** and **had ('d) better** are slightly less common in negative and question form.

Modal verbs of obligation, prohibition and advice – past

USE

- We use **had to** to talk about things which were obligatory or necessary.
- We use **didn't have to** to talk about things which were not obligatory or necessary.
- We use **needed to** to talk about things which were obligatory or necessary.
- We use **didn't need to** to talk about things which were not obligatory or necessary. Maybe we did them or maybe we didn't.
- We use **needn't have + past participle** to talk about things that were not obligatory or necessary, but we did them.
- We use **wasn't/weren't allowed to** to talk about past prohibitions.
- We use **couldn't** to talk about things that were prohibited or not possible.
- We use **should/ought to have + past participle** or **shouldn't have + past participle** to criticise past actions or to say that they were a mistake.

Modal verbs of speculation and deduction – present and future

USE

- We use **must** when we are 90% certain that something is true.
- We use **may**, **might**, **could**, **may not**, **mightn't** when there is a 50% possibility that something is true (or not).
- We use **can't** when we are 90% certain that something is not true.

Modal verbs of speculation and deduction – past

USE

- We use **must have** when we are 90% certain that something was true.
- We use **may have**, **might have**, **could have**, **may not have**, **mightn't have + past participle** when there is a 50% possibility that something was true (or not).
- We use **can't have** when we are 90% certain that something was not true.

Vocabulary

Buying and selling afford • bargain • cash • change • discount • receipt • refund • sale • value for money waste

Money and banking ATM/cashpoint • bank charges/fees • bill • current account • get into debt • interest lend money/give somebody a loan • overdraft • savings account • withdraw money

Phrasal verbs connected with money and shopping come to • cut back • get by • pay back • pick up sell out • set aside • splash out

Other words and phrases ➤ page 139

Grammar revision

Modal verbs of obligation, prohibition and advice – present
/ 6 points

1 Choose the correct alternative. In two sentences, both alternatives are correct.

1 You *needn't/don't need* come to class tomorrow.
2 You *mustn't/aren't allowed to* take your own food into a restaurant.
3 Usually at university you *mustn't/don't have to* go to classes all day.
4 You*'d better not/shouldn't* hand in your work late.
5 *Should/Ought* we leave at 6 o'clock?
6 You *don't have to/mustn't* leave your bags unattended at an airport.

Modals of obligation, prohibition and advice
/ 7 points

2 Make sentences with the correct form of the modal and verbs given.

1 Yesterday I .... (talk) to the bank manager. **HAVE TO**
2 I spent all night worrying about the exam, but I .... (worry) because it was easy. **NEED**
3 Students .... (write) their exam answers in red pen, only in black or blue. **MUST**
4 I .... (read) the instructions, but I didn't and I got the whole exercise wrong. **OUGHT TO**
5 I'm sorry. I .... (lie) to you. **SHOULD**
6 She .... (get) up early this morning so she stayed in bed. **NEED**
7 We .... (write) the essay this week, we can do it next week if we want. **HAVE TO**

Modals of speculation and deduction
/ 7 points

3 Match the pairs of sentences.

1 He looks exhausted.
2 Somebody is knocking at the door.
3 His lips are blue and he's shivering.
4 Somebody's taken my red pen.
5 My friend climbed a really high mountain.
6 I don't know when the cup final is.
7 Mike hasn't replied to my email.

a He must be really cold.
b He must have run all the way here.
c It can't be the postman because he's already been.
d It may be next week.
e That can't have been easy!
f He may not have received it.
g It might have been Jack because he lost his one.

Vocabulary revision

BUYING AND SELLING
/ 7 points

1 Match these words with the definitions.

afford • bargain • change • receipt
refund • sale • value for money

1 Money that you get back when you return something you have paid for.
2 A document that you get from someone showing that you have paid money.
3 The money you get back when you pay more than something costs.
4 Something that is of very good quality but relatively inexpensive.
5 A period of time when a shop reduces the price of some things it sells.
6 Something you buy that costs much less than normal.
7 Have enough money to buy something.

MONEY AND BANKING
/ 7 points

2 Match the words or parts of a word.

1	current	a	point
2	with	b	a loan
3	over	c	bill
4	cash	d	debt
5	give somebody	e	draft
6	get into	f	draw
7	pay a	g	account

PHRASAL VERBS: MONEY AND SHOPPING
/ 6 points

3 Rewrite these sentences without the phrasal verb.

1 Last week we **splashed out** on lunch in a restaurant.
2 They **get by** on £500 a month.
3 People are **cutting back** on holidays abroad this year.
4 The bill **comes to** £24.
5 I couldn't get that new game because it had **sold out**.
6 I need to **pick up** something for dinner tonight.

Total: / 40 points

6 Healthy living

Vocabulary

Parts of the body

1 SPEAKING **Work with a partner to identify where the following parts of your body are.**

ankle • bone • brain • chest • chin • forehead
heart • heel • hip • kidney • liver • lungs • skin
thigh • throat • toe • tongue
veins and arteries • wrist

Words connected with health

1
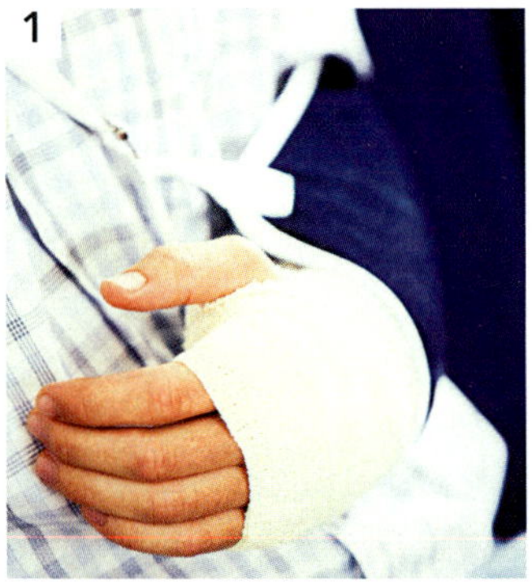

2

3

4
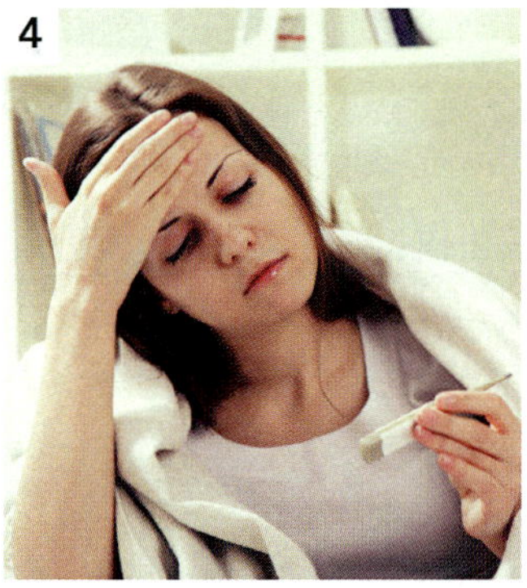

2 SPEAKING **Work with a partner. Take it in turns to talk about the photos.**

3 **Read the texts, ignoring the gaps. Match each text to the correct photo.**

A I think that generally I have quite a healthy lifestyle. I take regular exercise. I work out in a gym three or four times a week. I also have a (a) .... diet, including fresh fruit and vegetables. I go to the doctor's for a check-up every six months and I take my blood pressure regularly, too. The only problem I have is that I'm (b) .... to pollen, but I have a special injection from time to time and it relieves all the symptoms.

B Last year the doctor told me to stop eating so much fatty food and processed food that's high in salt and sugar. I was (c) .... a lot of weight and the doctor said I was in danger of becoming obese. My diet was increasing the risk of heart disease. To be honest, I think I was becoming (d) .... to junk food because I was eating it all the time, but I was able to stop and now I'm back to my ideal weight.

C Last week I picked up some sort of throat (e) .... I had a temperature and felt dizzy all the time. I couldn't stop shivering either. My doctor treated me for the illness. He wrote me a (f) .... which I took to the chemist's. As soon as I started taking the medicine, I got over the illness.

D Last month I fell down the stairs and injured myself quite badly. I twisted my ankle, sprained my wrist and (g) .... my shoulder. The only good news was that I didn't fracture or break any bones and I didn't need an operation or anything. But it was still really (h) ...., as you can imagine.

4a **Complete the texts with these words.**

addicted • allergic • balanced • dislocated
infection • painful • prescription • putting on

4b LISTENING 27 **Listen and check your answers. Then look again at the words in red and check that you understand what they mean. Use a dictionary if necessary.**

5a PRONUNCIATION **Where does the stress go in the words in 4a?**

5b LISTENING 28 **Listen and check your answers. Practise saying the words with the correct stress.**

6 SPEAKING **Work with a partner. Ask and answer these questions. Give details.**

1 Do you take regular exercise, for example working out in the gym?
2 Are you allergic to anything?
3 Have you ever injured yourself playing sport?
4 Are you afraid of injections?
5 Do you feel dizzy when you see blood?

1 SPEAKING **Work with a partner. Do you think these things are good or bad for us? Why?**

1 watching action films
2 eating ice cream quickly
3 drinking eight glasses of water a day
4 feeling pain

2 **Read the four articles from a health website and check your answers.**

Health news

SEARCH

Home | News | About | Top stories | Health A–Z | Videos | Nutrition

A We've heard it a million times. If you drink eight glasses (or two to three litres) of water a day, you'll have better skin, fewer headaches, healthier kidneys … People think that as long as they drink water all day they'll be much healthier. But is it actually true? Of course, we all know that if you don't drink, you die. But the truth is that, apart from extreme situations, the body adjusts very well to drinking either too much or too little water. It's also true that the water we need each day can be contained in other drinks such as coffee, tea or juice, or even in food. It certainly does not have to be mineral water. So where does this myth come from? When you look more closely at some 'scientific' articles, you realise that they are sponsored by mineral water manufacturers. What appears to be scientific research can sometimes be pure marketing.

B If you sit at home watching TV all the time the lack of exercise could increase your risk of heart disease. But new research has discovered that the type of programme you watch also makes a difference to your health. A team at Cornell University had three groups of volunteers. Some watched an action film, others watched the same action film but without sound, and the third group watched a talk show. Some had healthy snacks in front of them, and others had snacks high in salt and sugar. The result? The volunteers watching the action film with sound ate 98% more than those watching the talk show. Even those watching the action film without sound ate 36% more! It seems that faster programmes make you eat faster and pay less attention to how much food you're eating. Interestingly, the viewers who had healthy snacks also ate more. So next time you watch an action film, put away the snacks!

C If you dropped a heavy object on your big toe, you probably wouldn't enjoy the sensation. Pain is not something most of us like feeling. But the alternative, not feeling any pain, is much, much worse. Steven Pete was born with a rare genetic disorder which means he cannot feel pain. When he was a boy he broke his leg while roller skating. He only found out when somebody saw him and told him. The problem is that unless we sense pain, we don't pay attention to our body and what hurts us. Pain prevents us from injuring a body part even more. If it didn't hurt to walk on a broken leg or a sprained ankle, we would keep using it and cause more damage. If your throat is really sore, you'll probably go to the doctor, who can treat the infection before it becomes serious. As an adult, Steven Pete will have to have regular check-ups in case he becomes dangerously ill without knowing it. So, the next time you go 'ouch', just remember how lucky you are.

D The scientific term is 'sphenopalatine ganglioneuralgia', but we usually just call it 'brain freeze'. Brain freeze is when you eat ice cream too quickly and you get a short, sharp pain in your forehead. There is a rapid change of temperature at the back of your throat, close to two important arteries which feed blood to the brain. The brain doesn't like things to change. Brain freeze is a mechanism to prevent that from happening. The brain can't actually feel pain despite its billions of neurons. But the pain associated with brain freeze is sensed by receptors where the two arteries meet. Analysing brain freeze may seem like silly science to some, but it can help neuroscientists understand other types of headaches. And the cure for brain freeze? Provided you don't eat your ice cream quickly, you'll be fine. You can also put your tongue up to the roof of your mouth or drink something neither hot nor cold to normalise the temperature in your mouth.

3 **Read the articles again. Are the sentences True (T) or False (F)?**

1 The eight glasses we consume each day should be water, not juice, coffee or tea. T/F
2 Some companies that produce mineral water publish scientific magazines. T/F
3 When you watch an action film without sound, you eat less than when you watch it with sound. T/F
4 When you watch something exciting on TV, you don't think about how much you're eating. T/F
5 Pain helps you to stop making an injury worse. T/F
6 To stop brain freeze, you need to make your mouth warmer again. T/F

4 CRITICAL THINKING

Think! Then compare ideas in class.

- Do you believe everything you read in health articles? Why/Why not?

5 **What do the underlined words in the text mean? Guess and then check in your dictionary.**

6 SPEAKING **What about *you*?**

Which information from the articles could make a difference to you and your health?

Zero, first and second conditionals

1a Look at the sentences. Which type of conditional does each one use?

1 If you don't drink, you die.
2 If you dropped a heavy object on your big toe, you wouldn't enjoy it.
3 If you drink eight glasses of water a day, you'll have better skin.

1b Read the rules. Which type of conditional does each rule apply to?

1 It describes an improbable or imaginary situation in the present or future and its consequence.
2 It describes a possible situation in the present or future and its consequence.
3 It describes something that is generally true.
4 We use the present simple in the half of the sentence with *if*, and *will/won't* + infinitive in the other half.
5 We use the present simple in both halves of the sentence.
6 We use the past simple in the half of the sentence with *if*, and *would/wouldn't* + infinitive in the other half.

GRAMMAR REFERENCE ➤ PAGE 80

2 Complete each sentence to make a general statement using the zero conditional.

1 If you drink too much coffee, ...
2 If you never do any exercise, ...
3 If you only sleep a few hours a night, ...
4 If you eat a lot of junk food, ...
5 If you sit in front of a computer all day, ...

3 Decide if the sentences are correct. Rewrite the incorrect sentences.

1 If I am the Prime Minister, I would ban junk food.
2 We'll go to the concert if the tickets weren't too expensive.
3 I wouldn't do that if I were you.
4 What would you do if it rains all day tomorrow?
5 If I had a million pounds, I travelled around the world.
6 If you mix blue and yellow, you would get green.
7 If you don't water a plant, it dies.
8 What will you do if you lost the match?

4 Complete the questions with the correct form of the verbs given.

1 Which country .... you .... (live) in if you could choose any country in the world?
2 If you .... (have) the powers of a superhero, what powers would you like to have?
3 If you .... (go) out this weekend, where will you go?
4 If you were a journalist and could interview any famous person, who .... you .... (meet) and why?

5a SPEAKING Work with a partner. Ask and answer the questions in 4.

5b Tell the class something interesting you discovered about your partner.

unless, as long as, provided/providing (that), in case

6 Look at the sentences and match the words in blue with the expressions a–c.

1 Unless we sense pain, we don't pay attention to our bodies.
2 Why don't you take some sun cream in case there isn't any shade?
3 Provided/Providing (that) you stop eating quickly, you'll be fine.
4 As long as you drink water, you'll be much healthier.

a *if … not, except if*: ....
b *if, only if*: ...., ...
c *because maybe*: ....

GRAMMAR REFERENCE ➤ PAGE 80

7 Choose the correct alternative.

1 Don't forget to take a snack *in case/providing that* you're hungry.
2 She'll eat anything *as long as/unless* it's fresh and healthy.
3 I wouldn't speak to him *provided that/unless* he said he was sorry.
4 He'll work this weekend *as long as/unless* they pay him a bonus.
5 You can play that game all morning *in case/providing* you study in the afternoon.
6 I'll give you a key *as long as/in case* there's no one at home when you get back.
7 I don't care about money *as long as/unless* I'm fit and healthy.

✔ EXAM SUCCESS

In exercises where you have to rewrite sentences with the same meaning, do not add or change any words unnecessarily. They may change the meaning of the sentence or make you write too many words.

➤ EXAM SUCCESS page 146

8 Complete the second sentence so that it has a similar meaning to the first sentence, using the word given. Do not change the word given. You must use between three and five words, including the word given.

1 If you don't want to lose weight, don't go on a diet. **UNLESS**
Don't go on a diet ………………………… weight.

2 Bring something to eat and you can come to the party. **PROVIDED**
You can come to the party ………………………… something to eat.

3 I want to be a professional basketball player, but I'm not tall enough. **IF**
I would play basketball professionally ………………………… enough.

4 It's obvious that it won't work unless you switch it on. **IF**
It's obvious that ………………………… on, it won't work.

5 I'll only come if you promise to help me. **LONG**
I'll come ………………………… to help me.

6 I wouldn't say it if I didn't mean it. **UNLESS**
I wouldn't say it ………………………… it.

7 I'm not you, but I think you should go.
I ………………………… you. **WOULD**

8 Take an umbrella because it might rain. **CASE**
Take an umbrella ………………………… rains.

9 Complete these sentences in a logical way.

1 You should always make a copy of your computer files in case …
2 She'll go out with her friends this week providing …
3 Don't make any noise in case …
4 You can get into that club provided that …
5 I can go on holiday with my friends this year as long as …
6 I can't do my homework unless …

Developing vocabulary

Idioms connected with health and illness

1a Match the pictures to two of the idioms in red.

1 I think I'm **coming down with** a cold or something.
2 Phil has got a cold and he's feeling a bit **under the weather**.
3 I work out in the gym to **keep in shape**.
4 **A:** Are you sure you're OK?
B: Yes, I'm feeling **on top of the world**.
5 She's really dizzy. I think she's going to **black out**.
6 It's only a cold. You'll soon **be back on your feet**.
7 It was a bad accident, but he's going to **pull through**.

1b Match the idioms in 1a with the explanations a–g.

a lose consciousness …………
b keep fit, in good physical condition …………
c catch an illness, become sick with something …………
d recover from a serious illness or injury …………
e very healthy …………
f recover after an illness …………
g not feel very well …………

2 Correct the mistakes in these sentences.

1 Once you take this medicine you'll be back on your legs straight away.
2 My neighbour is 50, but he keeps in the weather by running every morning.
3 Our dog is really ill, but I'm sure he's going to pull over.
4 I don't feel well. I think I'm going to black down.
5 Are you feeling OK? You look a bit under the rain.

3 SPEAKING **Complete the questions with the correct word and then interview your partner.**

1 How do you ………………… in shape?
2 Have you ever blacked …………………?
3 What do you do when you start coming ………………… with a cold?
4 Do you know anybody who's ………………… the weather at the moment?

4 Draw a cartoon to represent one of the idioms. Can your partner guess the idiom?

Understanding NUTRITION

LIFE SKILLS OBJECTIVES

- To study the nutritional needs of teenagers.
- To look at the role of schools in promoting healthy eating.
- To plan a healthy eating campaign at school.

KEY CONCEPTS

intake [n]: *We should reduce our intake of salt to avoid high blood pressure.* **micronutrient [n]:** *The food we eat is full of micronutrients such as iron and zinc.* **saturated fat [n]:** *Hamburgers contain lots of saturated fats which are worse for us than the fat in nuts or fish.* **added sugars [n]:** *In many types of processed food there is added sugar that we don't realise is there.* **socially deprived [adj]:** *He comes from a poor, socially deprived part of the city.* **curriculum [n]:** *Maths and languages are basic elements in the school curriculum.*

1 SPEAKING **Work with a partner. Discuss these questions.**

1. What do you understand by a balanced diet?
2. What do you think are the advantages of a balanced diet?
3. Do you think you have a balanced diet? Why/Why not?
4. Do you think teenagers in general have healthy eating habits? Why/Why not?

2 READING **Read this summary of the results of a survey about British teenagers and nutrition. Complete the table with information from the text.**

SHORT-TERM BENEFITS OF HEALTHY EATING	LONG-TERM BENEFITS OF HEALTHY EATING

BRITISH TEENAGERS EAT TOO MUCH/MANY …	BRITISH TEENAGERS EAT TOO LITTLE/FEW …

3 Read the text again and answer these questions.

1. According to the survey, is nutrition better, worse or the same for UK teenagers as it was ten years ago?
2. Which group of teenagers doesn't consume enough micronutrients such as iron or zinc?
3. Which children in the UK eat more fruit and vegetables?
4. How many British girls between 11 and 15 do physical activity for at least an hour a day?
5. Does obesity affect all 11-year-olds in the UK in the same way? How do we know?
6. What does the text say about the role of schools in teenagers' nutrition?
7. How positive are the final conclusions of the survey?

NUTRITION AND TEENAGERS IN THE UK:

Home | **About** | Healthy recipes | Workouts

Adolescents need a healthy varied diet, incorporating all the major food groups. In the short term, this will help with general appearance (for example, shiny hair and healthy skin) as well as energy levels, while in the long term, it will help prevent chronic diseases such as heart disease, diabetes and osteoporosis.

It appears that some improvements to nutrient intakes have been made in the past decade. But there remains considerable room for improvement in the diets of British schoolchildren, according to the results of the government's National Diet and Nutrition Survey (NDNS).

On the positive side, average contribution of fat to total energy intake has dropped below the recommended maximum level of 35%. But intakes of saturated fat and added sugars are too high. For saturated fat, average intakes are 12.6% of energy in 11–18-year-olds, compared to the recommended maximum level of 11%. For added sugars, intakes are 15.3% in those aged 11–18 years, compared to the recommended maximum level of 11% of energy. In addition, average fibre intakes are lower than recommended.

There is evidence of inadequate micronutrient intakes in some groups in the UK, especially teenagers. For example, many teenage girls (11–18 years) are consuming low amounts of iron and there is also evidence of low intakes of vitamin A, riboflavin, calcium, magnesium, potassium, selenium, iodine and zinc.

There is some evidence of socioeconomic inequalities; for example, children from families with lower incomes tend to have lower intakes of fruit and vegetables (2.9 portions a day) compared with children from families with higher incomes (3.9 portions per day).

4 SPEAKING **Work with a partner. Discuss these questions.**

1 What do you think of the information found in the survey?

2 Do you think the results would be similar in your country? Why/Why not?

3 What specific things do you think schools can do to help students eat healthy food? Make a list.

Stop serving junk food at lunchtime.

SURVEY RESULTS

Lifestyles | Diets | Articles | Message board

As for physical activity, in data from the Health Survey for England, only 7% of boys aged 11–15 years achieved the recommendation of at least 60 minutes a day. In girls aged 11–15 years, none achieved the target and 96% had low activity levels.

Obesity remains a major problem among British schoolchildren and there is a clear socioeconomic difference, with levels of obesity being highest in the most socially deprived children. 13.7% of 11-year-olds are obese in the least deprived group and 24.3% in the most deprived. Almost 1 in 10 English children are obese when they start school and 2 in 10 are obese by age 11. These findings emphasise the importance of highlighting good nutrition through the school curriculum and through the food and drink available in schools. School food standards were introduced in 2007 and evaluations of the impact of these standards have shown improvements in the diets of schoolchildren since their introduction, not only at school but in their diets overall. However, there still remains room for improvement.

> “Almost 1 in 10 English children are obese when they start school.”

5 LISTENING 29 **Watch the video or listen to four students in the UK talking about how their university and the government help to encourage good nutrition. Tick (✓) any of the ideas in your list in 4 that they mention.**

6 29 **Watch or listen again. Copy and complete the table with notes about what each student says. Write between one and five words. Compare your tables in pairs.**

STUDENT	SAM	VANESSA	BEA	CHRIS
HEALTHY OPTIONS AT UNI				
UK GOVERNMENT				
HOW TO ENCOURAGE HEALTHY EATING				

7 SPEAKING **Work with a partner. Compare what the speakers say about healthy eating in the UK with the situation in your country.**

LIFE TASK

Your school wants to promote healthy eating for teenagers. They want you to think of ideas that could help teenagers to eat well, in and outside school. They also want you to think of a way to present those ideas to other students.

Work in a small group and follow this plan:

1 Discuss the ideas on these two pages that you think would be useful.

2 Think of other ideas that you think could work, e.g. making people pay extra for fizzy drinks.

3 Plan and prepare a healthy eating campaign for your school. This could include a poster, a video, a presentation and/or an information leaflet.

4 Present your ideas to the class.

a

b

c

1 SPEAKING **Work with a partner. Look at these sports. Have you ever tried them? If not, would you like to? Why/Why not?**

2 LISTENING 30 **Listen to five people talking about sport. Which sport does each person do?**

Speaker	Sport	Statement (A–F)
1		
2		
3		
4		
5		

3 30 **Listen again. Match the statements A–F with each speaker. There is one extra statement.**

A You have to learn theory and practice before you can do this sport.

B I want to get better at my favourite sport so that I can win matches.

C I couldn't start my favourite sport when I was younger.

D To do my favourite sport well I should have started earlier.

E My favourite sport is more tiring than it looks.

F In the past I took my favourite sport too seriously.

4 SPEAKING **What about *you*?**

1 What sport(s) do you do?
2 How tiring/expensive/difficult is it to learn?
3 How seriously do you take it? Why?

Grammar in context

Third conditional

1 **Look at these sentences and answer the questions.**

a If I'**d lived** closer to the sea, I **would have begun** surfing much earlier.

b If I **hadn't passed** my exams, they **wouldn't have let** me do the course.

1 In third conditional sentences, what tense is the verb in the half of the sentence containing *if*?
2 What verb form do we use in the other half of the sentence?
3 Do we use the third conditional for imaginary situations in the present or the past?

GRAMMAR REFERENCE ➤ PAGE 80

2 **Complete the sentences with the correct form of the verb given.**

1 I would have played better if I .... (practise) more.
2 She .... (become) ill if she hadn't taken the medicine.
3 If I .... (be) able to buy tickets, I would have gone to the match.
4 We .... (get) wet yesterday if it had rained.
5 If you .... (not explain) the rules, I wouldn't have known how to play.
6 If he hadn't lived near the mountains as a child, he .... (not learn) to ski.
7 If she .... (injure) herself, she wouldn't have finished the race.

3 **Make sentences about these past situations using the third conditional.**

1 She/not catch a cold/if/she/not go running in the rain.
She ....
2 If/I/know how to play tennis properly/I/not injure/ myself last week.
If I ....
3 The stadium/be full/if/the match/be important.
The stadium ....
4 She/win the race/if/she/not twist her ankle.
She ....
5 If/we/drink water before the race/we/not be so thirsty.
If ....
6 If/the sun/shone/we/swim in the sea.
If ....
7 If/he/need extra vitamins/he/take them.
If ....

4 **Look at the situations and write third conditional sentences.**

1 She won the race because she had trained hard.
If she hadn't trained hard, she wouldn't have won the race.
2 He didn't do sport because he didn't have enough time yesterday.
3 She missed the bus because she got up late.
4 I didn't swim because the water was cold.
5 We didn't play because we didn't have rackets.
6 I didn't sunbathe because I didn't have any sun cream.
7 He didn't learn to surf because he was afraid of water.
8 She didn't go for a run because her knee hurt.

I wish/If only

5 **Look at these sentences and answer the questions.**

a **I wish/If only I'd learnt** to swim properly when I was a kid
b **I wish/If only** I **was** taller.
c **I wish/If only** people **wouldn't** make fun of my favourite sport.

1 What tense appears after ***I wish/If only*** in sentence a?
2 Does this sentence talk about a present or past situation that we would like to be different?
3 What tense appears after ***I wish/If only*** in sentence b?
4 Does this sentence talk about an imaginary wish for a present or past situation?
5 What verb form appears after ***I wish/If only*** in sentence c?
6 Do we use sentence c to talk about habitual behaviour that we like, or we want to change?

GRAMMAR REFERENCE ➤ PAGE 80

Flipped classroom: watch the grammar presentation video.

6 **Complete the sentences with the correct form of the verb given.**

1 I wish I .... (go) to Spain for my holidays last summer, but I went to France.
2 I wish you .... (listen) to me when I'm talking!
3 If only I .... (know) how to surf! I'd spend every day in the sea!
4 If only he .... (make) less noise. I can't concentrate when he plays the guitar.
5 I wish we .... (see) the match yesterday. They say it was brilliant.
6 If only I .... (have) more free time. I'm always busy.

7 **Complete the text with one word for each space.**

'If **(a)** .... I was fitter! The thing is that I work really long hours in my new job. Sometimes I wish I **(b)** .... accepted the job. Basically, I took it because I really needed the money. If I hadn't needed the money, I **(c)** .... have taken it. One thing is clear though. **(d)** .... I find more time to do sport, I'll soon become very unfit. Another problem is my diet. If only I **(e)** .... like fast food so much, but I love it! But as **(f)** .... as I only eat it from time to time, I'll be OK. At work, some people bring cakes and sweets to share. I wish they **(g)** .... because I always end up eating them and I know I shouldn't. Anyway, like I say, provided that I **(h)** .... up a new sport like running or cycling, I'll get fit again in no time!'

8 **Rewrite the incorrect sentences.**

1 I wish I'm on a beach right now.
2 I wish you didn't interrupt me when I'm talking.
3 If only I studied more last night.
4 If only I'd won that competition last week.
5 I wish today was Saturday.
6 If only I can pass my exams without studying.

9a **Write three true sentences with *I wish*. Use each of the tenses/situations in 5.**

9b SPEAKING **Compare your sentences in small groups. Ask follow-up questions to find out more information.**

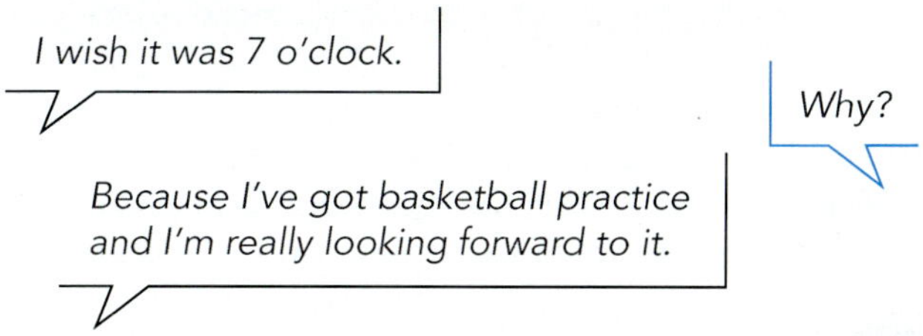

Negotiating and collaborating – 2

1 SPEAKING **Work with a partner. Look at both parts of the task. Make a list of advice on how to do this type of task. Look at Exam success for Unit 2 on page 144 if necessary.**

Your school wants to encourage students to live healthier lives. Here are some ideas that they are thinking about and a question for you to discuss. Talk to each other about how these ideas could encourage students to live healthier lives.

How could these ideas encourage students to live healthier lives?

- Cookery classes at school
- A week's free membership of a gym or sports club
- A school sports day
- A weekend in the country
- A talk by a doctor

Now you have a minute to decide which two ideas you think are the best.

2 SPEAKING **Do both parts of the task with your partner.**

3 LISTENING 31 **Listen to two students doing the task. Do you think they do the task well? Why/Why not? How do you think you did in comparison?**

4a Complete the expressions in section 4 of the Speaking bank with these words.

best • better • choice • choose • let's

4b Work with a partner. Make a list of expressions for sections 1–3 of the Speaking bank. Compare your answers with the Speaking bank on page 26.

SPEAKING BANK

Useful expressions for negotiating and collaborating – 2

1 Asking your partner's opinion
2 Agreeing
3 Disagreeing
4 Making choices

- *I think this is a good* **(a)** ....
- *I think we should* **(b)** .... …
- *I think the* **(c)** .... *option is* …
- *In my opinion,* … *is a* **(d)** .... *option than* …
- **(e)** .... *choose* …

PRACTICE MAKES PERFECT

5 SPEAKING **Work with a partner and do this task together. Remember to use expressions from the Speaking bank.**

I'd like you to imagine that your teachers want to introduce some new ideas at school to help young people to beat stress. Here are some ideas that they are thinking about and a question for you to discuss. Talk to each other about how these ideas could help students to beat stress.

How can these ideas help to beat stress?

- Later school starts
- Table tennis tables
- Outdoor pianos
- Relaxation rooms with sofas
- Regular yoga classes

Now you have a minute to decide which two ideas you think are the best.

A for-and-against essay

1 SPEAKING **Work with a partner. Describe what you can see in the photo. What does it say about modern life?**

2 Read this essay title. With your partner, make notes with your ideas.

'Life today is unhealthier than 50 years ago.' Write an essay giving arguments for and against this statement.

Ideas for	Ideas against

3 Read this essay. Are any of your ideas in it? Do you agree with the writer and their conclusion? Why/Why not?

In the last 50 years or so, new technology has made massive changes to the world. Mobile phones, computers and the Internet have all made the world faster, and so have cars and other types of transport. But not everybody agrees on whether these changes have had a positive or negative effect on our health.

Our health has certainly improved in some ways. Firstly, medical science has improved, which means that doctors are better at curing and preventing illnesses now than in the past. What is more, new technology has made our lives easier, for example by making it less necessary to use physical strength.

On the other hand, technology has possibly made our lives too easy. For example, some people go everywhere by car and so they never get any exercise. Furthermore, today's diet has changed greatly. Nowadays, people eat a lot of processed food whereas in the past they ate fresh, natural ingredients. In addition, today's lifestyle is very stressful because of work and faster communication. As a result, the risk of heart problems is greater now.

All in all, I think that, despite the advantages that modern technology has brought, today's world is unhealthier than in the past. However, it is up to us as individuals to be aware of the dangers and to take measures to make sure our own lives are as healthy as possible, by eating well and getting sufficient exercise.

4 Look again at the essay and answer the questions.

1 What is the purpose of each paragraph?
2 How are for-and-against essays different from opinion essays?

5 Put the underlined words in the essay in the correct place in the Writing bank.

WRITING BANK

Useful expressions in for-and-against essays

- Introducing and sequencing arguments
  ....
  Secondly,
  Lastly,
- Adding arguments
  ....
  ....
  ....
  not only … but also
- Making contrasts
  On the one hand,
  ....
  In contrast,
  ....
  In spite of (+ noun/gerund/the fact that …)
  ....
- Expressing consequences
  Therefore,
  and so
  ....
- Expressing opinions
  In my opinion,
  Personally, ...
  As far as I'm concerned
- Concluding
  In conclusion,
  ....
  To sum up

6 Work with a partner and read the essay task. Make a paragraph plan and write down notes with ideas for each paragraph.

'We should not use animals for testing new medical products.' Write an essay giving arguments for and against this statement.

✓ EXAM SUCCESS

Remember that in for-and-against essays, you must think of points for both sides of the argument. You can express your own view in the conclusion.

➤ EXAM SUCCESS page 146

7 PRACTICE MAKES PERFECT **Write your essay. Use your notes and the expressions in the Writing bank.**

WRITING BANK ➤ PAGE 155

Grammar reference

Zero, first, second and third conditionals

We use the **zero conditional** to talk about situations that are generally or always true.

If + **present simple**, … **present simple**

If you don't water plants, they die.

We use the **first conditional** to talk about possible and probable situations in the future, and their consequences.

If + **present simple**, … **will** + infinitive

If you eat junk food, you will put on weight.

We use the **second conditional** to talk about imaginary or improbable situations in the present or future and their consequences.

If + **past simple**, … **would/wouldn't** + infinitive

If I had a beard, I'd look older.

We use the **third conditional** to talk about imaginary or impossible situations in the past and their consequences. The situations are impossible because we cannot change them now that they have happened.

If + **past perfect**, … **would/wouldn't have** + past participle

If I had studied, I would have passed the exam.

unless, as long as, provided/providing (that), in case

Unless = if … not, except if

We won't be able to swim unless the swimming pool is open.

As long as, provided/providing (that) = if, only if

We'll be able to swim as long as/provided the swimming pool is open.

In case = because maybe

We'll take our swimming costumes in case the swimming pool is open.

I wish/If only

We use ***I wish/If only*** + **the past** to talk about imaginary situations in the present. It expresses wishes for things to be different in the present.

I wish I was on the beach right now.

We use ***I wish/If only*** + **the past perfect** to talk about past situations that we would have liked to be different. It expresses regrets.

If only I hadn't spent all my money last weekend.

We use ***I wish/If only*** with **would/wouldn't + infinitive** to talk about somebody's habitual behaviour that we want to criticise and change.

My dad smokes. I wish he wouldn't do it.

Vocabulary

Parts of the body ankle • bone • brain • chest • chin • forehead • heart • heel • hip • kidney • liver lungs • skin • thigh • throat • toe • tongue • veins and arteries • wrist

Words connected with health be/become addicted to • be allergic to • be in danger of • be/become obese be painful • break • dislocate • eat fatty food/food high in salt • feel dizzy • fracture • get/catch an infection get/give a prescription • get over an illness • go for a check-up • have a balanced diet • have/give an injection have an operation • have a temperature • increase the risk of • injure yourself • put on/lose weight relieve symptoms • shiver • sprain your wrist/ankle • suffer from heart disease • take your blood pressure treat somebody for • twist your ankle • work out

Idioms connected with health and illness be back on your feet • be/feel on top of the world be/feel under the weather • black out • come down with • keep in shape • pull through

Other words and phrases ➤ page 139

Grammar revision

Conditionals
/ 8 points

1 Put the verbs in the correct form. Which type of conditional is each sentence?

1 If I were you, I .... (not eat) that!
2 I would've prepared something special for dinner, if I .... (know) you were coming.
3 If she had told me your number, I .... (call) you last night.
4 If you multiply two by five, the answer .... (be) ten.
5 .... you .... (give) Matt this message if you see him tomorrow?
6 I would have had a good time if I .... (go) out last night.
7 If you find it, ... you .... (tell) me?
8 I .... (get) some food if I had any money.

unless, as long as, provided/providing (that), in case
/ 6 points

2 Rewrite the sentences using the words given.

1 They'll let you in, but only if you have your ID card. PROVIDING THAT
They ....
2 Take your mobile phone because you may need to call me. IN CASE
Take ....
3 We will win the match if we do our best. PROVIDED
We ....
4 They wouldn't need Danny in the team except if someone was ill. UNLESS
They ....
5 We'll be able to make sandwiches if Kate remembers to bring the bread. AS LONG AS
We ....
6 You won't finish in time if you don't hurry. UNLESS
You ....

I wish/If only
/ 6 points

3 Make sentences with *I wish* or *If only* for these situations.

1 You aren't fit but you would like to be.
I wish ....
2 Your sister always takes a long time in the bathroom.
I wish my sister ....
3 You didn't buy tickets for a concert yesterday and now they're sold out.
If only ....
4 Your parents don't let you have parties at home and you're not happy about it.
If only my parents ....
5 You ate a big lunch and now you regret it.
I wish ....
6 You're allergic to cats but you really like them.
I wish ....

Vocabulary revision

PARTS OF THE BODY
/ 7 points

1 Reorder the letters to make parts of the body.

1 phi .... 2 gnusl .... 3 ghiht .... 4 nidkye ....
5 nirba .... 6 reedhofa .... 7 notuge ....

WORDS CONNECTED WITH HEALTH
/ 7 points

2 Complete the sentences with words connected with health.

1 His head was spinning. He felt really ....
2 She's .... to gluten so she can't eat bread.
3 The doctor gave me a .... for some tablets.
4 She's got very high blood ....
5 He didn't completely break his arm. He .... it.
6 She had flu but she's starting to get .... it.
7 If you take this medicine, it will .... the symptoms.

IDIOMS: HEALTH AND ILLNESS
/ 6 points

3 Complete the idioms with the correct word.

1 My dog was ill, but he .... through and is OK now.
2 I've been feeling a little under the .... recently.
3 I walk to school to keep in ....
4 I'm fine. I'm on .... of the world.
5 I'm hot. I think I'm coming .... with something.
6 He isn't well now, but I hope he'll be back on his .... soon.

Total: / 40 points

Speaking

➤ TIP FOR SPEAKING EXAMS

In exams where you have to talk about photos, remember …
Before the exam, revise words and expressions you will need to compare and contrast photos, to make speculations about them, to introduce your personal opinion of them, and to say where things are in the photos.

➤ EXAM SUCCESS page 145

1 SPEAKING **Work with a partner. Look at these words and expressions. When would we use each one? What other words and expressions do you know for the same uses?**

at the top • can't be • in both photos
in the background • might have • personally • whereas

2 **Student A, look at photos 1a and 1b. Student B, look at photos 2a and 2b. Think about the similarities and differences between your photos and what you could say about them.**

1a

1b

2a

2b

3 SPEAKING **Student A, read this task and talk about your photos.**

Compare the two photos and say why you think the people have chosen to do these activities at the weekend.

4 SPEAKING **Student B, read this task and talk about your photos.**

Compare the two photos and say why you think the people like doing these different hobbies.

5 SPEAKING **What about *you*?**

Which of the activities in the photos do you like or would you like to try?

Listening

➤ TIP FOR LISTENING EXAMS

In activities where you have to complete notes, remember …
Always read the incomplete notes before you listen. Think about what type of word is missing, but be careful: if you know that you need a number, for example, do not simply write the first number that you hear.

➤ EXAM SUCCESS page 145

6 SPEAKING **Work with a partner. Discuss these questions.**

1 Do you ever consume 'energy drinks'? When? Why?
2 What might some of the dangers of energy drinks be?

7 **Read the text and predict what word or type of word could fill each gap.**

Expert Norma Robins says that energy drinks are not the same as sports drinks. Sports drinks replace liquid, carbohydrates and **(a)** .... Energy drinks are very different from sports drinks because they contain caffeine. Caffeine **(b)** .... be a danger for people under 16 and it is definitely bad for people who are under **(c)** .... Another effect of caffeine is that it **(d)** .... you.

A teenage boy died because he drank four cans of energy drink and then he played **(e)** ....

One report seemed to show that energy drinks can help **(f)** .... to concentrate more.

One 250ml can of energy drink can contain five **(g)** .... of sugar.

(h) .... is an amino acid which often comes in energy drinks.

This amino acid helps you to eliminate **(i)** .... from the body.

Norman thinks you don't really need energy drinks. You just need a healthy **(j)** ....

8 LISTENING ▶ 32 **Listen to a radio programme about energy drinks. Complete the text with one word or a number in each gap.**

Writing

➤ TIP FOR WRITING EXAMS

In for-and-against and opinion essays, remember ...
You must present both sides of the argument, whatever your personal opinion is. You can give your own opinion in the conclusion. In opinion essays you can just give your own side of the argument.

➤ EXAM SUCCESS page 146

9a SPEAKING **Work with a partner. Look at the essay title. Are the ideas below for or against the statement?**

'There is a tax on cigarettes and alcohol because we know that they are bad for us. Now we urgently need a tax on fast food.' Write an essay giving arguments for and against this statement.

1 We have to spend a lot of money curing people with health problems related to fast food.
2 What you eat should just be a personal choice.
3 We need to encourage people to eat healthier food.
4 Any food can be unhealthy if you eat too much of it, so this wouldn't help the situation.

9b With your partner, make notes with other ideas for and against the statement.

10 How many paragraphs do you think you should write? What should be the content of each paragraph?

11 Write your essay. Use linkers to introduce and sequence arguments and to make contrasts.

Use of English

➤ TIP FOR USE OF ENGLISH

In sentence transformation activities, remember ...
When you finish, check that you have not changed the meaning of the original sentence, or changed the form of the word they gave you, or written more than the maximum number of words permitted.

➤ EXAM SUCCESS page 146

12 Complete the second sentence so that it has a similar meaning to the first sentence, using the word given. Do not change the word given. You must use between three and five words.

1 I wouldn't have an energy drink if I didn't really need it.
UNLESS
I wouldn't have an energy drink .... it.

2 I made a real mistake not drinking any water during the race.
WISH
I .... some water during the race.

3 If you eat all your salad I'll get you an ice cream.
PROVIDED
I'll get you an ice cream .... all your salad.

4 I shouldn't go to bed late tonight.
BETTER
I .... to bed late tonight.

5 I didn't know kids could drink that.
ALLOWED
I didn't know kids .... that.

6 She bought some orange juice on the way to school.
PICKED
She .... on her way to school.

7 What's the matter? You don't look well.
WEATHER
What's the matter? You ....

8 I'll go to the gym but only if you come with me.
LONG
I'll go to the gym .... with me.

7 Creative arts

Vocabulary

Music and film

1 SPEAKING **Write down different types of music. Compare your answers with a partner. Now do the same with different types of films.**

2 **Complete the blog texts with the words. Use a dictionary if necessary.**

acting • crowd • gig • lighting • live (adv) • lyrics
performance • plot • recorded • role • scene • soundtrack
stage • starred • tracks

Posted 26th April | About | Updates | Follow me

I love music, especially rock and pop. Last summer I went to a brilliant (a) .... by Imagine Dragons. I knew all their songs, but I hadn't seen them play (b) .... before. When they appeared on (c) ...., the (d) .... went wild. They'd just (e) .... a brand new album with about 20 (f) .... on it, so they had lots of new songs to perform. The (g) .... was spectacular – you could see them really well from a distance. The sound was brilliant, too. You could hear all the words really clearly. That's important because I love their (h) ....

The film we saw last Saturday was amazing. It (i) .... Anne Hathaway in the (j) .... of an astronaut. Hathaway's (k) .... was brilliant. She was really convincing. In general, the (l) .... was really good – maybe one of the actors will win an Oscar. What I liked the most was the (m) .... because I think a good film should tell an interesting story. I remember that there was one (n) .... that was really emotional where the characters realise the consequences of their journey through space. The (o) .... was great too – the music went perfectly with the images.

3 LISTENING 33 **Listen to the definitions. Write the correct form of the words in 2 that match them. Change the tense of verbs if necessary.**

1 ....
2 ....
3 ....
4 ....
5 ....
6 ....
7 ....
8 ....

Media habits

4 **Match words or expressions in red in the questionnaire below with these definitions.**

1 move information from the Internet to your computer
2 watch or listen to something from the Internet without needing to put it in your computer
3 images or sounds that you can see and hear on your computer at the same time as they are happening
4 a phone, tablet or other small computer that you can hold in your hand
5 buy/pay money for
6 places on the Net where they distribute digitally stored information
7 going from one person's computer to another without any central controller
8 move music, information or images from one object or place to another

MEDIA HABITS QUESTIONNAIRE

HOW OFTEN DO YOU ...

1 purchase DVDs or CDs?
2 watch films or listen to music on a mobile device?
3 stream films or music?
4 watch live streams of gigs or other events?
5 download films or music that you have paid for or that are legally free?
6 transfer films or music from one device to another?
7 use peer-to-peer or other online file-sharing sites?

5 SPEAKING **Work with a partner. Take it in turns to ask and answer the questions in the questionnaire.**

1 SPEAKING **Work with a partner and answer this question.**

Do you like using streaming music services? Why/Why not?

2 **Read the article. What is the author complaining about and why?**

▶ MY VIEW

ALOE BLACC

If songwriters can't afford to make music then who will?

"At our core, **songwriters are creators**. We challenge ourselves and others to reflect on the world around us. And the work we produce has power – power to capture people's emotions and imaginations like few other art forms, power to transcend traditional barriers of age, language and culture, and power to generate positive social change.

But does our work as songwriters have value? Coming from someone who has spent his life working hard to master his craft in order to touch the lives of others, that may seem like an absurd question. But in today's rapidly changing music marketplace, the answer is increasingly unclear. Just this week, Taylor Swift removed her music from Spotify – not because she doesn't want you to stream her songs, but because she wants to be **compensated fairly** for her work. She wants Spotify to treat her work as though it has value. This problem ought to cause anyone who cares about the **future of music** – professionals and fans alike – to stand up and take note.

> I am many things ... But above all, I am a songwriter.

First, unlike most people in creative industries, songwriters seem to have less control over our work than ever before. If you copy a handbag design from a high-end fashion house or use a sports team's logo in your new T-shirt line, you can soon expect problems with the law. And just try copying a big tech company's patented innovation. You need express permission from the original creators to use or copy their work before you resell it. That's how they **protect the value** of their work.

But the world doesn't work that way for songwriters. We have no power to protect the value of the music we create. The ridiculously low rates songwriters are paid by streaming services are yet another indication our work is being devalued in today's marketplace.

Consider the fact that it takes roughly one million spins on Pandora for a songwriter to earn just $90. Avicii's release *Wake Me Up!* that I co-wrote and sing, for example, was the most streamed song in Spotify history and the 13th most played song on Pandora since its release in 2013, with more than 168 million streams in the US. And yet, that made only $12,359 in Pandora domestic royalties – which were then divided between three songwriters and our publishers. If that's what's now considered a streaming 'success story', is it any wonder that so many songwriters are now **struggling to get by**?

The reality is that purchasing and downloading songs have given way to streaming, and as a result, the money that songwriters depended on for years to make a living is now drying up.

But the irony of the situation is that our music is actually being enjoyed by more people in more places than ever before. Our work clearly does have value, of course, or else it would not be in such high demand. So why aren't songwriters compensated more fairly in the marketplace?

I, for one, can no longer stand and just watch as songwriters are left out in the cold, while streaming company executives build their fortunes thanks to our hard work. Songwriting is truly a **labour of love**, one that often does not result in wealth. But I know the work we create has real value. And I believe people will one day recognise that a system that allows digital streaming services to enjoy enormous profits while music creators struggle is imbalanced and broken.

You can also do your part to protect the music you love by **buying albums** and encouraging streaming services to respect the value of songwriting. After all, if songwriters can't afford to make music, then who will?"

3 **Read the article again and answer the questions.**

1. According to Blacc, what different types of power does a songwriter's work have?
2. Why did Taylor Swift remove her music from Spotify?
3. How are important fashion or technology companies different from songwriters?
4. In what way was Avicii's song *Wake Me Up!* a success?
5. Why does Blacc think that today's system is 'imbalanced and broken'?
6. What does Blacc want fans to do and what does he think will happen if they don't do it?

4 CRITICAL THINKING

Think! Then compare ideas with your class.

- Do you agree with Blacc's arguments? Why/ Why not?

5 **What do the underlined words in the text mean? Guess and then check in your dictionary.**

6 SPEAKING **What about *you*?**

Where and how do you prefer to listen to music?

Grammar in context

Reported speech – statements

1 Read the sentences and answer the questions below.

1a He said: 'I **am** many things.'
1b He said that he **was** many things.
2a He told them: '**I believe** people will one day recognise that the system **is** broken.'
2b He told them **he believed** people would one day recognise that the system **was** broken.
3a He said: 'Just **this** week, Taylor Swift **removed** her music from Spotify.'
3b He said that just **that** week Taylor Swift **had removed** her music from Spotify.

1 How do tenses change when we go from direct to reported speech?
2 Do you think tenses change when the reporting verb is in the present or present perfect (e.g. *He says, He has said*)?
3 What happens to the pronoun **I** when we put sentence 1a into reported speech?
4 What is the difference between **say** and **tell**?
5 Do we always need to use **that** after **say** or **tell**?

GRAMMAR REFERENCE ➤ PAGE 94

2 How do these tenses change when they go into reported speech? Do they all change?

Direct speech	Reported speech
present simple →	*past simple*
present continuous →	1 ....
past simple →	2 ....
past continuous →	3 ....
present perfect →	4 ....
past perfect →	5 ....
will →	6 ....
would →	7 ....
can →	8 ....
may →	9 ....
must/have to →	10 ....

3 How do these words change when they go into reported speech?

Direct speech	Reported speech
this/these	*that/those*
here	1 ....
today	2 ....
yesterday	3 ....
tomorrow	4 ....
tonight	5 ....
next (week/month/year)	6 ....
last (week/month/year)	7 ....
a (week/month/year) ago	8 ....

4 Complete the sentences with *said* or *told*.

1 She .... she hadn't downloaded any songs the day before.
2 They .... their computer was slower than ours.
3 We .... Josh that we'd meet him at the cinema that night.
4 He .... her the concert was the following day.
5 He .... he was sorry for what he'd done.
6 I .... you couldn't speak Russian.

5 Put the sentences in direct speech into reported speech.

1 'I never buy DVDs.'
Steve says ....
2 'We must leave if we want to get to the cinema on time.'
Sam told ....
3 'These books are mine.'
Emma said ....
4 'I'm going to record a new album.'
Alicia said ....
5 'The crowd were screaming throughout the concert.'
Juliet said ....
6 'I'll see you tomorrow, Simon.'
Dave told ....

Reported speech – questions

6 Read the sentences and answer questions 1–5 below.

1a 'Why **aren't** songwriters compensated more fairly?'
1b He asked his readers why songwriters **weren't** compensated more fairly.
2a 'Does our work **have** value?'
2b He wondered whether their work **had** value.
3a 'Is it any wonder that songwriters **are struggling**?'
3b He asked us if it was any wonder that songwriters **were struggling**.

1 Do tenses and pronouns change in reported questions in the same way as in reported statements?
2 Do we use the auxiliary verb *do* in reported questions?
3 Do we put the subject before the verb in reported questions?
4 Do we use question marks in reported questions?
5 What words do we use when we report questions that do not begin with a question word?

GRAMMAR REFERENCE ➤ PAGE 94

7 **Report the conversation using *said, told, asked* and *wanted to know*.**

Olivia: Have you ever been to a music festival?
Tom: Yes, I have. I went to one last year.
Olivia: Who was the best band?
Tom: I really enjoyed the Foo Fighters. I'm going to see them again later this year.
Olivia: I may go if it's not too expensive. When are they playing?
Tom: I think the concert will be in July. Are you going to be here in July?
Olivia: I think so. I've been saving up money to go to the US, but I still haven't got enough.
Tom: When do you think you'll be able to go?
Olivia: I'm probably going to go next year. I'd love to go to a festival there.

8a **Write five questions to ask people in your class about music.**

8b SPEAKING **Ask as many people your questions as possible and make a note of their answers.**

8c **Write a report about some of the questions you asked and the answers people gave.**

I asked people whether they listened to music while they were doing their homework. Three people told me they did, but the rest said they couldn't concentrate with music.

Compound nouns and adjectives

1 **Look at these compounds. Which are compound nouns and which are compound adjectives?**

brand new • download • fast-moving • file-sharing
marketplace • songwriter • soundtrack • thought-provoking

2 PRONUNCIATION 34 **Listen to the words. Where is the stress in the compound nouns – on the first word, the last word or both? And in the compound adjectives?**

3 **Match the compound nouns 1–8 with their definitions a–h.**

1 screenplay
2 blockbuster
3 box office
4 drawback
5 feedback
6 turnout
7 outcome
8 page-turner

a a book that is very interesting or exciting
b a film or show that is very successful
c a story that someone writes for a film
d the final result of a process or a meeting
e the number of people who come to an event
f comments about how well or badly someone is doing something
g the place in a theatre where you buy tickets, or the number of tickets a film sells
h a disadvantage

4 **Complete the sentences with the compound nouns in 3.**

1 It's a typical Hollywood .... with lots of special effects but not very good acting.
2 The .... of the report was that they decided not to invest in the Internet.
3 I can't put this book down – it's a real ....
4 One .... of downloading films is that often the quality is terrible.
5 We'd like your .... on our website so we can make it perfect for you!
6 The critics loved the film, but it wasn't a success at the ....
7 Two thousand people is a big .... for a new band.
8 When the director read the original ...., she knew it would make a great film.

Bringing IDEAS TO LIFE

21ST CENTURY SKILLS OBJECTIVES	KEY CONCEPTS
■ To learn about crowdfunding. ■ To look at how to make a crowdfunding video. ■ To create a crowdfunding campaign for a project.	**back [v]:** *The producer backed the director's plan to make a film and gave him the money to do it.* **pledge money [v]:** *They've pledged money for this project. They're promised £10,000, but only if the project actually happens.* **reward [n]:** *They're going to give her a reward for doing the project so well.* **entrepreneur [n]:** *We help entrepreneurs, people with ideas for new businesses.* **get something off the ground [phr]:** *He has a great idea for a new video game, but he needs money to get the idea off the ground.*

1 SPEAKING **Work with a partner. Imagine that you play in a band. You want to record an album. Think of ways that you could do this.**

2 READING **Read the answers to FAQs about 'crowdfunding'. How could it help you to make your album?**

MY RECORDING PLAN

1. Send a simple recording of one of our songs to a record company.

....

....

CROWDFUNDING FAQs

1 ....

Crowdfunding is a way to raise money for a particular project from a large group of people, usually via the Internet. There are usually three key elements in the crowdfunding process. Firstly, there is the artist, inventor or entrepreneur who has the idea for the project and who needs money to bring the project to life. Then, there is the crowd – the group of individuals who support the project and pledge money to it. These people are usually called the backers. In between these two is the platform, the organisation that makes it possible for the creator of the project to find backers. These are usually online services. Popular platforms include Kickstarter, Indiegogo and PledgeMusic.

2 ....

Any type. It could be to make an album, a book, a film, a video game, a new piece of technology. Basically, if you have an idea that's new and original and that excites people, you're sure to find people to pledge money and back the project.

3 ....

Anybody can be a backer. Usually you can pledge as little as $10 to back a project. With crowdfunding the idea is to get as many people behind the project as possible. Millions of people visit crowdfunding websites each week. The basic principle of crowdfunding is that if thousands of individuals offer even just a small amount of money, that can often be enough to get a project off the ground.

4 ....

Imagine that you're in a band and you want to make an album. The usual way to do that is to find a record company to help you to record your songs. If you find one and they offer you a contract, you'll probably have to record your songs according to the instructions or guidance of the record company. With crowdfunding, your band can show the type of songs that they want to record. If people like them, they offer money and your band is free to make the album the way you, and your fans, want. So there is a more direct relationship between artist and fans.

5 ....

Backers are usually offered special 'rewards' for supporting a project. Remember the example of a band making a new album with money from crowdfunding? By pledging the same amount of money as for a normal download, the band might offer you different rewards. For example, maybe you get exclusive videos from the studio showing the band recording the new songs. Or maybe you get a free T-shirt, or even a copy of the lyrics of one of the songs, written by hand by the artist. The backer can feel as if they are part of the new project, knowing that if you hadn't given money, maybe the album would never have existed.

3 Match the questions to answers 1–8 in the text.

a Do you need to have a lot of money to be a backer?

b What are some of the most successful projects to come from crowdfunding?

c What sort of projects can you get crowdfunding for?

d What are the advantages of crowdfunding for the artist or creator of the project?

e What can you do if you have an idea for a project?

f What is crowdfunding?

g What are the advantages of crowdfunding for the backer?

h How successful is crowdfunding?

4 SPEAKING **Work with a partner. Take it in turns to answer the questions in 3 in your own words. Try to answer without looking at the text.**

You don't have to be rich to be a backer. You can back a project with just $10, for example.

5 SPEAKING **Work with a partner. What do you think of the idea of crowdfunding? Explain why.**

6 .... In 2013, the crowdfunding industry grew to over $5.1 billion worldwide. And if early data is any indication, it's just getting started and should present major growth in the years to come.

7 .... A video game called 'Star Citizen' aimed to raise $500,000. By the end of 2014 it had already raised over $68 million, with over 697,000 backers! Neil Young, a famous singer-songwriter, raised over $6 million to create a brand new digital music player. But there have been smartwatches, movies, even charities that have successfully generated enough money from crowdfunding to become a reality.

8 .... Your project can be big or small, but you need to decide what exactly you are aiming to do, how you are going to do it, and how much money and time you need. One of the best ways to attract people to back your project is by making a video where you explain your project and where you give details of the rewards that backers can get, according to how much money they pledge.

6 SPEAKING **For crowdfunding, it is a good idea to make a video to attract backers. How important do you think the following are for a successful video? Discuss with a partner.**

1 A description of the project

2 Information about the creator(s) of the project

3 Examples of the project (e.g. a short section of a song, images from a video game, a short sequence from the film)

4 Information about the rewards you can get

5 Humour and originality

7 LISTENING ▶ 35 **Watch the video or listen to James talking about his experience of crowdfunding. What did he use crowdfunding for? How many people were involved in funding his project?**

8 ▶ 35 **Watch or listen and answer the questions. Compare your answers with a partner.**

1 How did James choose a host for his campaign?

2 How did he use the money?

3 What was James's crowdfunding video like?

4 How effective was the video?

5 What would James change if he did it again?

6 Does James recommend crowdfunding? Why/Why not?

21ST CENTURY TASK

You want to create a crowdfunding campaign.

Work in a group and follow this plan:

1 *Decide on a project that you would like to bring to life, e.g. a movie, video game, new technology, work of art, fashion item.*

2 *Outline the crowdfunding campaign for your project: What will you create to publicise your project and attract backers? (e.g. a video, a poster, a presentation) What rewards could you offer?*

3 *Create the publicity for your crowdfunding campaign. Make it as informative and attractive as possible. Use ideas from 6.*

4 *Present your crowdfunding campaign to the other groups. Each group must choose another project to back. Which got the most backers?*

1 SPEAKING **Work with a partner. Who and what can you see in the photo? What do you think a 'superfan' is?**

2 LISTENING 36 **Listen to a radio programme about superfans and answer the questions.**

1 What are 'superfans'?
2 How important are superfans to the creative industries?
3 Who is the world's most famous superfan?

3 36 **Listen again. Are the statements True (T), False (F) or is the information Not Mentioned (NM)?**

1 Ahmed bin Fahad only collects Super Mario computer games. T/F/NM
2 Ahmed has to spend more money to have games in his collection that have never been played. T/F/NM
3 Katie Aiani began her collection at a younger age than Ahmed. T/F/NM
4 Katie's sister helped to make her a superfan of Harry Potter. T/F/NM
5 Katie's parents didn't want her to become a Harry Potter superfan. T/F/NM
6 A key to Sarah M's success with celebrities is not insisting on taking their photo. T/F/NM
7 Sarah M moved home to be closer to the places where celebrities meet up and go out. T/F/NM
8 Usually Sarah M meets famous people by coincidence. T/F/NM
9 Sarah M doesn't only take photos with A-list celebrities. T/F/NM
10 Sarah M enjoys her own fame. T/F/NM

4 SPEAKING **What about *you*?**

1 What or who are you a fan of?
2 Do you think you could ever become a superfan? Why/Why not?

Grammar in context

Reported speech – other reporting verbs

1a Look at the sentences. Which reporting verbs have a person (like *told*) and which don't (like *said*)?

1a 'Superfans start young. Ahmed started at the age of five.'
1b He **explained** that superfans started young. He added that Ahmed had started at the age of five.
2a 'You have to be polite and respectful.'
2b She **warned** them that they had to be polite and respectful.
3a 'Don't forget collectors often buy two copies of each game.'
3b He **reminded** her that Ahmed needed to buy two copies of each game.
4a 'Sarah's become famous.'
4b He **claimed** that Sarah had become famous.

1b What is the meaning of these reporting verbs?

GRAMMAR REFERENCE ➤ PAGE 94

2a Choose the best alternative.

NEWS

At a press conference yesterday, Hollywood actor Jimmy Deep (a) *added/announced* that he was going to quit acting. He (b) *claimed/warned* that critics had destroyed his career with such negative reviews of his latest films. Deep (c) *agreed/complained* that he deserved criticism for his last film. He (d) *admitted/promised* not putting much effort into the role and (e) *added/announced* that it had been made too quickly. But Deep (f) *agreed/complained* that critics had been making personal insults about him in their reviews. He (g) *added/warned* them that he would do something if they continued. He (h) *complained/promised* that he would take legal action against them.

2b Rewrite the sentences in 2a in direct speech.

'I'm going to quit acting.'

3 Rewrite the sentences in reported speech using these verbs.

admit • announce • claim • complain • promise • remind • warn

1 Tom: 'The film was too short.'
2 Andy: 'I'm not very good at remembering film titles.'
3 Danny: 'I'll remember to give you your DVD back.'
4 The Prime Minister: 'The government is going to spend more money on the arts.'
5 Jack: 'I didn't know it was illegal to download that film.'
6 Kate: 'Josh, it's dangerous to sit too close to the screen.'
7 Jamie: 'Dave, don't forget. The match starts at 7 pm.'

Reported speech – other reporting structures

4a Check that you understand the reporting verbs and match them with the correct list (1–5) below.

a She suggested seeing a Harry Potter film.
b She apologised for disturbing the actor.
c I asked him to show me his collection of games.
d He refused to let me take his photo.
e They criticised him for not signing autographs.

1 verb + infinitive: ...., agree, claim, offer, promise
2 verb + object + infinitive: ...., advise, instruct, tell, order, invite, remind, warn, recommend
3 verb + gerund: ...., admit, advise, deny, regret, recommend
4 verb + preposition + gerund: ...., insist on, object to, confess to
5 verb + object + preposition + gerund: ...., congratulate somebody on, accuse somebody of, warn somebody against

4b Check that you understand the other reporting verbs in lists 1–5 above.

GRAMMAR REFERENCE ➤ PAGE 94

5 Choose the correct alternative.

1 My friend suggested to see/seeing a science fiction film.
2 They apologised for arrive/arriving late.
3 They criticised me to watch/for watching too many films.
4 We agreed to go/going at 8 o'clock.
5 She promised to not tell/not to tell me the end of the film.
6 I admitted to like/liking Harry Potter.
7 They refused to buy/buying the tickets.
8 She accused me of not know/knowing who the actor was.

6 Rewrite the sentences.

1 'I'm sorry I didn't wait for you, Emma.'
Connor apologised ....
2 'Don't come this way, Ashley, because it's dangerous.'
She warned ....
3 'Ella took the book from the library.'
She accused ....
4 'I'll tell you exactly what happened, Mum.'
Elizabeth promised ....
5 'I didn't take the CD.'
Taylor denied ....
6 'Don't go out with your friends this weekend, William.'
William's dad told ....
7 'OK, we'll help you with your homework tomorrow, Lara.'
Cathy and Lucas agreed ....
8 'No, I won't let them take my photo.'
The actor refused ....

7 Complete the sentences with information about yourself. You must use a verb.

1 Once somebody accused me ....
2 I once refused ....
3 When I was small, my parents insisted on ....
4 Once I promised ....
5 If you want to take up a new hobby, I suggest ....
6 Somebody once congratulated me on ....
7 My parents have always warned me ....
8 At school, they always tell you ....

8 SPEAKING **Work with a partner. Compare your sentences. Are any similar or the same?**

Discussions – 1

1 SPEAKING **Work with a partner. Look at the posters. Can you think of any other films where the star is female?**

2 **Read this website article. Does the information surprise you? Why/Why not?**

FILM ★★★★★

REVIEWS **MOVIE NEWS** BLOGS FEATURES PODCAST FORUMS

CHANGING THE WAY WE RATE FILMS

The Swedish cinema industry wants us to look at films in a different way. Four cinemas in the country have started using a simple test to evaluate films and other types of fiction. The test simply asks if there are at least two women in a film or a work of fiction who talk to each other about subjects other than men. If the film passes the test, it is given an 'A' rating. The problem is that apparently many famous films, including all the original *Star Wars* movies and all except one of the *Harry Potter* movies, fail the test. That doesn't mean that those films are bad, but the objective is to encourage more female stories and perspectives in the cinema. One Swedish TV channel had an 'A' rated Super Sunday when it only played films which pass the test, including *The Hunger Games* and the 2013 blockbuster *Gravity*, which stars Sandra Bullock. *Gravity* is unusual in having a female star. Recent research in the US showed that women only make up 33% of the characters in films, and only 11% of the main characters. Furthermore, the number of women appearing in films decreased in the previous five years.

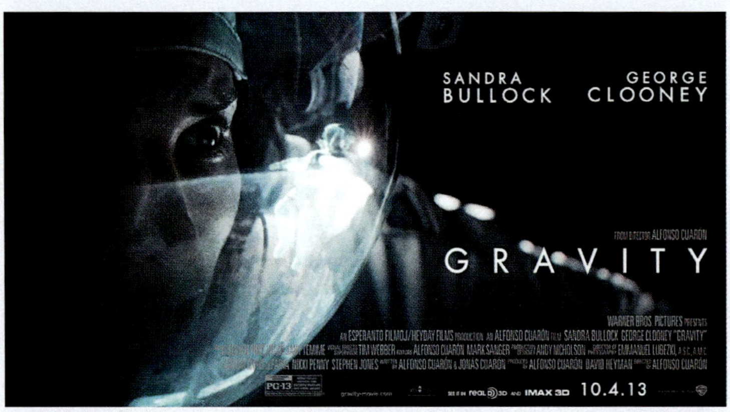

3 LISTENING 37 **Listen to two teenagers discussing the newspaper article and answer the questions.**

1 What is each person's opinion?

2 What examples do they give to support their arguments?

4 37 **Listen again and tick (✓) the expressions in the Speaking bank that you hear.**

SPEAKING BANK

Presenting a solid argument

Giving emphasis

- You have to remember that …
- Don't forget that …
- There's no doubt in my mind that …
- I really do think that …
- I'm totally convinced that …
- You can't deny that …

Giving examples

- For instance,
- Take …, for example
- What about the case of …?
- Look at …
- You only have to think of …
- … such as …
- A good example of that is …
- Just to give you an idea …

5 SPEAKING **Work in groups of three. Discuss your own opinions about the article in 2. Give examples.**

✓ EXAM SUCCESS

Remember that in discussions you must listen carefully to what other people say and react to it. Your mark will depend in part on how well you interact with others.

➤ EXAM SUCCESS page 146

PRACTICE MAKES PERFECT

6a SPEAKING **Look at these discussion topics. Decide what your opinion is for each one and make a note of your arguments and examples.**

1 Most video games are made for boys, not girls.

2 Violent films and video games create violent teenagers.

3 Sales of video games are now higher than sales of DVDs because they don't make good films anymore.

6b **Work in groups of three. Discuss the different topics. Remember to use expressions from the Speaking bank.**

6c **Share your ideas with the whole class. Do you have similar opinions or not?**

A review

1 SPEAKING **Work with a partner. Look at this notice on a website. Which book(s) would you recommend and why?**

from BOOKREVIEWS **REVIEWS WANTED**

We are always looking for reviews of great books for teenagers!

Which book would you recommend to readers of your age? Write a review telling us what happens in the book and explain why you think it's a good book for teenagers.

2 **Read this review of a book for teenagers. Would you want to read this book after reading the review? Why/ Why not?**

BOOKREVIEWS.COM SEARCH

HOME GENRE NEWS WIN! SUBSCRIBE TO OUR NEWSLETTER

Legend by Marie Lu ★★★★★

1 *Legend* is a really good book for teenagers written by an American writer called Marie Lu. It's a fantasy novel set in a dystopian future. The book first appeared in 2011. It's the first part of a trilogy.

2 The plot of the story is very good because you're never really sure what is going to happen next. The two main characters are both 15. One is a girl called June and the other is a boy called Day. June works for the Republic as a type of police officer. But Day is a rebel who is fighting against the Republic. June has to find and capture Day, but when she meets him, she realises the truth about the Republic. One good thing about the book is both June and Day are narrators, so you know exactly what each of them thinks. There are some good scenes where June and Day's feelings for each other change and the plot takes lots of good turns that you don't expect.

3 In my opinion, this book is really good for teenagers because there is action and romance, but it also makes good points about loyalty to family, friends and your country. I also like the good descriptions of how our world might be in the future.

4 All things considered, this is a great book for teenagers because it's both exciting and thought-provoking. If you're a fan of stories that combine action, good characters and good descriptions, you'll love *Legend*.

3 **Read the review again and decide what the purpose of each paragraph is.**

Paragraph 1: ....

Paragraph 2: ....

Paragraph 3: ....

Paragraph 4: ....

4 **What do you think of the use of adjectives in the book review? Why?**

5a **Work with a partner. Look at the adjectives in the Writing bank. Which ones do you know? Use a dictionary to check the meaning of any you don't know.**

5b **Which adjectives do you think are positive and which are negative?**

WRITING BANK

Using adjectives in reviews

amazing • amusing • appealing • awful
brilliant • clever • clichéd • convincing
credible • deep • fascinating • fast-moving
gripping • hilarious • incredible • inspiring
intricate • intriguing • lively • moving
mysterious • perceptive • predictable
realistic • relaxing • scary • sensitive
spectacular • stunning • stupid • terrible
thought-provoking • thrilling
unconvincing • uninspiring • vivid
well-produced

6 **Use adjectives from the Writing bank to replace the adjective *good* in the review in 2.**

✓ EXAM SUCCESS

To make reviews interesting for the reader, use a variety of adjectives and adverbs. Don't forget to use expressions of opinion (see page 27) and to make it clear what your recommendation is.

➤ EXAM SUCCESS page 146

PRACTICE MAKES PERFECT

7a **Make notes about one of the books you thought about in 1. Organise your notes into paragraphs. Follow the paragraph plan in 3.**

7b **Write your review.**

7c **Exchange reviews with other students. Which of the books do you want to read?**

WRITING BANK ➤ PAGE 156

Grammar reference

Reported speech – statements

When the reporting verb (e.g. **say**, **tell**) is in the past, the tense of the verb in reported speech usually changes, going one tense 'back'. Some tenses cannot go any further back and so stay the same.

Could, **would**, **should** and **might** do not change from direct to reported speech.

When the reporting verb is in the present simple or present perfect, the tense of the verb in reported speech usually stays the same.

'I enjoy watching films.' → He says he enjoys watching films.

When the reporting verb is in the past but the statement is something which is still true, or is and will always be true, the tense of the verb in reported speech usually stays the same.

'I'm American.' → Hayden said he's American.

'They make lots of films in India.' → The guide told us that they make lots of films in India.

In reported speech, pronouns and possessive adjectives also change.

*'I love **your** smile.' → Brad said **he** loved **her** smile.*

With **say** you do not need to use a personal object to say who you are talking to.

He said it was going to be a great film.

~~*He said me it was going to be a great film.*~~

With **tell** you use a personal object to say who you are talking to.

He told me it was going to be a great film.

~~*He told that it was going to be a great film.*~~

Reported speech – questions

The same changes occur with tenses, pronouns and other words as with reported statements.

We do not use the auxiliary verb **do** in reported questions.

'Do you like rap music?' → She asked me if I liked rap music.

There is no inversion of subject and verb in reported questions.

'Where are you?' → He asked me where I was.

Reported questions are not real questions so they do not need question marks.

~~*She asked me what I needed?*~~

When there is no question word (*who*, *what*, *how*, *why*, etc.), we use **if** or **whether**.

'Can you do it?' → They asked me if I could do it.

Reported speech – other reporting verbs

- ***add***, ***admit***, ***agree***, ***announce***, ***claim***, ***complain***, ***explain***, ***promise***
  These work like **say** – you do not need to use a personal object with them.
- ***remind***, ***warn***
  These work like **tell** – you need to use a personal object with them.

Reported speech – other reporting structures

- verb + infinitive: agree, claim, offer, promise, refuse
  *He **agreed** to go with them.*
- verb + object + infinitive: advise, ask, instruct, invite, order, recommend, remind, tell, warn
  *She **advised** him to buy tickets in advance.*
- verb + gerund: admit, advise, deny, recommend, regret, suggest
  *They **admitted** stealing the watch.*
- verb + preposition + gerund: apologise for, confess to, insist on, object to
  *We **apologised** for arriving late.*
- verb + object + preposition + gerund: accuse somebody of, congratulate somebody on, criticise somebody for, warn somebody against
  *They **accused** him of cheating in the exam.*

Vocabulary

Music and film acting • crowd • gig • lighting • live (adv) • lyrics • performance • plot • record (v) • role scene • soundtrack • stage • star (v) • track

Media habits download • file-sharing site • live stream (n) • mobile device • peer-to-peer • purchase stream (n, v) • transfer

Compound nouns and adjectives **Nouns:** blockbuster • box office • download • drawback • feedback file-sharing • marketplace • outcome • page-turner • screenplay • songwriter • soundtrack • turnout
Adjectives: brand new • fast-moving • thought-provoking

Other words and phrases ➤ page 140

Grammar revision

Reported speech – statements / 6 points

1 Complete the second sentence so that it has a similar meaning to the first. Use between two and five words, including the word given.

1 'I can't do this exercise,' Ethan said. ABLE
Ethan said .... do the exercise.
2 'You must bring your ID,' the teacher said to me. TO
The teacher told .... bring my ID.
3 'It's on TV tonight on Channel 4,' said Ava. THAT
Ava explained it .... on Channel 4.
4 'I failed the exam,' said Daniel. PASSED
Daniel admitted .... the exam.
5 'I'm sure these are our seats,' said Chloe. WAS
Chloe claimed she .... seats.
6 'We might have made a mistake,' Ben said. MAYBE
Ben warned them that .... a mistake.

Reported speech – questions / 7 points

2 Complete the sentences with reported speech.

1 'Where have you just been?' Charlie asked Holly.
Charlie asked ....
2 'Do you want to out tonight, Jo?' He asked her.
He asked Jo ....
3 'Can you speak English?' Lucy asked the boy.
Lucy asked ....
4 'Will it rain next week?' wondered Dave.
Dave wondered ....
5 'How did they do that stunt?' Sophie wanted to know.
Sophie wanted to know ....
6 'Are you going to buy a car?' Grace asked Jack.
Grace asked ....
7 'What have you been doing this morning?' Mum asked us.
Mum asked ....

Reported speech – other reporting structures / 7 points

3 Complete the text with the correct form of the verbs given. Add prepositions if necessary.

Last year the police (a) .... (promise/do) something about people downloading films illegally. They (b) .... (accuse/one man/make) hundreds of illegal copies of a recent Hollywood blockbuster. They arrested him, but he (c) .... (refuse/answer) any of their questions. In the end, he (d) .... (admit/do) it. He (e) .... (confess/copy) nearly 1,000 films. He (f) .... (apologise/cause) any problems. The police (g) .... (tell/him/not do) it again.

Vocabulary revision

MUSIC AND FILM / 6 points

1 Complete the sentences with the correct words.

1 Their albums are good, but I prefer hearing them l.................... .
2 I thought the film was good, but the last s.................... was too long.
3 I like the music in this song, but I don't understand any of the l.................... .
4 He's appeared as a minor character in lots of films, but this is the first time he's s.................... in one.
5 He loves recording, but he's so shy he hates getting up on s.................... .
6 He usually plays the r.................... of a criminal.

COMPOUND NOUNS/ADJECTIVES / 7 points

2 Match the words in the two columns. Is each word an adjective or a noun?

1 block	a new
2 box	b moving
3 brand-	c buster
4 draw	d come
5 fast-	e out
6 turn	f office
7 out	g back

MEDIA HABITS / 7 points

3 Reorder the letters in the words in red.

1 I'm going to watch a evil meatrs of the match.
2 I usually listen to music on a bileom cedive.
3 I sometimes fernasrt songs from my laptop to my MP3 player so that I have them on both.
4 I couldn't tremas the song or oldwodna a film because the connection was so slow.
5 To rushpace things on the Net use a credit card.
6 Not all the music life-granish isset are illegal.

Total: / 40 points

8 Surviving disaster

Vocabulary

Natural disasters

a

b

c

d

e

1a Match the photos to these words. There are five extra words.

avalanche • drought • earthquake
epidemic • flood • forest fire • hurricane
landslide • tsunami • volcanic eruption

1b Match the extra words in 1a with these definitions.

1 a situation in which a disease spreads very quickly and infects many people
2 a very large wave or series of waves caused when something such as an earthquake happens underwater
3 a large amount of snow and ice that suddenly falls down a mountain
4 a situation in which a large area with trees burns
5 a violent storm with extremely strong winds and heavy rain

2 PRONUNCIATION 38 **Where does the stress go in the words in 1a? Listen and check your answers.**

3 SPEAKING **Work with a partner. Which parts of the world do you associate with the natural disasters in 1a? Which ones could happen in your country?**

Words connected with natural disasters

4 SPEAKING **Work in groups of three. Each person reads one of the texts A–C. Check the words in red in a dictionary if necessary. Explain the words to the others in your group.**

A There are hundreds of **casualties** after last night's earthquake and its **aftershock**. Many of the **victims** are young or elderly. The **survivors** of the earthquake are camping out in the street because it is safer than being indoors. Many **injuries** have been caused by **collapsing** walls since the earthquake has caused terrible damage to many buildings in the city. Firefighters have been working hard to **put out** fires caused by the **tremors**.

B First the volcano threw up a cloud of **ash**. Then **molten lava** started to come down the side of the mountain. Right now, the lava is **heading towards** the most populated village on the island. **Panic** had already been **spreading** through the village over the past few weeks. The neighbouring island has already set up camps for the hundreds of **refugees** who are arriving.

C The **torrential** rain that has **swept across** the country in the last few days has caused terrible floods. Three major rivers have **burst their banks**. Many people have been **evacuated** from their homes. **Mud** and water have destroyed many houses. The **destruction** has been much worse in western areas where the rain has been heavier.

5 Complete the sentences with the correct form of words in 4.

1 We need to .... the area immediately.
2 A hurricane is quickly .... across the ocean.
3 Experts think the hurricane is .... towards land.
4 The disease is .... quickly. Doctors fear that thousands more people will catch it in the next few weeks.
5 Nothing was left after the fire, only ....
6 The .... of the earthquake are being offered food, drink and blankets at the town hall.

6 LISTENING 39 **Listen to three short reports on natural disasters and complete the notes.**

	1	2	3
Type of disaster			
Where			
Casualties			
Damage			

7 SPEAKING **Work with a partner. Talk about a natural disaster that has happened recently or that is very famous.**

1 SPEAKING **Work with a partner. Look at the photo at the bottom of the page and discuss what it could be.**

2 **Read the article and answer the questions.**

1 What is the name of the object in the photo?
2 What exactly is it for?

3 **Read again and choose the best answer.**

1 Julian Sharpe thinks the problem in Japan in 2011 was that people …
  a had made no plans for a natural disaster.
  b were not ready for the size of this disaster.
  c didn't know where to go to be evacuated.
2 Sharpe had his idea when he …
  a was in Indonesia during the 2004 tsunami.
  b saw a sphere floating in the water.
  c realised that with long, gradual slopes it isn't easy to get away from a tsunami.
3 The company has designed …
  a different models of the Survival Capsule for different types of disaster.
  b just one model of the Survival Capsule but in varying sizes.
  c only capsules that have the most basic survival facilities.
4 The capsule …
  a needs to be rescued by helicopter when the tsunami eventually ends.
  b starts off tied to the ground.
  c could be trapped under deep water.
5 The article says that …
  a they haven't made any capsules yet.
  b the cost of the spheres is too high.
  c the cost is OK if they save lives.

✓ EXAM SUCCESS

Remember that if you find the same words in the text and in one of the options, this does not mean it is the correct option. The correct option will probably express the information in the text using different words.

➤ EXAM SUCCESS page 146

4 **CRITICAL THINKING**

Think! Then compare ideas with your class.

- Do you think this is a useful, practical invention? Why/Why not?

5 **What do the underlined words in the text mean? Guess and then check in your dictionary.**

6 SPEAKING **What about *you*?**

What can we do to prepare for such events? Do you know any security procedures?

TSUNAMI!

A 21st century survival solution

The 2011 Tohoku earthquake and the tsunami that followed count as one of the worst natural disasters of the 21st century. When the earthquake struck with a force of magnitude 9, it was the most powerful ever to hit Japan and its consequences were catastrophic. In anticipation of a similar disaster, an American company called Survival Capsules LCC turned their design for a sphere to protect people from both fire and flood into reality.

> *… the tsunami was a terrible learning experience for the Japanese.*

According to Julian Sharpe, president of Survival Capsules LCC, the tsunami was a terrible learning experience for the Japanese. The different regions had evacuation towers and the local population knew what to do in case of a tsunami. But in the end the evacuation towers that they relied on for survival turned out to be far too low. The tsunami was much higher than expected, with a maximum height of just over 40 metres. It resulted in nearly 16,000 deaths, over 6,000 casualties, and more than 2,500 people missing.

Sharpe says he came up with the initial concept for the Survival Capsule while on holiday with his family in a coastal town in Oregon in the US in 2004. While he was there, he couldn't help thinking about the tsunami that had just swept across the Indian Ocean and the East Indies. He noticed that many coastal areas with beaches have a similar landscape, with long, gradual slopes. Even when residents are given a tsunami alert, it's impossible to get to sufficiently high ground fast enough.

That was when Sharpe came up with the idea of something more flexible. He thought of capsules that could float above the approaching wave. According to Sharpe, his personal safety system (PSS) is designed to protect survivors not only in tsunamis, but also in hurricanes, earthquakes and tornadoes. It was designed by aircraft engineers in consultation with tsunami experts.

There are currently five versions of the capsule. They range in size from a basic two-person model with a diameter of 1.4m to one capable of holding ten adults. The capsules have been built for use in homes, businesses, schools and airports. The brightly-painted spherical capsule is built to survive impacts, and the shape allows it to roll out from beneath the debris of collapsed buildings. The capsules can also be made with one or two windows.

> *Mobile phone use is possible, to communicate with the outside world.*

Access to the capsule is by a round door that can be opened from inside or outside. Inside, there are seats, water containers, GPS equipment, storage facilities for food and 60 minutes of oxygen. Mobile phone use is possible, to communicate with the outside world. The capsule weighs only about 136kg, so it's easy to move. It has a handle so that it can be recovered by a crane or helicopter. Optional extras are also offered, including a toilet, a music system and solar panels.

The idea is for capsules to be placed along coastlines. If the sea rises, the line tying the capsule to the ground gets longer. When the water recedes, the capsule floats back to the ground. If the water gets too deep, the line disconnects and the capsule floats to the surface.

The current cost of the spheres is between $13,000 and $20,000. This is a small price to pay if, as Sharpe hopes, the Survival Capsules increase people's chances of surviving the next tsunami.

The passive

1a Look at the sentences and answer the questions below.

a It **was designed** by aircraft engineers.
b It **can be recovered** by a crane or helicopter.
c Optional extras **are** also **offered**.
d The capsules **have been built** for use in private homes.

1 Are all the sentences in the passive?
2 What tense is each sentence?
3 How do we form the passive?
4 What does *by* introduce?

1b Are these statements True (T) or False (F)?

1 We use the passive when we are interested mainly in an action, not the person who does the action. T/F
2 We use the passive when we don't know the person who does the action. T/F
3 We use the passive when it is obvious who does the action. T/F

GRAMMAR REFERENCE ➤ PAGE 106

2 Complete the sentences with the correct passive form of the verbs given.

1 New Orleans .... (hit) by Hurricane Katrina in 2005.
2 Throughout history, a number of cities .... (destroy) by volcanoes.
3 Some experts think the weather .... (control) by humans one day.
4 Some forest fires can .... (see) from space.
5 The strength of earthquakes .... (measure) using the Richter Scale.
6 In areas where earthquakes are common, houses and flats should .... (build) in a special way so that they don't collapse easily.
7 When the tsunami hit Indonesia in 2004, people .... (not warn) of the possible danger.

Flooding in New Orleans, 2005

3 Find the mistakes in these sentences and rewrite them correctly.

1 Some areas of Africa have being affected by a terrible drought.
2 Twenty people were save in the mountains by a rescue team yesterday.
3 A huge landslide was hit a small town in Peru last week.
4 Some people think that one day the Earth will be destroyed for a big meteorite.
5 Our house was been damaged by torrential rain last year.
6 More hurricanes have predicted for this summer.
7 Have been any people injured in the fire?
8 In rescue situations I think children must helped first.

The passive – verbs with two objects

4a Look at the sentences and read the explanation below.

1 They give residents a tsunami alert.
2a A tsunami alert **is given** to residents.
2b Residents **are given** a tsunami alert.

Some verbs are followed by two objects, one usually a thing and the other a person. When this happens, we can make two different **passive** sentences (2a/2b).

4b Is it more common to use the thing (2a) or the person (2b) as the subject?

4c These verbs can be followed by two objects. Check their meanings in a dictionary if necessary.

bring • buy • lend • offer • owe • pay
promise • refuse • send • show
teach • tell

GRAMMAR REFERENCE ➤ PAGE 106

5 Which sentence in each pair is more natural?

1a The survivors were given water.
1b Water was given to the survivors.
2a Help was promised to them.
2b They were promised help.
3a I was taught first aid by my grandmother.
3b First aid was taught to me by my grandmother.
4a The president was sent an urgent message.
4b An urgent message was sent to the president.
5a A prize was given to Taylor Swift for her charity work.
5b Taylor Swift was given a prize for her charity work.

Typhoon damage in Leyte Province, Philippines, 2013

6 Rewrite the sentences using the passive. Use the person or people as the subject.

1 The government has sent food and medicine to the victims of the earthquake.
The victims of the earthquake have been sent food and medicine by the government.
2 They paid the president of the company $40,000 for two Survival Capsules.
3 They're offering the survivors financial aid.
4 My teacher has given me information about surviving earthquakes.
5 Perhaps they'll offer the casualties medical help.
6 They told her the news when she arrived.
7 They are not going to refuse the refugees entrance into the country.
8 The government has promised the scientists money for research.

7 SPEAKING Find somebody in your class for each of the squares and write their name. Do not write the same person twice. Ignore the 'details' section.

Find someone who has been …

given a prize *Name:* *Details:*	*given a special present* *Name:* *Details:*
taught to do something by a member of their family *Name:* *Details:*	*offered a job or a special responsibility* *Name:* *Details:*
sent an important email *Name:* *Details:*	*told a secret* *Name:* *Details:*
paid for doing something *Name:* *Details:*	*owed money* *Name:* *Details:*

8 SPEAKING Now ask questions to find out more details about each activity.

Why were you given a prize?
What were you taught?

Prepositional phrases with verbs

1 Look at the verbs in these sentences. Which prepositions do they need?

1 People **relied** .... evacuation towers for survival.
2 The capsule **protects** people .... fire and flood.

2 Complete the sentences with these prepositions.

about • for • for • in • of • on • on • to • to • with

1 Residents **listened** .... the experts.
2 Most people **agree** .... my theory.
3 People used to **believe** .... supernatural causes for natural disasters.
4 The strength of a volcano **depends** .... different factors.
5 The experts **apologised** .... not warning people about the possibilities of a tsunami.
6 The residents **complained** .... not being informed.
7 Nobody **dreamt** .... something as big as a 40-metre wave.
8 The government **waited** .... a team of experts to send their report.
9 Nobody knew who the dog **belonged** ....
10 You can **spend** money .... optional extras.

3 Complete the sentences so they are true for you. Use a preposition.

1 I occasionally spend money …
2 I hate waiting …
3 For the future, I dream …
4 I know I can rely …
5 I never listen …
6 Once I had to apologise …
7 I nearly always agree …
8 I don't usually complain …

4 SPEAKING Work in small groups. Compare your sentences in 3. Tell the class any sentences that you have in common.

Helping a CHARITY

LIFE SKILLS OBJECTIVES

- To learn about the work of a humanitarian organisation.
- To consider reasons for helping with charity work.
- To investigate a current disaster or problem and how we can help.

KEY CONCEPTS

aid [n, v]: *After an earthquake, people need urgent medical aid.* **relief [n]:** *Relief services are helping victims of the flood.* **aid/relief worker [n]:** *Thousands of relief workers are arriving to help the victims.* **in need [phr]:** *There are many people in need in this country, people who need money, clothes or a home.* **donate [v]:** *People are donating money and clothes to help the victims.*

1 SPEAKING **Work with a partner. What do you know about ...**

1 Ebola?
2 the organisation Médecins Sans Frontières/Doctors Without Borders (MSF)?

2 Look at this Médecins Sans Frontières (MSF) poster about Ebola. Read the introduction and answer the questions.

1 What does the text say about Ebola?
2 What does it say about what MSF has done?
3 What information will appear in the rest of the poster?

HOW WE TREAT EBOLA

MEDECINS SANS FRONTIERES
DOCTORS WITHOUT BORDERS

When Ebola haemorrhagic fever broke out recently in Guinea, West Africa, MSF set up three specialised treatment centres in the worst-hit areas. Ebola is so infectious – and so deadly – that patients need to be treated in isolation by staff wearing special protective clothing. Emergency coordinator Henry Gray and logistician Pascal Piguet, both just back from Guinea, explain why, with Ebola, every little detail counts.

1 Protective clothing
"The suits are so stifling that it's hard to stay inside for more than 40 minutes. You sweat a lot – up to two litres each time – but you don't cool down because the sweat doesn't evaporate," says Pascal.

2 Changing area
Before entering the high-risk zone, staff help each other put on their protective suits, while respecting the strict 'no body-to-body contact' rule.

3 Staff entrance to high-risk zone
"Each time we go in, we have to plan it down to the finest detail. To prepare, we have a 30-minute briefing about what we are going to do, and we get all the equipment ready beforehand," says Pascal.

4 High-risk zone: confirmed cases
After doing their rounds in the zone for suspected cases, staff enter the zone for confirmed cases. "There's a gradation of risk all the time – you don't want to recontaminate a zone," says Henry. "The high-risk zone's not an easy place to be – you're isolated, you've got no access to the outside world, so we try and make it as friendly as possible, with a TV, radios, plastic chairs and shaded areas to sit," says Henry.

5 Staff exit from high-risk zone
On leaving the high-risk area, staff remove their protective suits and disinfect themselves.

6 Laundry
All recyclable items of clothing are washed in chlorinated water every day and reused.

7 Incinerator
Everything used in the high-risk area which can't be disinfected is burnt.

8 Triage tent
Patients with Ebola symptoms are admitted to the zone for suspected cases.

9 High-risk zone: suspected cases
Many of the early symptoms of Ebola are similar to diseases such as malaria and TB. "It's really important that there are separate zones for suspected and confirmed cases, because you don't want to contaminate someone with TB with Ebola – that's basically a death sentence," says Henry.

10 Treatment ward
"With a mortality rate of up to 90 percent, we know that most people in the treatment ward will not come out. We do the most we can for them: whatever the patient wants, the patient gets – special food, new items of clothing … it's easy to do and it does them good," says Pascal.

3 SPEAKING **Work with a partner. Look at the map of the centre and answer these questions.**

1 What is the purpose of each different area?
2 What is the purple route through the treatment centre? What happens on this route?
3 Why do you think the poster gives the price of the protective clothes which the relief workers have to wear?
4 What do you think are the aims of this poster?

4 Read texts 1–12 and answer the questions.

1 What do you think the 'no body-to-body contact' rule means, and why do they have it?
2 Apart from putting on their suits, what do the aid workers do before they go into the high-risk zone?
3 What do they do when they leave the high-risk zones?
4 Why is it essential to have different zones for suspected and confirmed cases?
5 What is the process followed before patients can leave the treatment centre?
6 What happens to cured patients after they leave?

11 Visitors' area

Family members talk with patients through the fence, local religious leaders offer moral support, and MSF psychologists provide counselling.

12 Exit for cured patients

When a patient is feeling better and has had two negative lab tests in a row, they are allowed home. Before leaving, they shower in chlorinated water and receive clean clothes and a package containing therapeutic food and vitamins to build up their strength.

Returning home isn't always easy, due to the stigma and fear associated with Ebola. Survivors receive continued support from psychologists after they leave, while health promoters help educate their communities about the disease.

5 SPEAKING **Work with a partner. How successful do you think the poster is? Explain why or why not.**

6 LISTENING ▶ 40 **Watch or listen to four students discussing charity fundraising. Answer questions a–d. Tick (✓) below.**

a Who prefers charities with a personal connection to them?
b Who has raised funds for more than one charity?
c Who thinks putting on events is a good way to raise money?
d Who believes that any method for collecting money is OK?

Speaker	a	b	c	d
Sam				
Vanessa				
Bea				
Chris				

7 ▶ 40 **Watch or listen again. What does each speaker say about their own experiences of raising money for charity? Discuss your answers in pairs.**

LIFE TASK

You want to investigate a problem and ways you can help.

Work in a group and follow this plan:

1 *Choose a current or recent disaster or a typical problem affecting people in any part of the world.*
2 *Research the problem. Find out the causes, effects and importance of the problem.*
3 *Find out what type of help could be given to the people suffering the problem.*
4 *Make a poster to inform members of the public about the problem and how they can help.*

Listening

The tsunami survivor who is an example to us all

1 SPEAKING **Work with a partner. Look at the photo and caption.**

Why do you think the woman in the photo might be an example to others?

2 LISTENING 41 **Listen to a radio programme about the woman in the photo and check your predictions in 1.**

3 41 **Listen again. Are these statements True (T), False (F) or is the information Not Mentioned (NM)?**

1 Petra's friend did not survive the tsunami. T/F/NM
2 Petra's organisation builds brand new schools around the world. T/F/NM
3 Tilly Smith was a hero of the 2004 tsunami. T/F/NM
4 Petra has met Tilly Smith in person. T/F/NM
5 Petra keeps her job and her charity work completely separate. T/F/NM
6 Petra finds it very painful to talk about her survival story. T/F/NM
7 The aim of Petra's organisation is not to offer aid in the first few days after a natural disaster. T/F/NM
8 Petra would like to make more of an impact by becoming a politician one day. T/F/NM

✓ EXAM SUCCESS

In some True/False activities, such as this one, there are three possibilities: True/False/Not Mentioned. Choose Not Mentioned if you cannot hear the information when you listen to the text.

➤ EXAM SUCCESS page 146

4 SPEAKING **What about you?**

What do you think of the story of Petra Němcová?

Grammar in context

The passive with say, know, believe, etc. – 1

1a Look at the sentences and answer the questions below.

a It **was reported that** she saved people thanks to a geography lesson.
b It **is thought that** Tilly saved around 100 lives.
c It **has been claimed that** more than 280,000 people died.
d It**'s believed that** children are the worst victims.

1 What is the subject in the first part of these sentences?
2 Why do we use the passive in the first part of these sentences?
3 Why are different tenses used in the first part of the sentences?

1b Here is a list of verbs which are frequently used in this way. Check their meaning in a dictionary if necessary.

believe • claim • expect • know • report
say • think

GRAMMAR REFERENCE ➤ PAGE 106

2 Make complete sentences with the structures in 1.

1 'The Sun goes round the Earth.' – past belief
It *was believed that the Sun went round the Earth.*
2 'The Earth is flat' – past thought
It ....
3 'Natural disasters are becoming more frequent.' – present claim
It ....
4 'An asteroid will destroy the world one day.' – something people have said
It ....
5 'A big volcano will erupt in Iceland soon.' – present expectation
It ....
6 'Volcanic ash can have a terrible effect on planes.' – present knowledge
It ....
7 'People heard the eruption of Krakatoa over 3,000 km away.' – past report
It ....
8 'One day an enormous earthquake will strike Los Angeles.' – something people say
It ....

The passive with say, know, believe, etc. – 2

3 Look at the sentences and decide if the statements below are True (T) or False (F).

a Each school **is said to cost** around £110,000.

b Petra **is known to have been** impressed by the story.

c At first, she **was thought to have died**, but then they found her.

d Twelve thousand children **are said to be** benefitting from the project.

e Animals **are said to know** when a natural disaster is coming.

1 In each sentence, the subject of the first part of the sentence is the subject of the rest of the second verb. T/F

2 After the verbs *reported*, *known*, *believed*, etc. we use *to* + infinitive to talk about things in the present, or things that are always true. T/F

3 After the verbs *reported*, *known*, *believed*, etc. we use *to have* + past participle to talk about past events. T/F

4 We use *is/are believed/thought*, etc. to talk about present beliefs and thoughts. T/F

5 We use *was/were believed/thought*, etc. to talk about past beliefs and thoughts. T/F

GRAMMAR REFERENCE ➤ PAGE 106

4 Rewrite the sentences.

1 They say that toads sense earthquakes.
Toads ……………………………………………………

2 They know that bees are very important for the environment.
Bees ……………………………………………………

3 People claim that global warming is responsible for many natural disasters.
Global warming ……………………………………………………

4 They reported that many people had gone missing after the eruption.
Many people ……………………………………………………

5 People believed that the Titanic was unsinkable.
The Titanic ……………………………………………………

6 People didn't know Everest was the highest mountain until 1852.
Everest ……………………………………………………

7 It is said that Pompeii is one of the most popular tourist attractions in Italy.
Pompeii ……………………………………………………

8 It's believed that a meteorite caused the extinction of dinosaurs.
A meteorite ……………………………………………………

5 Read the text and choose the correct alternative.

ANIMAL SENSES

Very few animals were reported to (a) die/have died in the tsunami in December 2004. For example, in an area of Sri Lanka that was hit by the disaster, there is a very popular national park called Yala National Park. It has hundreds of wild animals, including elephants, leopards and monkeys. But (b) it was/they were said that the only animals that died that day were two or three water buffalos. Flamingos are (c) reporting/reported to have flown to higher ground. Bats were seen flying away, too. Three wild elephants were seen running away from a beach before any humans knew anything about the coming tsunami. Unfortunately, the animals' warning had no effect on the people watching. How did all these animals know what was going to happen? It is (d) think/thought that animals have a sixth sense. (e) It is known/Some animals are known to be able to hear things that humans cannot hear, and this may be one way that several different types of animal may spot danger before we can. It is also believed (f) animals to be/that animals are much more sensitive to vibrations of the Earth than humans. For example, it (g) is/was thought that even large elephants can detect minor movements. It has been (h) claimed/known by some people that humans used to possess the same highly developed senses that animals have, but that over time we have lost our 'sixth sense'.

6 Complete the sentences in a logical way.

1 People from my country are said …
2 It's well known …
3 In the past, it was believed …
4 Last week in the news it was reported …
5 Students are expected …
6 Sometimes I'm known …

7 SPEAKING Compare sentences with a partner. Do you agree with your partner's sentences?

Talking about statistics

1 Look at the pie chart. It shows the percentage of people affected by different disasters in Oceania between 1980 and 2008. According to the pie chart, are these statements True (T) or False (F)?

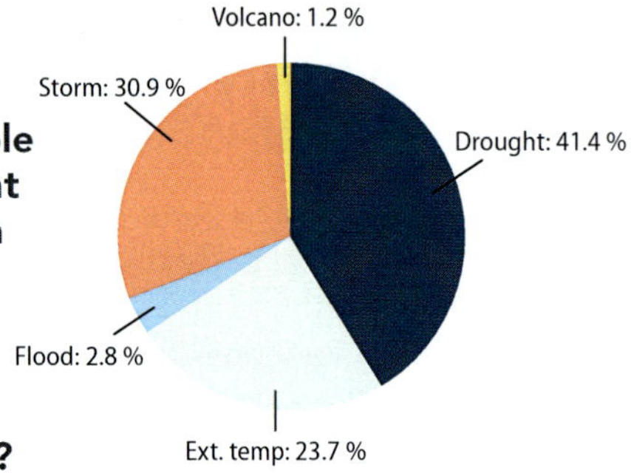

1 Over one-third of people were affected by drought. T/F
2 Just under one-fifth of people were affected by extreme temperatures. T/F
3 Fewer people were affected by extreme temperatures than by storms. T/F
4 Only about one in a hundred people were affected by volcanoes. T/F
5 Just over a quarter of people were affected by extreme temperatures and floods combined. T/F
6 The majority of people were affected by drought. T/F

2a Express the fractions as percentages and vice versa.

1 ¼ = 3 10% = 5 ½ =
2 20% = 4 66.6% = 6 80% =

2b LISTENING 42 **Listen and check. Then practise saying the fractions and percentages.**

3 Look at this graph. It shows the number of storms around the world between 1980 and 2011. Read the text below and check that you understand the words in bold.

Number of storms around the world between 1980 and 2011

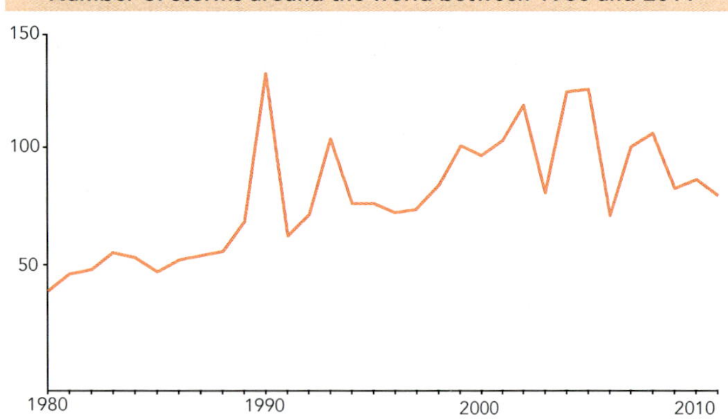

The number of storms around the world **rose gradually** between 1980 and 1988. There was **a sharp increase** in the number of storms between 1988 and 1990. Between 1980 and 1990 the number more than **tripled**. However, the number of storms **fell sharply** the year after. Between 1996 and 1998 there was only **a slight increase**. The number of storms then **fluctuated** between 2000 and 2011. It rarely **stayed the same**. There was **a dramatic rise** in numbers in 2004, but in 2006 there was **a significant decrease**.

4 Find a word or words in the Speaking bank which mean …

1 go up.
2 go from 20,000 to 40,000, for example.
3 go from 40,000 to 20,000, for example.
4 one in three.
5 slowly and in small amounts.
6 important.
7 in a sudden and surprising way.
8 most of the people or things in a group.

SPEAKING BANK

Talking about statistics

Numbers and proportions

- *a half/third/quarter/fifth/sixth*, etc.
- *one in two/three/five/ten*, etc.
- *the majority*

Trends

- *rise/fall* (n, v)
- *increase/decrease* (n, v)
- *stay the same/change little* (adj/adv)
- *slow(ly)/gradual(ly)/slight(ly)* (adj/adv)
- *steady* (adj), *steadily* (adv)
- *significant(ly)/sharp(ly)/dramatic(ally)* (adj/adv)
- *double/triple/half* (n), *halve* (v)

PRACTICE MAKES PERFECT

5a SPEAKING **Work with a partner. Student A, describe the pie chart using words and expressions in the Speaking bank.**

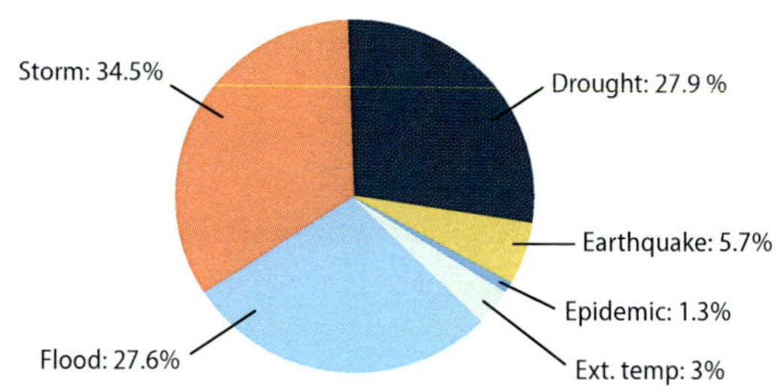

5b Student B, describe the graph using words and expressions in the Speaking bank.

Number of floods around the world between 1980 and 2011

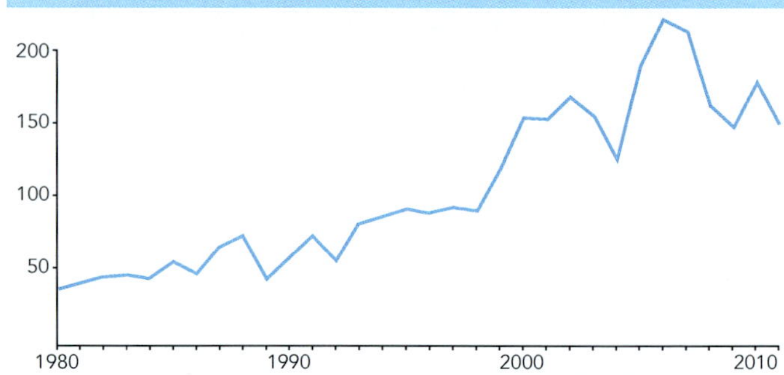

5c Work together. Compare the two pie charts on this page. Then compare the two graphs. What information do you find surprising, interesting or worrying?

An opinion essay – 2

1 SPEAKING **Work with a partner. Look at the task. Complete point 3 and discuss two ideas for each of the points 1–3.**

At school you have been talking about climate change and extreme weather. Now your English teacher has asked you to write an essay for homework.
Write your essay using all the notes and giving reasons for your point of view.

> **How can we help to save the planet?**
>
> Notes
>
> Write about: 1 recycling 2 saving energy
>
> 3 .... (your own idea)

2 Read this essay. Does it include any of your ideas in 1?

Each year there are more and more storms and floods, and temperatures are changing dramatically. In my opinion, this is partly because of the effect that humans are having on the planet. I believe that we all can and should do something about this.

The first point to make is that if we all recycled more, we could make a big difference to the environment. By recycling paper, for example, we could protect our forests. What is more, if we reused items such as plastic bags and bottles, we could also save precious natural resources. However, not enough people do this.

Another thing to bear in mind is that people use energy unnecessarily. For instance, they forget to switch computers or lights off and make their houses too warm in the winter even though by saving some of this energy, we could reduce environmental damage.

Although many students live near school, their parents take them by car each day. If we all walked, cycled or used public transport, we could help to minimise the pollution caused by exhaust fumes. Furthermore, walking or cycling would help to keep us healthy.

In conclusion, some people say that there is nothing that we can do to save the planet. I disagree. If we all take small steps to change simple daily habits, those millions of small actions can have a major impact on the planet.

3 Read the essay again. What is the purpose of each paragraph?

4 Put the underlined words and expressions in the text in the correct list.

Expressing opinions: ....

Adding ideas: ....

Putting ideas in order: ....

Contrasting ideas: ....

Concluding: ....

5 Look at how *although*, *even though* and *however* are used in the text. Which words join two halves of a sentence? Which words introduce a new sentence? Read the information in the Writing bank and check that you understand the meaning of all the linkers.

> **WRITING BANK**
>
> **Using linkers correctly**
>
> - Some linkers join two halves of a sentence. They can go at the start of the sentence or in the middle of the sentence.
>
>   *Although the country is a long way away, we must help it.*
>
>   *We must help the country although it is a long way away.*
>
>   Linkers which join two halves of a sentence:
>   *although, and, and so, because, despite, even though, since, so that, when, whereas, while*
>
> - Other linkers introduce a new sentence which refers to the previous sentence. These words are usually followed by commas.
>
>   *The country is a long way away. However, we must help it.*
>
>   Linkers which join two sentences:
>   *all things considered, as a result, as far as I am concerned, consequently, finally, firstly, furthermore, however, in addition, in conclusion, in my opinion, in the end, meanwhile, moreover, nevertheless, on the one hand, on the other hand, personally, secondly, therefore, to sum up, what is more*

PRACTICE MAKES PERFECT

6a Work with a partner. Look at the task and think about ideas and information that you could include.

At school you have been talking about problems facing the world in the 21st century. Now your English teacher has asked you to write an essay for homework.
Write your essay using all the notes and giving reasons for your point of view.

> **What are the biggest problems facing the world in the 21st century?**
>
> Notes
>
> Write about:
>
> 1 epidemics
>
> 2 changing weather conditions
>
> 3 .... (your own idea)

WRITING BANK ➤ PAGE 151

6b Write your essay. Include linkers and remember to use the Writing bank to help you.

Grammar reference

The passive

FORM

subject + **be** + **past participle** (+ **by** + agent)

Warnings are given. (present simple)

The hospital has been built by the government. (present perfect)

This programme is being watched by millions of people. (present continuous)

Volcanoes weren't understood in the middle ages. (past simple)

New types of energy will be used in the future. (*will*)

We make the passive with the appropriate tense and form of the verb **to be** and the past participle of the verb.

To make questions in the passive, we put the first auxiliary verb before the subject.

Is the news being given on TV?

Has the earthquake been shown on TV?

We use the preposition **by** to introduce the agent, that is, the person or thing doing the action.

USE

We use the passive when:

1 we are more interested in the action than who or what does the action.
The city was destroyed in 1755.

2 we do not know who exactly does the action.
Many objects have been stolen.

3 it is obvious or understood who did the action.
The patient was cured.

The passive – verbs with two objects

FORM

Some verbs are followed by two objects, one usually a thing and the other a person. *They told me the truth.*

When this happens, we can make two different passive sentences.

I was told the truth.

The truth was told to me.

It is more common to make passive sentences with the **person** or **people** as the subject.

Here is a list of common verbs which are followed by two objects:

bring, buy, give, lend, offer, owe, pay, promise, refuse, send, show, teach, tell

The passive with say, know, believe, etc.

FORM

It + **be** + **past participle** (of *believe, claim, expect, know, report, say, think*) + ***that***

It is said that dolphins can communicate.

It was claimed that the president knew about the situation.

We use the present of **to be** to talk about present beliefs and thoughts.

We use the past of **to be** to talk about past beliefs and thoughts.

Instead of using the impersonal pronoun ***it***, we can use this structure:

Subject + **be** + **past participle** (of *believe, claim, expect, know, report, say, think*) + **to** + ***infinitive*/*have*** + **past participle**

Dolphins are said to be able to communicate.

The president was claimed to have known about the situation.

With this structure, we use **to** + infinitive to talk about things in the present, or things that are always true.

We use to ***have*** + past participle to talk about past events.

USE

We use these structures to talk about what people in general say, think or believe about something.

Vocabulary

Natural disasters avalanche • drought • earthquake • epidemic • flood • forest fire • hurricane • landslide tsunami • volcanic eruption

Words connected with natural disasters aftershock • ash • (of a river) burst its banks • casualty • collapse destruction • evacuate • head towards • injury • molten lava • mud • panic • put out • refugee • spread survivor • sweep across • torrential (rain) • tremor • victim

Prepositional phrases with verbs agree with (somebody) • apologise for (something) • believe in • belong to complain about (something) • depend on • dream of • listen to • protect (somebody) from (something) • rely on spend on • wait for

Other words and phrases ➤ page 141

Grammar revision

The passive — / 7 points

1 Rewrite the sentences. Change the form from active to passive or passive to active.

1 A boat rescued the boy and girl.
2 A Japanese company is going to rebuild the damaged towers.
3 The airport had been designed by a famous architect.
4 The waves won't have destroyed the port.
5 Petra Němcová is presenting the awards tonight.
6 They should have written a report about the catastrophe.
7 The school might be opened by a local politician.

The passive – verbs with two objects — / 7 points

2 Put the words in the correct order. Then make the sentences active.

1 will sent be an email You important
You will be sent an important email. We will send you an important email.
2 was a birthday camera given for I my
3 disasters They being shown a are about natural film
4 parents stories children Young often are told their by
5 has million been a actor dollars The paid
6 sister lent I by money was some my
7 We taught mathematics a were teacher by new
8 a job He has offered government been the by

The passive with say, know, believe, etc. — / 6 points

3 Find the mistakes in these sentences and rewrite them correctly.

1 It is often claimed Paris to be one of the most beautiful cities in the world.
2 Galileo Galilei is said to invent the telescope.
3 It was reported to have started the fire an accident.
4 Avalanches are said that they are caused by loud noises.
5 A long time ago the Moon is believed to be made of cheese.
6 The eruption of Krakatoa is thought to turn the skies orange in 1883.

Vocabulary revision

NATURAL DISASTERS — / 5 points

1 Make simple definitions or explanations for these words.

1 flood
2 epidemic
3 landslide
4 drought
5 forest fire

WORDS CONNECTED WITH NATURAL DISASTERS — / 8 points

2 Match the definitions to words on page 106.

1 very strong and heavy, talking about rain
2 someone who is injured or killed in an accident
3 make a fire stop
4 gradually cover or affect a larger area
5 move in the direction of something or someone
6 leave a place because it is dangerous
7 when something does this it breaks suddenly because of the pressure of water or air
8 grey powder left after something has burnt

PREPOSITIONAL PHRASES WITH VERBS — / 7 points

3 Match the verbs and prepositions.

Verb	Preposition
1 apologise	a about
2 belong	b to
3 rely	c with
4 complain	d on
5 dream	e for
6 agree	f of
7 spend	g on

Total: / 40 points

Reading

➤ TIP FOR READING EXAMS

In multiple-choice activities, remember …

If you aren't 100% sure which answer is best, take away any answers which you know are not correct.

➤ EXAM SUCCESS page 146

1 SPEAKING **Work with a partner. Would you ever go on holiday to an area where a natural disaster was happening? Why/Why not?**

2 **Read the text and choose the best answer.**

OUR TRIP OF A LIFETIME

In the early hours of the morning of the 21st March I was woken by a text message from Iceland – an eruption had occurred close to the Eyjafjallajökull glacier.

I knew this could cause serious disruption for some school groups and individual travellers either in Iceland or about to leave, so the rest of the night was spent trying to find out the extent of the eruption. By 9 o'clock on Sunday morning our team was in the office, making sure everyone travelling with us in Iceland and those who were about to travel were fully briefed on the situation. Luckily, by midday it was established the eruption was located on a small deserted pass between two glaciers and there was no danger outside the immediate area. Roads were then reopened, flights were allowed to leave – our website was updated and our team was free to enjoy what was left of the weekend!

On the Monday we contacted all those on our Volcano Hotline and started making travel plans for those wanting to see the eruption. The first passenger left that evening. As the week went on we found there was a great deal of interest in going to see the eruption – which was understandable as it is truly one of nature's most impressive spectacles – something Iceland has more than its fair share of!

Ten days later I found myself on a plane bound for Keflavik with two of my children Ben (16) and Gemma (13) – we had also been bitten by the volcano bug. After a comfortable night in the Northern Light Inn we had a relaxing dip in the famous Blue Lagoon. The weather was a little chilly but wonderfully bright and we took the seldom travelled southern route along the Reykjanes Peninsula – which I would really recommend. By mid afternoon we arrived at my favourite hotel in Iceland – the ranch-style Hotel Ranga. It is from here that our visits to the volcano would start the next day. That night in the restaurant we enjoyed some wonderful food with more views of the eruption, which as darkness fell became even more spectacular.

Just after lunch the next day we took one of the helicopters based at the hotel for the most amazing flight I have ever experienced in my life. We flew over spectacular plains, followed the edge of the glaciers and finally came to the site of the eruption we had come to see. It certainly did not disappoint and we landed on a hill close by the volcano and stood in awe as the volcano belched out molten lava and thundered away in an amazing display. All too soon it was time to go and the helicopter returned to collect us. We bid adieu to the volcano and returned to Hotel Ranga – but I had a little surprise arranged for later

in the day! A few hours later we boarded a Superjeep – which was to take us in comfort over the glacier to approach the volcano from the ground. Driving Superjeeps is an Icelandic art and our driver, Ragnar, was both skilled and great company.

> " … the volcano belched out molten lava and thundered away in an amazing display. "

1 Because of the start of the eruption …
- a all current trips to Iceland were disrupted.
- b the writer and his team had to explain to their customers what was happening.
- c the team told people not to go to Iceland.

2 The writer's company …
- a quickly organised trips to see the eruption.
- b didn't think people would be interested in trips to see the volcano.
- c had information about previous volcano visitors.

3 The writer went to Iceland …
- a out of curiosity.
- b because of his work.
- c to be with his children.

4 For the writer the helicopter flight was …
- a very frightening.
- b a once-in-a-lifetime experience.
- c disappointing.

5 After arriving at the volcano by helicopter, the writer and his children …
- a left almost immediately.
- b wanted to stay longer.
- c couldn't move because they were so amazed.

6 The Superjeep …
- a was something the writer didn't know about.
- b requires a very skillful driver.
- c was chosen because it was so comfortable.

Listening

➤ TIP FOR LISTENING EXAMS

In True/False/Not Mentioned activities, remember …

You can usually hear the recording twice. If you don't hear the answer to one question, start listening immediately for the answer to the next question. Use the second listening to find the answers you didn't hear the first time and to check the answers you already have.

➤ EXAM SUCCESS page 146

3 LISTENING 43 **Listen to two girls talking about different rescue services in the US. Are these statements True (T), False (F) or is the information Not Mentioned (NM)?**

1 One service is offering evacuation from areas hit by hurricanes by luxury helicopter. T/F/NM
2 The same service offers luxury vacations throughout the year. T/F/NM
3 The creator of this service got the idea when he couldn't find a seat on a normal plane. T/F/NM
4 The people who are likely to use this service usually book flights on normal planes. T/F/NM
5 The service is only for members. T/F/NM
6 You can pay for a service that can protect your house from forest fires. T/F/NM
7 One company they talk about runs your business while you escape a hurricane. T/F/NM

4 SPEAKING **Work with a partner. What do you think of the services they talk about? Are they fair or not?**

Writing

➤ TIP FOR WRITING EXAMS

In reviews, remember …

The important thing is to give a detailed picture of the thing that you are reviewing and to make your own opinion clear. To do this, use a wide variety of adjectives and adverbs and use expressions of opinion.

➤ EXAM SUCCESS page 146

5 SPEAKING **Work with a partner. Look at this notice. Which film would you choose and why?**

from **FILM**REVIEWS

REVIEWS WANTED

A film that all teenagers MUST see!

Which film would you recommend to your friends? It could be comedy, fantasy, science fiction, a disaster film … you decide! In your review describe what happens in the film and explain why you like it so much.

6 **Do the task in 5. Follow this paragraph plan.**

Paragraph 1: Introduction/Basic information about the film.
Paragraph 2: More detailed information about the film.
Paragraph 3: What you like about the film.
Paragraph 4: Who you would recommend the film to and briefly restate why.

Speaking

➤ TIP FOR SPEAKING EXAMS

In activities where you have to discuss something, remember …

If you are working with other students, be sensitive. Don't talk for too long without giving your partner a chance to speak.

➤ EXAM SUCCESS page 146

7 **Look at these expressions. Which do we use for giving emphasis and which do we use to give examples?**

1 Take …, for instance.
2 You have to remember that …
3 I really do think that …
4 You can't deny that …
5 You only have to think of …

8 **Look at this statement. Do you think this would be useful, fun, time-consuming, embarrassing, interesting? Make notes with ideas and examples.**

> *"All secondary school students should have lessons in First Aid at school so that they can help out in accidents and emergencies."*

9 SPEAKING **Work in groups of three. Discuss your opinions. Remember to use expressions to give emphasis and examples.**

9 Digital world

Vocabulary

Everyday technology

1 SPEAKING **Work with a partner. Match the words in the columns to make everyday items. What do you use each thing for?**

1	dish	a	control
2	washing	b	processor
3	web	c	wave
4	remote	d	board
5	head	e	phones
6	flash	f	washer
7	micro	g	cleaner
8	vacuum	h	nav
9	food	i	camera
10	digital	j	machine
11	sat	k	drive
12	key	l	cam

2 **Match the words with the definitions.**

broadband • charger • coverage • device
drop-down menu • glitch • network • plug
touch screen • wireless

1 a machine or piece of equipment that does a particular thing
2 when a set of similar things are connected to each other, for example computers or phones
3 a screen on a computer, tablet or phone that you touch in order to choose what you want to do next
4 a piece of equipment used for giving power to a battery
5 a type of connection to the Internet that allows you to receive or send a lot of information very quickly
6 this technology communicates using electronic signals, not with wires
7 the strength of the signal to your phone from your network
8 a list of options that appears on a screen when you press it
9 a small and sudden problem especially with technology
10 an object used to connect a piece of equipment to an electricity supply

Verbs connected with technology

3 **In each sentence, choose the correct alternative and then say what the other word means. In two sentences, both alternatives are correct.**

1 You switch the phone on by *pushing/pressing* the ON button.
2 Oh no! My battery has *recharged/gone dead*!
3 I'm not surprised you can't see the film. You've forgotten to *insert/plug in* the DVD into the machine!
4 My computer is really old. It keeps *crashing/freezing*.
5 I need to *install/upgrade* my phone so that I can do more with it.
6 Can you help me to *set/delete* the alarm on my phone so that I wake up early tomorrow?
7 You need to *select/adjust* this option from the drop-down menu.
8 You can make the image bigger or smaller by *pinching/swiping* it.
9 When your phone is fully charged, you should *connect/disconnect* it.
10 To switch the phone off you should press and *hold/tap* this button for a second or two.

4 LISTENING 44 **Listen to somebody giving instructions. What exactly are the instructions for?**

5 **Imagine that your mobile is switched off and the battery is dead. What do you need to do to be able to call a friend? Write the complete instructions.**

Plug in the charger and connect the phone. Or insert a USB cable into the phone and connect the phone to a computer via the USB port …

6 SPEAKING **Work with a partner. Read your instructions to your partner and compare them. Are they similar?**

7 SPEAKING **With your partner, think of something that you typically do with your phone or tablet (e.g. take a photo or send a message). Prepare instructions to describe the process. Read out your instructions to the class. Can they identify what the action is?**

1a SPEAKING **Work with a partner. What can you see in the photo? Look at the title of the article. What do you think a 'screenager' is?**

1b READING **Read the text, ignoring the gaps. Check your answer in 1a.**

GEN Z

A generation of 'screenagers'

Look around you. Are there any people of your age about? **1** .... They'll almost certainly be busy swiping, pinching or tapping some type of screen.

You only have to look at some of the statistics for this generation of 'screenagers'. It's said that 36% of children use electronic devices during family meals. Forty-nine per cent of 14- and 15-year-olds feel that they are addicted to the Internet and 77% take a phone or computer to bed. Their greatest fears? Not being able to pick up a wi-fi signal, a glitch with their latest app or their battery unexpectedly running out.

> Gen Z is possibly the smartest and most sophisticated generation in history.

Technology is clearly at the heart of Generation Z, or Gen Z, the generation which is made up of the youngsters born between 1995 and 2010. It's the first generation to have grown up with the touch screen as the norm. Some say that Gen Z doesn't just represent the future. **2** ....

Is there a positive side to this generation of connected teenagers? The answer is yes. Take Ann Makosinski. She was just 16 when she came up with an ingenious device – a flashlight which is charged and powered by the heat of a human hand. **3** .... It was the fact that Makosinski, who was born in Canada, took her inspiration from the difficulties of a friend in the Philippines who had failed her school exams because she had no electricity to study at night.

An advertising agency called Sparks & Honey, which is based in New York, has been investigating Gen Z and has come up with some interesting findings. On the whole, perhaps surprisingly, the overall picture is quite optimistic and positive. In fact, it has been claimed that, thanks to technology, Gen Z is possibly the smartest and most sophisticated generation in history. **4** .... They are bright thinkers like Ann Makosinski. Other examples include Jack Andraka, who at the age of just 15 created a cheap device to detect pancreatic cancer, or Angela Zhang, who helped to improve cancer detection when she was just 17.

Meanwhile, people of older generations tend to warn of the negative effects of computers and technology. **5** .... They also say that touch screens and keyboards, which teenagers use all the time, are responsible for students gradually losing the ability to write. Certainly, statistics seem to justify another claim: that young people cannot concentrate for long periods. Sparks & Honey state that the average attention span of American teenagers in 2014 was just 8 seconds, down from 12 seconds in 2000.

But, while some of these concerns do seem valid, it is also true that Gen Z appears to be acquiring new skills to replace those skills which they are losing. Today's teens are totally at ease switching from screen to screen and adjusting from task to task within seconds. **6** ....

Of course, any generation reflects the society that it has grown up in. Gen Z has not had it easy. Its members are very aware of the impact of global warming, for example. And the economic recession has also had an impact. **7** ....

According to Sparks & Honey, nine out of ten feel optimistic about their own future. Instead of depending on other people to offer them a job or waiting for opportunities to appear, Gen Z makes things happen. Rather than wanting to work for a big company, 71% want to start their own business.

Although it can be worrying to see teenagers burying their heads in screens, paradoxically it would appear that modern technology is creating more communication and solidarity between people around the world. Sparks & Honey claim that 78% are concerned about world hunger and 77% are concerned about children around the world dying of preventable diseases. Meanwhile, 26% would need to fly to visit most of the friends they've made through social networking. Technology has made Gen Z a truly connected, worldwide phenomenon.

2 **Read the text again. Complete with A–G.**

- **A** Some claim that, because of easy access to information on the Internet, young people are no longer exercising their memories.
- **B** But it wasn't just the invention that was impressive.
- **C** In fact, this generation is actively creating it.
- **D** However, adversity has not made this generation negative.
- **E** If there are, they probably aren't talking to one another.
- **F** Their stars are not teen singers and actors.
- **G** This is something which previous generations find more difficult.

3 CRITICAL THINKING

Think! Then compare ideas with your class.

- Do you agree with the description of Gen Z? Why/Why not?

4 **What do the underlined words in the text mean? Guess and then check in your dictionary.**

5 SPEAKING **What about *you*?**

1. How long do you spend looking at a screen per day?
2. What device do you use the most, and for what?

Relative clauses

1 Look at the sentences and answer the questions below.

a She invented a torch **which** is powered by the heat of your hand.

b Makosinski, **who** was born in Canada, invented the device for a friend.

c This is something **which** other generations find difficult.

d She had a friend **who** failed her exams because she had no electricity.

e The agency, **which** is based in New York, has been investigating Gen Z.

f Touch screens, **which** teenagers use all the time, may be responsible for students gradually losing the ability to write.

1 Which **relative clauses** are **defining**, giving us essential information about someone or something? Do they have commas?

2 Which **relative clauses** are **non-defining**, giving us extra, non-essential information about someone or something? Do they have commas?

3 When do we use the **relative pronoun *which*** and when do we use ***who***?

4 When do we use ***whose***, ***when***, ***where*** or ***why***?

5 Can we replace ***which*** with ***that*** in sentences a or c?

6 Can we replace ***which*** with ***that*** in sentences e or f? Why/Why not?

7 Can we omit the **relative pronoun** in sentences b, e or f? Why/Why not?

8 Can we omit the **relative pronouns** in sentences a or d? Why/Why not?

9 Can we omit the **relative pronoun** in sentence c? Why/Why not?

GRAMMAR REFERENCE ➤ PAGE 120

2 Decide if the sentences are correct. Rewrite the incorrect sentences.

1 My tablet, that I bought last week, is already broken!

2 I think that's the phone that I saw it.

3 Here is the room that we study in.

4 She's the person who I spoke to on the phone.

5 They're the two people who's invention became really popular.

6 I've got a new phone that takes great pictures.

7 I've downloaded the app that you recommended.

8 This is the friend which I told you about.

3 Omit the relative pronouns where possible.

It sounds like something **(a) that** James Bond would use or **(b) that** would appear in spy movies like *Mission Impossible*. It's a new smartphone **(c) which** self-destructs when somebody tries to use it without permission. The customers **(d) who** they are designing the phone for are mainly people **(e) who** work for government agencies. The self-destruct is being designed by two companies. One of them is BlackBerry and the other is Boeing, **(f) whose** main business is manufacturing planes. John Chen, **(g) who** is the CEO of BlackBerry, announced the existence of the phone but wanted to keep the details secret. However, we do know that the phone **(h) which** they are developing does not actually explode or catch fire. But if somebody tries to open the case **(i) that** covers the phone, all of the data and software **(j) which** is inside will be deleted. At the moment, these phones are only for people **(k) who** have very special safety needs. But experts predict that one day all phones may use the technology **(l) which** the two companies are developing.

4 Rewrite the sentences as one sentence using a non-defining relative clause.

1 The inventor of the remote control didn't like watching TV. His name was Robert Adler.

2 Remote controls were originally called 'space commands'. They first appeared in 1956.

3 Robert Adler went to university in Vienna. He was born there.

4 Adler was a brilliant physicist. He invented more than 180 different things.

5 Adler was especially proud of his work on touch screens. His most successful invention was the remote control.

6 His remote control used ultrasonic frequencies. It was replaced by infrared systems in the 1980s.

7 In 2007 Robert Adler died. He was ninety-three.

8 Adler wasn't very interested in his own invention. It changed the way we live.

5 **Read the text. Who is the boy in the photo and what did he do? What was so surprising about what he did?**

At the age of just 19, Adam Cudworth sent a camera (1) …… he had bought for just £30 up into space. The camera, (2) …… went up to a height of over 33,000 metres, took amazing photos of the Earth. A two metre balloon carried the box (3) …… he had placed the camera. The other things he put in the box were a satnav, radio, video camera and microprocessor. The amazing thing is that the photos that Adam took look like they could be images from NASA. But Adam, (4) …… scientific qualifications only consisted of a physics A level at the time, spent a total of just £200 (5) …… his photos. NASA, (6) …… the other hand, depend (7) …… expensive satellites for their photos, spending millions of pounds for similar results to Adam's. Adam, (8) …… went on to study engineering at university, said that he had just wanted to set himself a challenge. He himself was amazed at the quality of the photos that he managed to take. (9) ……, he wasn't the only one who was impressed. Since then, he has appeared in newspapers, magazines and TV programmes all round the world. It is said (10) …… he is currently working on a new experiment to make his photos even better.

6 **Read the text again. Choose which answer (A, B, C or D) best fits each gap.**

	A	B	C	D
1	A what	B –	C where	D when
2	A what	B which	C that	D –
3	A in	B –	C which	D where
4	A who	B whose	C his	D that
5	A in	B on	C at	D with
6	A in	B for	C on	D with
7	A of	B on	C for	D to
8	A that	B –	C who	D which
9	A However	B Although	C Even	D Despite
10	A to	B that	C what	D which

✔ EXAM SUCCESS

If you aren't sure which answer is correct, think about why other answers are definitely wrong and eliminate them first.

➤ EXAM SUCCESS page 147

Phrasal verbs connected with technology and computers

1 **Look at the sentences. Match the phrasal verbs in red with their meanings a–j.**

1 I'll have to call you back later because my battery's **running out**.
2 My phone isn't **picking up** a signal.
3 Don't forget to **back up** all your documents.
4 An alarm **goes off** when you press this button.
5 Can you **print out** a copy for me?
6 This device **runs on** batteries.
7 To buy this app, you have to **set up** an account.
8 The image is really small so you need to **zoom in**.
9 Use the mouse to **scroll up**, **down** or **across**.
10 A box suddenly **popped up** on the screen.

a make something appear bigger and closer
b receive
c use something for power or energy
d produce a copy of a document from a printer
e make a copy of information that is on your computer
f move information on a screen in order to read it
g use all of something and have nothing left
h start making a noise
i appear very quickly
j start, create

2 SPEAKING **Work with a partner. Look at the pictures and answer the questions using a phrasal verb.**

1

2

3

4

5

6

1 Why would you click on this icon?
……
2 And this one?
……
3 What happens if you have an image and you click here?
……
4 What's the problem with the mobile phone?
……
5 What's the problem with the battery?
……
6 What's happening with the alarm?
……

Using technology for STUDY

ACADEMIC SKILLS OBJECTIVES	KEY CONCEPTS
■ To reflect on the uses of technology for study. ■ To consider some advantages and disadvantages of using technology in your studies. ■ To plan how to integrate technology into your future study plan.	**blend [n], blended [adj]:** *Her course is a blend of learning online and attending class.* **collaborate [v]:** *In group work, you need to collaborate with other students.* **face-to-face [adj]:** *Most students enjoy face-to-face lessons with their teacher.* **virtual learning environment (VLE) [n phr]:** *We have a VLE, an online site where we can get information, exercises and other materials to help us with our course.* **resource [n]:** *There are lots of useful resources in the library – ebooks, magazines, music, films, computers, printers …*

1 READING **Look at these statistics about university students and technology. Do any of the statistics surprise you? If so, which ones and why?**

STUDENTS AND TECHNOLOGY

SURVEY CONDUCTED 2014

75,306 STUDENT RESPONDENTS

FROM **213** CAMPUSES

IN 16 COUNTRIES, INCLUDING US, FRANCE, EGYPT, IRELAND, UNITED ARAB EMIRATES

EXPERIENCES

Technology is part of students' lives, and students are generally happy to use technology.

ATTITUDE TO TECHNOLOGY:

70% positive

2 IN 3 STUDENTS feel prepared to use the technology needed in their courses

TECHNOLOGY MAKES ME FEEL MORE CONNECTED TO …

Other students	Instructors	The institution
51% AGREE	54% AGREE	65% AGREE

9 IN 10 STUDENTS ARE AT LEAST MODERATELY INTERESTED IN ONLINE COMMUNICATION SUCH AS …

ALERTS if it appears that their progress in a course is going down

SUGGESTIONS about courses they might consider taking in the future

GUIDANCE for how to improve their performance in a course

93% of students are at least quite interested in receiving personalised online support and information about progress towards their final learning goals

LEARNING ENVIRONMENTS

More students than ever have experienced a digital or virtual learning environment (VLE). The majority say that they learn best with a blend of online and face-to-face work.

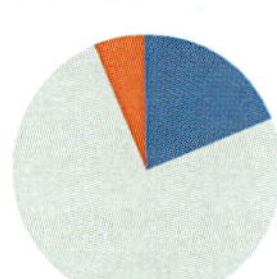

NO ONLINE COMPONENTS 19% in favour
PARTIALLY ONLINE 75% in favour
COMPLETELY ONLINE 6% in favour

54% of students typically connect to the network with at least two devices at a time.

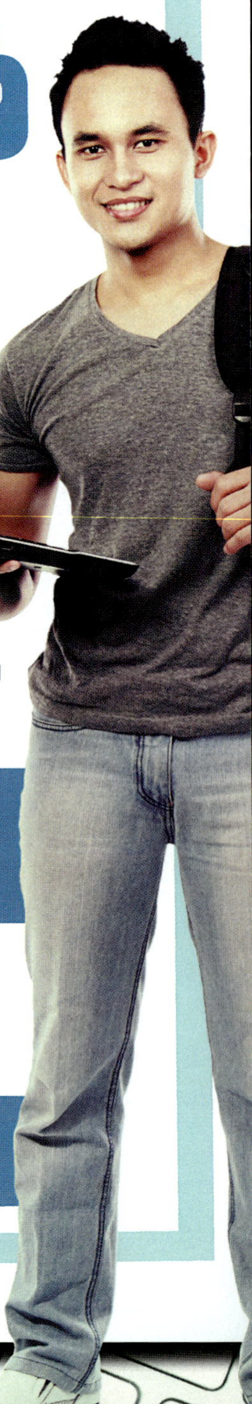

Information provided by EDUCAUSE

2 SPEAKING **Work with a partner. Answer the questions below. Do your answers coincide with the most common answers in the statistics in 1?**

1 Are you happy about using technology for study? Why/Why not?
2 Do you feel prepared to use technology for study? Why/Why not?
3 Does technology make you feel more connected to other students, teachers or your school? How?
4 Do/Would you like personalised online support and information about your progress?
5 Which would you prefer – to have only face-to-face classes, only online classes or a mix of both? Why?
6 Which different devices do you use for study?

3 Work individually. Do the questionnaire below.

4 SPEAKING **Work with a partner. Compare your answers in 3 and discuss ...**

1 what hardware (computer, laptop, tablet, smartphone, webcam) you use to do these different things.
2 what programs you use for them.
3 what websites and blogs you find useful.

DO YOU USE TECHNOLOGY TO ...

1 communicate with other people about schoolwork, to collaborate or ask for help?
Always / Sometimes / Never

2 do research and find information needed for schoolwork?
Always / Sometimes / Never

3 do extra reading and investigation to find out more about the things you are studying at school?
Always / Sometimes / Never

4 find and do practice activities?
Always / Sometimes / Never

5 write essays, assignments or projects?
Always / Sometimes / Never

6 take notes in class or write up notes after class?
Always / Sometimes / Never

7 revise before tests and exams?
Always / Sometimes / Never

8 prepare and give presentations?
Always / Sometimes / Never

5 Work with a partner. Make two lists, one with the advantages of using technology for study and one with the disadvantages.

6 LISTENING 45 **Watch or listen to four students talking about using technology for study. Do they mention any of your ideas in 5?**

7 45 **Watch or listen again. In groups of four choose one speaker each and write notes on what they say about the seven questions. Compare your notes. Do you agree more with your speaker or with the others? Why/ Why not?**

Sam
Vanessa
Bea
Chris

8 SPEAKING **Work with a partner. Ask and answer these questions.**

1 Do you agree or disagree with the advantages and disadvantages mentioned for teachers and students using technology? Why?
2 Can you think of solutions for any of the problems mentioned?

ACADEMIC TASK

You want to integrate technology into your English studies.

Work in a group and follow this plan:

1 *Discuss which hardware, programs or websites you could use to study English, either inside the classroom or out. Use the general ideas on these two pages for ideas.*
2 *Find out what topics, areas and tasks you are going to do in English in the next two or three weeks.*
3 *Write up a plan with suggestions for using technology to help with these tasks and then try some of your suggestions out. Evaluate how successful each experience is and why.*

Listening

1 SPEAKING **Work with a partner. What is the problem in each picture a–d? What could or should you do in each case?**

2 LISTENING ▶ 46 **Listen and match the problems a–d to speakers 1–4. Are any of the ideas similar to yours?**

Speaker 1: ....
Speaker 2: ....
Speaker 3: ....
Speaker 4: ....

3 ▶ 46 **Listen again. Which problem do the statements refer to?**

1 You need a type of food to solve the problem. a/b/c/d
2 You need a change in temperature to solve the problem. a/b/c/d
3 You should quickly disconnect the device from an electrical source. a/b/c/d
4 You need to make something to solve the problem. a/b/c/d
5 Warmth is not helpful in this situation. a/b/c/d
6 This problem is extremely common and happened to the speaker. a/b/c/d
7 The speaker warns us not to touch parts of the device directly because it can make the situation worse. a/b/c/d
8 You should wait at least two days to make the situation better. a/b/c/d
9 You may not be able to solve the problem completely on your own. a/b/c/d
10 The solution was suggested by someone close to the speaker. a/b/c/d

4 SPEAKING ▶ 46 **Work in groups. Make notes about one of the problems. Then explain it to the rest of the class. Does everybody agree that the information is correct? Listen again to check if necessary.**

5 SPEAKING **What about *you*?**

1 Have any of these things happened to you? What did you do?
2 Do you have any tips about what to do when you have a problem with a device?

Grammar in context

Gerunds and infinitives – 2

1a Read the pairs of sentences. In which pair do the two sentences have the same meaning?

1a I stopped **to use** my phone.
1b I stopped **using** my phone.
2a It started **to vibrate**.
2b It started **vibrating**.
3a I remember **to switch** it off.
3b I remember **switching** it off.
4a I forgot **to do** it.
4b I forgot **doing** it.
5a I like **to read** tech blogs.
5b I like **reading** tech blogs.

1b Match the verbs + gerund/infinitive with the correct meaning (a or b).

1 stop to do ....
2 stop doing ....
   a you stop one activity because you want or need to do another activity
   b you are doing something and then you stop

3 remember to do ....
4 remember doing ....
   a you do something and then you remember it later
   b you remember you need to do something and then you do it

5 forget to do ....
6 forget doing ....
   a you don't do something that you intended to do
   b you did something, but now you don't remember it

7 like to do ....
8 like doing ....
   a you do something because you enjoy doing it
   b you do something because you think it's a good idea

GRAMMAR REFERENCE ➤ PAGE 120

2 Choose the correct alternative.

1 I remember *to play/playing* with a tablet when I was young.
2 The teacher's angry because I forgot *to do/doing* my homework.
3 I like *to go/going* to the dentist twice a year.
4 We stopped *to eat/eating* because we were hungry.
5 Did you forget *to bring/bringing* a pen? Don't worry. I've got a spare one.
6 Can you remember *to give/giving* this to Dan when you see him tomorrow?
7 You look really healthy now that you've stopped *to eat/eating* junk food.
8 My dad likes *to get/getting* up early because that means he can finish work early, too.

3 Complete the second sentence so that it has a similar meaning to the first sentence, using the word given. Do not change the word given. You must use between two and five words, including the word given.

1 I didn't send that email yesterday because I didn't remember.
FORGOT
I .... yesterday.
2 He thinks it's important to wear a tie for interviews.
LIKES
He .... for interviews.
3 You always interrupt me when I'm on the phone. Please don't!
STOP
Please .... when I'm on the phone!
4 Don't worry. I sent the message. I didn't forget.
REMEMBERED
Don't worry. .... the message.
5 I think making videos is really good fun.
LIKE
I .... videos.
6 My mum stopped work and had a coffee.
TO
My mum stopped .... a coffee.
7 I lost my first mobile phone. I'll never forget.
REMEMBER
I .... my first mobile phone.
8 Meet me after school. Please don't forget!
REMEMBER
Please .... after school.
9 I became silent when the film started.
STOPPED
I .... when the film started.
10 I spilt orange juice on my laptop. I'll always remember it.
FORGET
I'll .... on my laptop.

4 Decide if the sentences are correct. Rewrite the incorrect sentences.

1 I have to go back home because I forgot switching the oven off.
2 Can you remember bringing me my book tomorrow because I need it?
3 I think it's time to start to revise for the exam.
4 Stop to play that song because it's awful.
5 I like getting up early when I have an exam.
6 Don't worry. I won't forget to send you emails when you're away.
7 I'll always remember to meet you for the first time last summer.
8 I love video games so much that I don't think I'll ever stop playing them.

5 Write complete sentences about these things.

1 something unusual you remember doing when you were young
2 something that you remembered to do last week
3 something important that you once forgot to do
4 something that you like doing
5 something that you like to do because you think it's a good idea
6 something that you did when you were younger but that you stopped
7 something that you were doing yesterday and then you stopped to do something else

6 SPEAKING **Work with a partner. Compare your sentences. Ask follow-up questions.**

I remember playing with remote control cars when I was young.

Who did you play with?

I usually played with my dad.

Discussions – 2

a

b

1 SPEAKING **Work with a partner. Compare and contrast the two photos.**

2a With your partner, make two lists – one with arguments in favour of using smartphones in the classroom and one with arguments against.

For	Against

2b Do you have more arguments for or against smartphones in the classroom? Overall, do you think it is a good idea or a bad idea?

3 LISTENING 47 **Listen to two people discussing whether students should be allowed to take mobile phones into class. What is each person's opinion?**

	Opinion
Man	
Woman	

4 Look at the expressions in the Speaking bank. Complete the headings with the uses a–b below.

a asking someone to clarify something

b checking someone has understood you

SPEAKING BANK

Clarifying and checking understanding

Useful expressions for:

1 ....

- Do you see what I mean?
- Do you get what I'm saying?
- Are you following me?
- Are you with me?
- What I mean/meant is/was …
- Yes, that's exactly what I mean/meant.
- No, that's not quite what I mean/meant.

Useful expressions for:

2 ....

- Are you saying that …?
- If I understand you correctly, …
- In other words …
- What do you mean when you say …?
- I'm not sure what you mean by …
- Could you go over that again?
- Sorry, I'm not with you.
- I don't understand what you're getting at.

5a PRONUNCIATION **Look at the first sentence from the Speaking bank. What do you think the circles represent?**

● ●

Do you see what I mean?

5b Where does the stress go in the other sentences in the Speaking bank?

5c LISTENING 48 **Listen and check.**

5d 48 **Listen again and repeat. Pay attention to the stress and intonation.**

PRACTICE MAKES PERFECT

6 Look at this statement. Prepare some notes, giving your opinion and arguments to support it.

Many young people today spend over ten hours a day in front of a screen. There should be a limit to young people's screen time because too much of it could create serious physical and psychological problems in the future.

7 SPEAKING **Work in a small group. Discuss the statement. Remember to use expressions from the Speaking bank.**

A report

1 SPEAKING **Work with a partner and answer these questions.**

1 Does your school have a website? If so, what can you find on the website? Do you like it? Why/Why not?

2 If your school doesn't have a website, imagine that it is going to have one in the future. What would be good to have on the website? How could you make it attractive?

2 Read this writing task. What style do you think you should use to do this task – formal or informal?

Your school has a website, but not many people visit it. The head of your school has asked you to speak to as many students as possible and then write a report saying:

- why the current website is not very popular
- how the website could be improved to attract more visitors in the future

Write your **report**.

3 Read this student's report. What style is it written in? Does the student mention any of the things you talked about in 1?

Improvements to the school website

Introduction

The aim of this report is to outline our opinion of the current school website and to suggest how we could improve the school website in order to attract more visitors in the future.

The current website

At the moment, the website has a very old, traditional design which is not very attractive or dynamic. Furthermore, nearly all the students that we interviewed said that they found it difficult to navigate. Another problem with the current website is that not all of the information there is up-to-date, which a large number of people feel is a major problem.

Suggested improvements

Nearly all the students we spoke to suggested a new, brighter design for the website. There should be a section for school news, including news about trips, concerts and sports events. This section should be updated every week, so that people revisit the website regularly. A few people suggested that the website could also include a blog written by students. This could be attractive to both students and parents.

Conclusion

In conclusion, most of the students we spoke to think the website has to be both more attractive and more informative. We also believe that the key to a popular website is making sure that the information there is fresh and frequently updated.

✓ EXAM SUCCESS

When you write reports, give the report a title. Divide the report into paragraphs and give each paragraph a heading.

➤ EXAM SUCCESS page 147

4 Are the words in orange used correctly? Rewrite the incorrect sentences. Use the information in the Writing bank to help you.

1 Each students think that it is important.
2 All of the students are happy with the website.
3 None students wanted to visit the website.
4 Every student in the class was interested in writing a blog.
5 A good website needs a large number of time and effort.
6 No students visited the website.
7 We update the website every day.
8 Most of the people in our class finds the website boring.

WRITING BANK

Using determiners and quantifiers

- a (large/small) number of *(+ plural countable nouns)*
- all, all of *(+ singular countable, plural countable and uncountable nouns)*
- most, most of *(+ singular countable, plural countable and uncountable nouns)*
- each, every *(+ singular countable nouns)*
- each of, every one of *(+ plural countable nouns)*
- no *(+ singular countable, plural countable and uncountable nouns)*
- none *(without of this is a pronoun and cannot go with another noun)*
- none of *(+ plural countable and uncountable nouns)*

Remember also: some, any, (a) few, (a) little, many, much, a lot (of), lots (of)

PRACTICE MAKES PERFECT

5 Read the task below and write your report. Remember to use words and expressions from the Writing bank.

An international company wants to know which websites are popular with teenagers in your country. You have been asked to write a report about:

- which websites you and your friends like
- what it is that you like about them

Write your **report**.

WRITING BANK ➤ PAGE 157

Grammar reference

Defining relative clauses

FORM

William Gilbert was the first person ***who/that*** *investigated electricity scientifically.*

We use **who** and **that** for people, **which** and **that** for things, **whose** for possessions, **where** for places, **when** for times and **why** for reasons.

In defining **relative clauses** we can omit **who**, **which** or **that** when followed immediately by a noun or pronoun.

That's the device that she invented. = That's the device she invented.

That's the device which I use the most. = That's the device I use the most.

but

That's the device that is popular. NOT ~~*That's the device is popular.*~~

That's the device that helps me the most. NOT ~~*That's the device helps me the most.*~~

Instead of **when** or **where** we can use **which/that ...** .

That's the year when I was born.

That's the year which I was born in.

That's the city where I was born.

That's the city that I was born in.

We do not use commas in defining relative clauses.

USE

We use **defining relative clauses** to give essential information about the person, thing, place, time or reason in the other half of the sentence.

Non-defining relative clauses

FORM

William Gilbert, ***who*** *was born in 1544, investigated electricity scientifically.*

We use **who** for people, **which** for things, **whose** for possessions, **where** for places and **when** for times.

We do not use **that** in **non-defining relative clauses**.

In non-defining relative clauses we cannot omit the relative pronoun or adverb.

~~*That device, she invented ten years ago, is really useful.*~~

We always use commas in non-defining relative clauses.

We can use **which** to refer back to the whole of the sentence.

People spend all their money on mobile phones, which I think is ridiculous.

USE

We use **non-defining relative clauses** to give extra, non-essential information about the person, thing, place or time in the first half of the sentence. The commas work in a similar way to parentheses, showing that the information is not vital to the sentence.

Gerunds and infinitives – 2

Some verbs go with the **gerund** or the **infinitive** and there is no difference in meaning.

She started to work there in 2014. = She started working there in 2014.

Other verbs: *begin, can't bear, can't stand, continue, hate, love, prefer*

Some verbs go with the gerund or the infinitive, but there is an important difference in meaning, e.g.

stop *to do*: you stop one activity because you want or need to do another activity

stop *doing*: you are doing something and then you stop

remember *to do*: you remember you need to do something and then you do it

remember *doing*: you do something and then you remember it later

forget *to do*: you don't do something that you intended to do

forget *doing*: you did something, but now you don't remember it

like *to do*: you do something because you think it's a good idea

like *doing*: you do something because you enjoy doing it

Vocabulary

Everyday technology broadband • charger • coverage • device • digital camera • dishwasher drop-down menu • flash drive • food processor • glitch • headphones • keyboard • microwave • network • plug remote control • satnav • touch screen • vacuum cleaner • washing machine • webcam • wireless

Verbs connected with technology adjust • connect • crash • delete • disconnect • freeze • go dead • hold insert • install • pinch • plug in • press • push • recharge • select • set • swipe • tap • upgrade

Phrasal verbs connected with technology and computers back up • go off • pick up • pop up • print out run out • scroll up/down/across • set up • zoom in

Other words and phrases ➤ page 142

Grammar revision

Relative clauses

/ 6 points

1 Choose the correct alternative. If you think both are possible, you must choose both.

1 The man *who/–* came to fix the TV knew about computers, too.
2 The other day, *when/which* I saw you in the shopping centre, I bought a new DVD.
3 The classroom *where/which* we leave our bags in is only used by the English department.
4 This unusual invention, *that/which* comes from Japan, could be really popular one day.
5 The blog *that/–* she writes is really interesting.
6 Does anybody know *who's/whose* pen this is?

/ 7 points

2 Write definitions with defining relative clauses for these people, places, times or things.

1 Argentina is a country …
2 2014 was the year …
3 Caviar is a type of food …
4 Ice hockey is a sport …
5 Marie Curie was a scientist …
6 Tea is a drink …
7 Glass is a material which …

Gerunds and infinitives – 2

/ 7 points

3 Put the verbs in the correct form.

1 Can you remember .... (switch) off the light when you leave?
2 She really likes .... (paint). It's her favourite hobby.
3 We stopped .... (write) when the exam finished.
4 Don't forget .... (go) to the meeting tomorrow.
5 I know Harry was at school yesterday because I remember .... (see) him.
6 I like .... (do) homework on Friday evening so that I'm free at the weekend.
7 The musicians stopped .... (play) because they'd already been playing for two hours.

Vocabulary revision

EVERYDAY TECHNOLOGY

/ 6 points

1 Complete the words.

1 net ....
2 drop - .... menu
3 web ....
4 head ....
5 broad ....
6 wire ....

VERBS CONNECTED WITH TECHNOLOGY

/ 7 points

2 Match these words with the definitions. There are four extra words.

adjust • delete • freeze • hold • insert • pinch • press • recharge • swipe • tap • upgrade

1 keep your finger on a button for a few seconds
2 use your fingers to make an image bigger or smaller
3 put something into something else
4 when a computer stops working
5 change or move something slightly so that it's better
6 remove information stored in a computer
7 give power back to a battery

PHRASAL VERBS CONNECTED WITH TECHNOLOGY AND COMPUTERS

/ 7 points

3 Choose the correct alternative.

1 He backed *off/up* the files on a flash drive in case he lost them.
2 It's strange that my mobile can't *pick/run* up a signal here because there must be coverage.
3 Can you print *out/up* a copy of those lyrics so I can keep them?
4 An advert suddenly *popped/set* up on the screen.
5 All cars will run *on/up* electricity one day.
6 You need to zoom *in/up* to see the image more clearly.
7 That sound is the alarm on my mobile. Why is it going *off/out* if I didn't set it?

Total: / 40 points

10 News feed

Vocabulary

News sections

1 SPEAKING **Work with a partner. Look at different sections that often appear on a news website or in a newspaper. Discuss what you think each one is. Group any that you think are similar.**

arts • business • comment • editor's blog
entertainment • features • finance • gossip
have your say • health • life and style • obituaries
opinion • showbiz • sport
weather forecast • world news

2 SPEAKING **Work with a partner and discuss these questions.**

1 What stories are in the news at the moment? In which section would you expect to read about them?
2 Which sections in 1 do you prefer to look at? Why?

News headlines

3 **News headlines need to catch people's attention quickly using little space. Look at how they do this.**

Grammar

Articles and auxiliary verbs are omitted.

Man arrested in busy supermarket

The present simple is used for current or recent events.

Prince opens high tech school

The infinitive is used for future events.

Britain to help Mali

The headlines are not usually complete sentences. Nouns are used as adjectives and are often put one after another.

Volcano eruption fear

Direct speech can be used without inverted commas.

I'm not quitting, says United boss

Vocabulary

Headlines use words that are short and dramatic. Look at this list of frequently used words. Many of the words can be nouns and verbs.

aid = help
axe = cut
back = support
ban = make illegal
blast = explosion
blaze = fire
boost = increase, encourage
boss/head = manager, director
clash = disagree violently
cut = reduce
drama = tense situation
hit = affect badly
key = important, essential
link = connection
move = step towards a goal
plea = request
pledge = promise
PM = Prime Minister
probe = investigation
quit = leave, resign
riddle = mystery
spark = cause
wed = marry

4 **Match the headlines 1–4 with the topics a–d.**

1 PM pledges flood aid
2 Bank boss to wed in style
3 Phone company axes 1,000 jobs
4 Hospital blaze kills 10

a A promise made by a politician
b A tragic fire
c A future marriage
d Bad news for a group of workers

5 SPEAKING **Work with a partner. Explain what these newspaper stories are about.**

a Government plan backed by universities
b I quit, says football star following clash with boss
c New virus sparks safety fears
d Police probe corruption claims
e Spy riddle behind city centre blast
f Government moves for fast-food advertising ban
g Key politician in plane drama

6 LISTENING 49 **Listen to three stories. Match each story to a headline in 5.**

1 .... 2 .... 3 ....

7 SPEAKING **Work with a partner. Invent a headline using the grammar and vocabulary in 3. Then write a short explanation of your news story. Read it to another pair. Can they guess the headline?**

The Prime Minister asked the public to support him.

PM pleas for public backing

1 SPEAKING **Work with a partner. Look at the headlines. What do you think each news story will be about?**

2 **Read the news stories. Are they similar to your predictions?**

NEWS 24/7

Cookie Policy Enable location services

University zoos spark debate

There's nothing like chasing farm animals around to take a person's mind off their problems.

Students in their petting zoo

That probably explains the recent trend for universities to set up petting zoos for their students just around exam time. At Australia's University of Canberra, goats, kittens, rabbits, lambs, puppies, chickens and more are all available to students for a week before the exam period, and the students take full advantage of it. The petting zoo programme is part of the University of Canberra's 'stress less week', which includes a barbecue, music, free breakfast and other activities.

However, the animal rights group People for the Ethical Treatment of Animals (PETA) have contacted students unions to make them aware of the poor treatment of animals in petting zoos, and the potential health risks to students. They believe that if students knew the facts, these zoos wouldn't have become so popular on campuses.

PETA argue that although students may get rid of their stress with a petting zoo, these zoos actually cause stress for the animals in them. PETA's Dan Howe said: 'Petting zoos are a bad bet for students and for animals. Travel, confinement to small cages and rough handling cause animals intense stress.'

Stirling University in Scotland was about to set up a petting zoo for their exam period. But after hearing PETA's arguments, they decided that they were going to try different methods to de-stress. Instead of animals, the student union has decided to go for bouncy castles, film nights and massages!

Have your say (221)

I think the animals in these zoos are happy. I wish we had a petting zoo at our school! *Kat*

Students solve sofa cash riddle

When a trio of New York college students bought a smelly, second-hand sofa from a charity store for $20, they had no idea what secrets it held.

One evening, flatmates Reese Werkhoven, Cally Guasti and Lara Russo decided to stay home and watch a movie. That was when they realised that they could feel something inside the couch. They had a look and found three envelopes full of cash. The students got excited. Reese already had plans – he was going to buy a car for his mum, and a boat!

However, the students' excitement was to turn to a moral dilemma when they found that one of the envelopes had a woman's name on it. The students knew that they hadn't earned the money, so the hunt for the real owner began, with the help of the students' parents.

Werkhoven's mother eventually found the woman in a phone book and the young man called her up. As soon as he told the woman that they had her sofa, she told him that she had left a lot of money in it. She kept the money there for 30 years, until she recently had a back operation. While she was in hospital, her doctors recommended her children replace the old sofa to aid her back pain. And that's how it ended up in the second-hand shop.

'We almost didn't pick that ugly couch,' Russo said 'but it was the only one with the right dimensions for our living room.'

If the three students hadn't found the woman's name, they would certainly be richer today. But the students didn't go home empty-handed. The woman gave them a thousand dollars to share between them as a reward.

Comments (319)

Their parents should be very proud. We need more honest people like these kids. *Aunt Sarah*

3 **Read the news stories again. Are these statements True (T), False (F) or is the information Not Mentioned (NM)?**

1 The University of Canberra was the first university to organise a petting zoo. T/F /NM
2 PETA argues that petting zoos are not effective for students. T/F /NM
3 PETA thinks the problem is that students are not given all the facts about petting zoos. T/F /NM
4 PETA claims that animals in petting zoos are often treated badly. T/F /NM
5 The three students were initially unhappy about finding the envelopes. T/F /NM
6 The students felt that they hadn't done anything to deserve the money. T/F /NM
7 The woman who owned the money did not want any publicity. T/F /NM

✓ EXAM SUCCESS

In True/False activities, read the text quickly. Then read the statements. Find the sections of the text where you think the answers come and read in more detail.

➤ EXAM SUCCESS page 147

4 **CRITICAL THINKING**

Think! Then compare ideas with your class.

- Do the writers of these articles judge people's actions? Give examples.

5 **What do the underlined words in the text mean? Guess and then check in your dictionary.**

6 SPEAKING **What about *you*?**

What comment would you add for each story?

Future activities in the past

1 Sometimes when we are talking about the past, we want to talk about something that was in the future at that time, something which had not happened yet (and perhaps never did happen). Look at the sentences and find the structures used to talk about future activities in the past.

1 They were about to discover something amazing.
2 He was going to buy a car for his mum.
3 Their excitement was to turn to a moral dilemma.
4 Thanks to the envelopes, she would have enough money to live off.
5 The rector of the university was opening the zoo the next day.

GRAMMAR REFERENCE ➤ PAGE 132

2 Complete the text with these words and expressions.

about • going to • playing • to • were • would
would survive

School baseball team in rescue drama

On Tuesday, a high school baseball team was doing training as usual. The next day they were (a) .... their last game of the season. Meanwhile, in the school car park, next to the baseball field, a mother was (b) .... to leave her daughter at school. She was (c) .... do an extracurricular activity. The girl got out of the car and walked behind it. She had no idea what (d) .... happen next. The mother accidentally put the car in reverse and knocked her daughter over. The team heard the accident and ran to the car park. They were (e) .... get a terrible shock. The girl was trapped under the back wheel of the car. Between 10 and 15 players immediately lifted the car up together, and the team coach pulled the girl out from under it. The girl (f) .... thanks to the boys' teamwork. Although the team (g) .... to lose their last match the following day, their coach said that they played one of their best games ever.

Many US teens play baseball

3 Decide if the sentences are correct. Rewrite the incorrect sentences.

1 The sky went black and it looked like it was about rain very soon.
2 She couldn't go to school the next morning because she was seeing the doctor.
3 They were to getting an incredible surprise the day after.
4 They thought it was snowing the next day, but it didn't.
5 He had no idea that he would win his next race.
6 They went to bed early because the next day was to be very busy.

4a Use your imagination to complete these sentences.

1 I knew it was going to be a great day because …
2 I was going to do my homework when …
3 I never thought it would happen, but one day …
4 I was meeting my friends the next day, but …
5 I was going to call my parents when …
6 The car was about to hit the dog when …

4b SPEAKING **Compare your sentences in groups. Choose the best sentence for each situation.**

Mixed conditionals

5 Look at these sentences and answer the questions.

a If the students **hadn't found** the woman's name, they **would be** richer today.
b If I **liked** animals, I **would have gone** with you to the petting zoo yesterday.

1 Are mixed conditionals a mixture of first and second conditionals, or second and third conditionals?
2 Which sentence describes an imaginary past situation and its present consequence?
3 Which sentence describes an imaginary present situation and its past consequence?

GRAMMAR REFERENCE ➤ PAGE 132

6 Which sentence endings are possible? How is the meaning of each sentence different?

1 If I'd studied photography …
 a I take photos for a newspaper.
 b I would take photos for a newspaper.
 c I would have taken photos for a newspaper.

2 I would have gone to the cinema if …
 a I like science fiction movies.
 b I liked science fiction movies.
 c I had liked science fiction movies.

3 She would be ill now if …
 a she doesn't take the medicine.
 b she didn't take the medicine.
 c she hadn't taken the medicine.

4 If penicillin didn't exist …
 a many people will die.
 b many people would die.
 c many people would have died.

5 I wouldn't be happy if …
 a you lie to me.
 b you lied to me.
 c you had lied to me.

7 Look at the situations and complete the sentences using mixed conditionals.

1 Jenna loves taking photos so she joined a camera club.
If Jenna didn't love taking photos, ...

2 Sam spent lots of time studying and now he's a journalist.
If Sam ....

3 Their new film is great because they spent years making it.
If they ....

4 They don't know where the key is. That's why they haven't opened the door.
If they ....

5 They didn't interview the actor because they can't speak English.
If they ....

6 I haven't got anything for you to eat because I didn't know you were coming.
If I ....

7 Liam has a new phone because he lost his old one.
He ....

8 I have to do my homework now because I didn't remember to do it yesterday.
If I ....

Developing vocabulary

Collocations connected with the news

1 SPEAKING Work with a partner. What do you think the expressions in red mean?

1 This new band is starting to **make the headlines** all over the world!
2 Read about the dog that became **front-page news**!
3 The PM has decided to **hold a press conference**.
4 The next **news item** is great news for drivers but terrible news for cyclists.
5 We **keep you informed** 24-hours a day!
6 There has been a very surprising **turn of events** in the peace talks.
7 Our website is the best for **breaking news**, bringing you **news updates** every moment of every day.
8 We're interrupting this programme for an important **newsflash**.

2 Match the expressions in red in 1 with their meanings a–i.

a piece of news, individual story or article
b organise a meeting where journalists get information and ask questions about a particular piece of news
c become famous by being reported in the news
d reports containing all the latest news
e news that is appearing for the first time
f become important enough to appear on the first page of a newspaper
g a short broadcast of an important piece of news in the middle of a TV or radio programme
h an unexpected change in a situation
i tell you all the essential information

3a Complete the sentences with the words in the box.

breaking • front • headlines • informed • items newsflash • press

1 How do you keep ....?
2 In your country, what type of news is important enough to get a .... and interrupt normal programmes?
3 Has your favourite actor, singer, sports person ever held a .... conference? Why?
4 What events became .... page news last week?
5 Which famous people are making the ....?
6 Are there any funny or silly .... of news at the moment?
7 How do you think you would first find out about any important .... news?

3b SPEAKING Work with a partner. Discuss the questions.

Analysing News Stories

GREAT NE
FRIDAY 23RD NOVEM

21ST CENTURY SKILLS OBJECTIVES

- To learn how to analyse news stories.
- To consider the advantages and disadvantages of citizen journalism.
- To practise analysing news stories from different sources and compare their treatment.

KEY CONCEPTS

portray [v], portrayal [n]: *Newspapers often portray young people as lazy.* **bias [n], biased [adj]:** *That football journalist is biased – he always says good things about that team because he used to play for them.* **neutral [adj]:** *The article was neutral because it didn't express arguments either for or against.* **objective [adj]:** *My opinion is totally objective, based on the facts and not on my personal beliefs or feelings.* **citizen journalism [n phr]:** *When members of the public send photos of incidents in the news, this is an example of citizen journalism.*

1a SPEAKING **There is a popular saying: 'Don't believe everything you read in the news.' Work with a partner. Do you agree with the statement?**

1b Make a list of questions that you could ask about a news article to help you to decide whether to believe it or not.

Is the article giving any facts or just opinions?

2 READING **Look at this guide to help students analyse news articles. How many of the questions did you think of?**

3a Use the questions to analyse the news stories on page 123.

3b SPEAKING **Compare your answers in 3a with a partner.**

NEWS ANALYSIS: A GUIDE

1. Who is the author of the article? Is it a famous person? Could they be biased for some reason? For example, do they belong to a particular organisation or have a personal connection with the people or events in the story?

2. Does the headline give a clear idea of what the article is about? Does it show any particular opinion about the topic?

3. What does the first paragraph tell you? Does it outline the main points of the story and/or give a summary of the most important ideas? If so, what are they?

4. What is the purpose of the article? Is it to describe and report facts? Is it to give you the writer's opinion or point of view on a particular question? Is it to entertain you or make you laugh? Is it to persuade you of something? Is it to teach or instruct you about something? Is it to explore and examine something in detail? Is it to shock you or create controversy?

5. Is the text giving you facts or opinions? Does the author use statistics, published studies or quotations from experts to support its arguments? Or does it just express personal emotions and experiences? Answering these questions can help you to answer the questions in number 4, too.

6. Does the writer give just one side of an argument, or do they give several?

7. Are there any diagrams, illustrations or photos with the article? Do they fairly and objectively represent the news in the article? Do they try to get a particular response from the reader (laughter, anger, sympathy, shock)?

8. Have you read information about the same story somewhere else? Was the treatment of the story similar or different?

9. How might different readers see this article? Is there a stereotypical portrayal of any groups of people? Could it offend somebody?

4 SPEAKING **Work with a partner and discuss these questions.**

1 How important do you think it is to analyse news stories in this way? Why?

2 Which three questions in 2 do you consider to be the most important?

5 **Work with a partner. Read this explanation of 'citizen journalism'. What could be the advantages and disadvantages of citizen journalism? Make two lists.**

CITIZEN JOURNALISM

FAQs

What exactly is citizen journalism?

In the past, most news was reported by professional journalists working for newspapers. In the 21st century, thanks to the Internet and social media networks, everybody and anybody can report the news. Citizen journalism is this recording, reporting and sharing of news events by members of the public using mobile technology and new media.

6 LISTENING 50 **Watch or listen to four students in a media studies class. They are debating whether citizen journalism is a good thing. Which of your ideas in 5 do they mention? Who would you vote for at the end of the debate?**

7 50 **Watch or listen again. Using your own words complete each sentence with between one and three words. Compare your answers with a partner.**

1 Increasingly news and events are now being provided by .... on websites uploaded by members of the public.

2 Citizen journalism might not be .... as it very often depends on personal opinion.

3 Major news providers make background checks about facts from many .... not just one or two.

4 You can sometimes get a better .... with a phone camera than with a camera crew.

5 Sometimes news on social media is uploaded for .... rather than as a public service.

6 As more varieties of news are broadcast there is also more online .... about events.

8 SPEAKING **Work with a partner. Do you agree with the statements in 7? Why/Why not?**

21ST CENTURY TASK

You want to analyse a news story from different sources.

Work in a small group and follow this plan:

1 *Choose a story that has been in the news recently.*

2 *Find two different sources for it, e.g. two different newspapers, or a newspaper and a news website.*

3 *Do the stories receive the same amount of space or attention? Do the journalists give the same facts or comment on the news in the same way? Use the questions in the guide in 2 to help you.*

4 *Work with your group and compare your opinions.*

5 *Write a report with your conclusions.*

6 *Present your report to the class.*

Listening

1 SPEAKING **Work with a partner. Read this headline. What questions would you ask the teenager to find out the full story of what happened? Make a list.**

TRAIN PASSENGER GIVES ARTWORK 'WORTH £20,000' TO HELPFUL TEENAGER

Who was the mystery passenger?

2 LISTENING 51 **Listen to two journalists interviewing the teenager. Tick (✓) any of your questions which they ask.**

3 51 **Listen again and choose the correct answers.**

1 The thing that stuck in the boy's memory was that …
   a the man on the train was quite old.
   b not all of the man's clothes were the right size.
   c the man had obviously just been painting.

2 The man gave the boy …
   a one of his most famous paintings.
   b a copy of one of his works which he added things to.
   c an unusual, signed drawing of some flowers.

3 The boy searched the Internet because …
   a he wanted to know the real value of the picture that he'd been given.
   b he suspected that he'd just met somebody famous.
   c the name Arthur Street was new to him, but the name Bootsy sounded familiar.

4 The boy's immediate plan is to …
   a find out more about the picture.
   b sell the picture and spend the cash.
   c keep the picture for the moment and maybe sell it for a higher price later on.

5 One of the reporters thinks that …
   a Bootsy gave the boy the picture to confuse everybody.
   b it's good to see people getting a reward for doing something good.
   c people should be kinder more often.

✓ EXAM SUCCESS

Remember that you may hear a word or words that come in one of the possible answers, but this does not mean it is definitely the answer. The word(s) may be there just to distract you.

➤ EXAM SUCCESS page 147

4 SPEAKING **What about *you*?**

What would you do if this happened to you? Would you keep the picture or sell it?

Grammar in context

Indirect questions

1a **Look at these sentences. They are all indirect questions. Write the direct questions.**

a I'd like to ask you what the man looked like.
b I wonder if you could tell us what he did then.
c I wonder what your reaction was when you found out.
d Have you got any idea why he gave you the picture?
e Do you know if you'd sell it?
f Can I ask what you'd do with the money?

1b **Answer these questions.**

1 In the underlined part of each sentence, does the subject come *before* the verb (like in a statement) or *after* the verb (like in a question)? Why?
2 Sentences a to c do not have a question mark at the end of the sentence, but sentences d to f do. Why?
3 Are indirect questions usually more formal and polite than direct questions or less formal and polite?

GRAMMAR REFERENCE ➤ PAGE 132

2 **Complete the second sentence so that it has a similar meaning to the first sentence, using the word given. Use between two and five words.**

1 How long did you take to discover his identity? TOOK
   Can you tell me how .... to discover his identity?
2 Was he talking to a friend? WHETHER
   I'd like to .... to a friend.
3 Why doesn't he want people to know his identity? IDEA
   Have you .... want people to know his identity?
4 What do other artists think of incidents like this? WONDER
   I .... of incidents like this.
5 Is it the first time this has happened? IF
   Do you know .... first time this has happened?
6 Why did you decide to give the picture to an expert? WHY
   Can I ask .... the picture to an expert?
7 How many paintings does he do each year? DOES
   I'd like to know how many paintings ....

3 **Write indirect questions using the words given.**

1 How long have you lived in this area? I'd like to know …
2 What do you think of graffiti? Can you tell me …
3 What are you going to do this summer? Have you any idea …
4 How often do you watch the news on TV? Can I ask …
5 Are you interested in sport? I wonder if you could tell me …
6 How many people read showbiz news? Do you know …
7 Have you ever met somebody famous? I'd like to ask …

4 SPEAKING **Work with a partner. Take it in turns to ask and answer the indirect questions in 3.**

5a SPEAKING **Look at this news headline. Work with a partner. You are reporters. Write six indirect questions to ask the teenager.**

Boy, 13, chases across city in taxi to follow bus

5b **One of you is the reporter and the other is the teenager from the story. Role-play your conversation for the class.**

Question tags

6 **Look at these sentences and the question tags they contain. Decide if the statements below are True (T) or False (F).**

a You were on a train, **weren't you**?
b He told you his name, **didn't he**?
c You'd never heard that name before, **had you**?
d You haven't seen any of his paintings, **have you**?
e This type of thing can't happen often, **can it**?
f I'm right in saying that, **aren't I**?
g Nobody is sure about his identity, **are they**?

1 We use question tags when we want somebody to confirm what we are saying. T/F
2 We use subject pronouns at the end of question tags. T/F
3 We use auxiliary or modal in question tags, not main verbs. T/F
4 Usually the question tag in an affirmative sentence is negative and the question tag in a negative sentence is affirmative. T/F
5 In sentences with *I am* the question tag is *am not I?* T/F
6 In sentences with *nobody, somebody, everybody*, we use the pronoun *they*. T/F

GRAMMAR REFERENCE ➤ PAGE 132

7 **Match sentences 1–8 with the correct question tags a–h.**

1	You love art,	a	have you?
2	You aren't interested in the news,	b	are you?
3	You haven't appeared on the news,	c	had you?
4	You will help me tomorrow,	d	can't you?
5	You told me that story,	e	didn't you?
6	You hadn't thought about that,	f	did you?
7	You didn't try to stop him,	g	won't you?
8	You can call an expert,	h	don't you?

8 **Complete the sentences with question tags.**

1 Everybody likes the summer, ...?
2 I'm right, ...?
3 We should use question tags, ...?
4 The news will be on soon, ...?
5 We're going to be on TV one day, ...?
6 You read the news yesterday, ...?
7 She never comes late, ...?
8 We've got homework tonight, ...?

9 LISTENING ▶ 52 **Listen and check your answers.**

10a PRONUNCIATION ▶ 53 **Listen to this sentence twice. What is the difference in pronunciation? In which case does the speaker seem very certain that they know the answer to their question?**

Everybody likes football, don't they?

10b ▶ 52 **Listen to the sentences in 8 again. Does the intonation go up or down? Write ↗ or ↘.**

10c ▶ 52 **Listen again and repeat. Pay special attention to the intonation.**

11a SPEAKING **Write three sentences about your partner that you know or think you know, and three things that you aren't sure about.**

You love watching sci-fi films.

11b **Add a question tag to each sentence.**

You love watching sci-fi films, don't you?

11c **Now ask your partner your questions. Remember to use falling intonation when you are quite certain of your partner's answer and rising intonation when you aren't so sure.**

Developing speaking

Presentations – 2

1 SPEAKING **Work with a partner and discuss these questions.**

1 Do you ever read stories about famous people? Why/Why not?

2 Why do you think so many people are interested in the private lives of celebrities?

2 SPEAKING **Look at this statement. Work with a partner and think of arguments for and against it.**

> *Celebrities do not deserve privacy. They use the press to become famous, so it's normal that the press continues to follow them around when they are famous.*

3 LISTENING 54 **Listen to somebody giving a presentation on this topic. Do you agree with what they say? Why/Why not?**

4 54 **Listen again and complete the expressions in the Speaking bank.**

SPEAKING BANK

Giving your point of view

Presenting opposing points of view

- It is true that …
- You can't deny that …
- There's no .... that …
- You can't .... with the fact that …
- I accept that …

Responding to opposing points of view

- But that doesn't mean that …
- However, …
- Let's not .... that …
- I would still say that …
- Even so, I still believe that …
- Having .... that,
- That doesn't alter my opinion that …

5 Choose one of these statements. Think of arguments for and against. Then decide what your opinion is.

> *If you don't read the newspaper, you are uninformed. If you do read the newspaper, you are misinformed.*
> (Mark Twain)

> *The press should always be free to write what they like.*

> *Famous politicians, scientists or writers have more right to privacy than famous actors or singers.*

6 Make notes for a presentation. Follow this guide.

1 Introduction: state your opinion.

2 Make your main points and justify them.

3 Present one or two opposing points.

4 Respond to the opposing point(s).

5 Conclusion: restate your opinion.

7 Think of expressions that are useful at each stage of your presentation and note them down.

8 **PRACTICE MAKES PERFECT** SPEAKING **Give your presentation to the class. Remember to use expressions from the Speaking bank and 7.**

An article – 2

1a SPEAKING **Work in groups. Brainstorm any people, stories or events that teenagers in your country are talking about right now.**

1b Compare answers with the rest of the class. Have you chosen similar things?

2 Look at this writing task. Find the key information that you need to include in your article.

Articles wanted
Trending topics

Write an article telling us who or what, in your opinion, people are talking about right now. Tell us why you think people are talking about them and give us your own opinion on these trending topics.

Write your article and send it to us today!

3 Read this article. Does it include all the necessary information?

TRENDING TOPICS

Nowadays, we are used to hearing about the latest news from social media networks. Trending topics change quickly and constantly. I am going to talk about just two topics that are very popular right now.

(a) Despite/Despite the fact that she has been acting for a while, one person who everybody is talking about right now is the American actress Emma Stone. She co-stars in a great film that has just appeared recently in the cinema, and she has been nominated for an Oscar for her performance. (b) Firstly/At first, I was not particularly interested in Emma Stone (c) since/whereas most of the films she had made before did not really appeal to me. (d) However/Although, I have just seen this new film and I have to say that I was very impressed.

The other topic that many of my friends are talking about right now is retrogaming. It used to be difficult and expensive to get the old, original games that people played in the 1980s. But some of the big companies have just started creating less expensive new editions of some of these games (e) as/therefore they have become so popular recently. (f) As far as I am concerned/Nevertheless, this is great news (g) as/and so I think the old games are really fun to play!

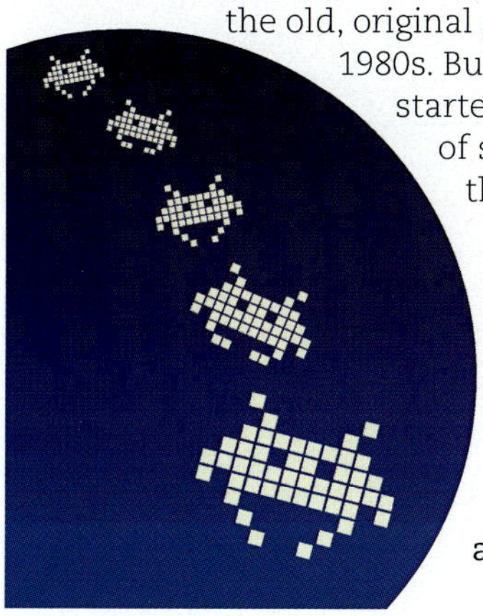

So, these are just two things that people are talking about right now. But everything changes so fast, doesn't it? Who knows what we will all be talking about tomorrow?!

4 Look again at the article and choose the correct alternative. Think about the meaning of the words and how they function in a sentence.

5 Put these titles in the correct places in the Writing bank.

a Addition
b Consequence
c Opinion
d Sequencing arguments
e Reason
f Contrast

WRITING BANK

Linkers – a review

1 ...d...
firstly, secondly, lastly

2 ....
however, nevertheless, although, despite, whereas, on the other hand

3 ....
what's more, furthermore, moreover, in addition, not only ... but also

4 ....
therefore, and so, as a result, consequently

5 ....
because, as, since

6 ....
as far as I'm concerned, personally, in my opinion

6 Work with a partner. Put these stages of writing a text in order.

a Organise your notes into logical paragraphs.
b Make notes.
c Check your text for mistakes, edit it, and check that you have answered the question.
d Write the first version of your text.
e Brainstorm ideas.
f Write the final version of your text.

1 – e

7 PRACTICE MAKES PERFECT **Write your article for the task in 2. Remember to use linkers from the Writing bank and follow the correct procedure in 6.**

WRITING BANK ➤ PAGE 153

Grammar reference

Future activities in the past

FORM

I **was going to** speak to him, but he ran away.
My American friend **was** arriv**ing** the next day.
I knew it **would** be a good day.
I **was about to** go out when my mum called.
The meeting **was to** take place on Tuesday.

USE

- We use *was/were to* when there was an arrangement for something to happen. It is usually formal.
- We use *was/were about to* for things that were going to happen very soon after.
- We use the past continuous for confirmed plans.

Mixed conditional

FORM

If + **past simple**, ... **would/wouldn't have** + past participle
If I wanted a coffee, I would have asked for one.
If + **past perfect**, ... **would/wouldn't** + infinitive
If I had passed my driving test, I'd drive to university.

USE

Mixed conditionals are a mixture of the second and third conditional. They can describe an imaginary present situation and its past consequence.
If I liked that group I would have gone to see them in concert.
Or they can describe an imaginary past situation and its present consequence. *If I'd had breakfast, I wouldn't be hungry now.*

Indirect questions

FORM

I'd like to know why you ***came****.*
I wonder what you ***prefer****.*
Do you know whether they ***won****?*
Could/Can you tell me what the problem ***is****?*
In the second part of these sentences we do not put the verb before the subject.
I wonder if you could tell us what you thought of the show.

We use question marks when the first part of the sentence is a question. *Have you any idea what time he's coming?*
When there is no question word (*who*, *what*, etc.), we use *if/whether*. *I'd like to know whether you agree.*

USE

We use **indirect questions** in more formal situations and to be more polite. We can also use indirect questions to ask a big favour from someone we know well.
Dad, I was wondering if I could take the car tonight.

Question tags

FORM

I'm late, ***aren't I?*** *I'm not late,* ***am I?***
You like rock music, ***don't you?***
You don't like classical music, ***do you?***
She could do the exercise, ***couldn't she?***
They enjoyed the party, ***didn't they?***
Everybody likes going to the cinema, ***don't they?***
In **question tags** we use pronouns, not nouns.
We make question tags with auxiliary or modal verbs. If there is no auxiliary or modal verb, we use the auxiliary *do*.
In affirmative sentences, the question tag is negative. In negative sentences, the question tag is affirmative.

With *everybody*, *nobody* and *somebody*, we use *they*.
We reply using the auxiliary or modal verb.
You don't like classical music, do you? No, I don't./Yes, I do.

USE

We use **question tags** to change a statement into a question. The question is to confirm what we are saying.
When we are very certain of the answer that somebody is going to give us, the intonation falls in the question tag.
You're Mike's sister, aren't ↘you?
When we aren't so sure of the answer, the intonation rises in the question tag.
The film has just started, hasn't ↗it?

Vocabulary

News sections arts • business • comment • editor's blog • entertainment • features • finance • gossip have your say • health • life and style • obituaries • opinion • showbiz • sport • weather forecast • world news

News headlines aid • axe • back • ban • blast • blaze • boost • boss/head • clash • cut • drama • hit key • link • move • plea • pledge • PM • probe • quit • riddle • spark • wed

Collocations connected with the news breaking news • front page news • hold a press conference keep somebody informed • make the headlines • newsflash • news item • news updates • turn of events

Other words and phrases ➤ page 142

Grammar revision

Future activities in the past — / 5 points

1 Complete the sentences with these words.

going • to • to • was • would

1. He thought the sun .... shine the next day, but it was really cloudy.
2. They ran to catch the train because it was .... to leave at that moment.
3. The interview was .... start at 10 am, but she was late.
4. They thought the party .... starting at 9 pm, but they were wrong.
5. He was laughing so hard he was about .... cry.

Mixed conditionals — / 5 points

2 Put the verbs in the correct form.

1. I .... (be) tired now if I'd gone to bed late last night.
2. Dylan would be studying at university if he .... (pass) his exam last June.
3. If I knew your number, I .... (call) you last night.
4. If they .... (win) the lottery last week, they'd all be millionaires.
5. I .... (finish) my assignment last week if I were more organised.

Indirect questions — / 5 points

3 Put the words in the correct order and add question marks at the end of the sentence if necessary.

1. you can me tell want what you — Can ....
2. are I to would know how like you — I ....
3. know you what is time it do — Do ....
4. you idea coffee any whether have he drinks — Have ....
5. to how know want you I did that — I ....

Question tags — / 5 points

4 Choose the correct alternative.

1. Nobody knows how to do it, *does he/do they*?
2. You never arrive on time, *do/don't* you?
3. He's made a lot of mistakes, *hasn't/isn't* he?
4. I'm not ready to do the exam, *am/aren't* I?
5. There's a lot of good news in the paper today, isn't *it/there*?

Vocabulary revision

NEWS SECTIONS — / 6 points

1 Which news section would you look at if you want to …

1. read about somebody who has just died? o ....
2. read about the private life of a famous actor? g ....
3. find out if it will rain later? w .... f ....
4. find out about a new TV series? e ....
5. add comments on a news story? h ....
6. read a longer article that gives more detail? f ....

NEWSPAPER HEADLINES — / 8 points

2 Match the words.

1	axe	**2**	key	**3**	plea	**4**	clash
5	wed	**6**	quit	**7**	back	**8**	blaze

a	marry	**e**	important, essential
b	support	**f**	cut
c	request	**g**	leave, resign
d	fire	**h**	disagree violently

COLLOCATIONS CONNECTED WITH THE NEWS — / 6 points

3 Choose the correct alternative.

1. Tomorrow they're going to hold a *headline/press conference* about the increase in organised crime.
2. There has been an interesting turn of *events/news* in the negotiations.
3. We have an interesting *article/news item* coming up now.
4. You can get news *front pages/updates* on your phone.
5. We'll keep you *aware/informed* of any new developments in the situation.
6. Because of one stupid mistake he has become *front page/headline* news.

Total: / 40 points

Reading

➤ TIP FOR READING EXAMS

In True/False/Not Mentioned activities, remember … Choose *Not Mentioned* if you can't find any information in the text to prove or disprove the statements.

➤ EXAM SUCCESS page 147

1 SPEAKING **Work with a partner. Look at the headlines. Invent a short newspaper story that could fit each headline.**

A Polish dog becomes bilingual

B Honest taxi driver becomes national hero

2 READING **Read the real newspaper stories. Are they similar to your invented stories?**

1

A dog which only responded to commands in Polish has found a new home thanks to the RSPCA (Royal Society for the Prevention of Cruelty to Animals) animal protection organisation.

Cent has settled in with his new owners, the Mroz family from Chelmsford, after 16-year-old Dominic and his mum Jolanta saw the dog's unusual story on the television.

Staff at the RSPCA centre in Oldham were originally confused when Cent arrived with them back in September, when his previous owners could no longer look after him.

Since he did not react to commands such as 'sit' or 'come', they were worried that the dog may have been deaf.

After looking at Cent's records they found that he had come from a Polish family and could only understand Polish. If they had known this from the start, they would have spoken to him in his own language. When they realised, they looked up basic commands in Polish on the Internet, although they weren't very sure about their pronunciation.

The RSPCA spent four months training Cent, who is now able to respond to many commands in English. However, his language skills won't be wasted in his new home, where his new owners speak both English and Polish. Jolanta said: 'He understands Polish really well and he'll immediately react to a lot of commands. He's so clever though and he understands English as well now, so we speak to him in both languages. We had been looking for a dog already, but we spotted Cent on the television and because we are of Polish origin, his story really stuck with us.'

Having watched a clip of him on the Internet about 50 times, they already felt like they knew him by the time they actually got to meet him. Mandy Tierney, a manager for the RSPCA, said: 'He had been with us for four months and we spent so much time with him, so it was very sad to see him go. He couldn't have gone to a more perfect home though. The minute Jolanta started speaking to him in Polish he instantly responded and was doing whatever she said.'

2

An Argentinian taxi driver has made the headlines after returning a bag full of money to its owners. The taxi driver has received thousands of dollars in donations after returning the $32,500 cash he found in his taxi to the people who accidentally left it there.

After reading the story, people all over the world are calling Santiago Gori a hero. A website set up in his honour has so far received donations of over $14,580 to reward him.

Gori, who drives a taxi in the Argentinian city of La Plata, made his discovery after leaving at their destination an elderly couple who had travelled a short distance in his cab. According to reports, they had left a bag filled with thousands of dollars on the back seat.

Immediately after finding the money, Gori began to look for the couple. He finally managed to find them several days later and returned their bag to them with its contents complete.

The story made the headlines in many newspapers around the world and, unsurprisingly, it has made a huge impact on many people. Two young Argentines decided to set up a website to congratulate Santiago Gori for his principles and integrity. Thousands of people visited the site, leaving money, messages and offers of snowboarding lessons, satnavs, pizzas and kilos of ice cream. Thanks to another offer, the taxi driver could have recorded an album if he was interested in starting a music career. Most of the messages thank Gori and say that they wish that more people were like him.

Meanwhile, Gori is said to be confused by the whole thing. He always knew he wouldn't take the money for himself. He claims that he simply did what he thought was the right thing. The turn of events in his story clearly proves that old proverb: 'honesty is the best policy'.

3 **Read the stories again. Are these statements True (T), False (F) or is the information Not Mentioned (NM)?**

1 Cent had to leave his last home because his owners were getting too old. T/F/NM

2 By watching Cent's behaviour, the staff realised that he understood Polish. T/F/NM

3 The dog's background made the Mroz family particularly interested in him. T/F/NM

4 The RSPCA made TV adverts with Cent so that somebody would adopt him. T/F/NM

5 Santiago Gori was given a reward by the people whose money he found. T/F/NM

6 Gori would be richer now if he had kept the money he found. T/F/NM

7 Gori didn't want to make a record. T/F/NM

8 Returning the money was a long, hard choice for Gori to make. T/F/NM

4 SPEAKING **What about *you*?**

Do you think there are enough 'good news' stories in the news?

Listening

➤ TIP FOR LISTENING EXAMS

In multiple-choice activities, remember …
When you listen, you may hear the correct answer but expressed in different words from the ones used in the question.

➤ EXAM SUCCESS page 147

5 SPEAKING **Work with a partner. Read this headline. What do you think actually happened?**

BATMAN ARRESTS COMIC BOOK THIEF

SHOP OWNER DRESSED AS BATMAN STOPS ROBBERY

6 LISTENING 55 **Listen to some journalists interviewing the shop owner. Choose the correct answer.**

1 The comic book shop was celebrating …
- a a national holiday.
- b a day when comics are given to customers as presents.
- c Halloween, a day when everybody wears fancy dress.

2 The people wearing special costumes …
- a were all working in the shop.
- b got a free comic.
- c included staff and customers.

3 The shop owner paid special attention to one customer because …
- a the customer was acting suspiciously.
- b he had never seen this customer before.
- c the customer was older than most of the regular customers.

4 The thief was trying to steal …
- a about $200 in cash.
- b somewhere between $600 and $800 in goods.
- c a whole collection of rare Batman comics.

5 When he first saw the shop owner, the thief was …
- a surprised.
- b angry and violent.
- c calm and resigned.

6 When the shop owner first asked for help …
- a a big group of 'superheroes' came to help him.
- b people didn't believe him.
- c everybody laughed.

7 The police officers who came to the shop …
- a saw the funny side of the situation.
- b didn't arrest the thief.
- c didn't want to give the shop free publicity.

Use of English

➤ TIP FOR USE OF ENGLISH

In cloze activities, remember …
Look closely at the words and expressions which come just before and after the gap. Think about the type of word you need and the general meaning.

➤ EXAM SUCCESS page 147

7 Read this news story and invent a good headline for it.

NEWS

In the US, a teenager has **(1)** .... the headlines by helping the police to catch a gang **(2)** .... stole his smartphone. Dustin Simantob, 15, had set **(3)** .... the special 'Find my phone' feature on his new device. This service allows you to discover **(4)** .... your phone is in case you lose it. When the device **(5)** .... stolen from his father's car in Colorado, he was able to use the service and track it down. That day, Dustin and his dad had been on a river trip. When they returned to their cars, they were **(6)** .... get an unpleasant surprise. All the windows had been broken and all their valuables had been taken. Dustin remembered the 'Find my phone' service and discovered that it was at a house close to where it had been stolen. Dustin called the police and told them the address. The police went straight to the house and found the phones, money and satnav **(7)** .... the criminals had stolen from their cars. Thanks to Dustin, the police were finally able to arrest the family of criminals. And thanks to technology, too. Let's hope that technology can help to reduce crime in the future. That'd certainly be good news, **(8)** .... it?

8 Read the text again. Decide which answer (A, B, C, D) best fits each gap.

	A	B	C	D
1	caught	done	had	made
2	–	that	what	when
3	at	on	to	up
4	–	that	where	which
5	was	has	is	had
6	about	for	really	to
7	when	where	which	who
8	hadn't	won't	would	wouldn't

Writing

➤ TIP FOR WRITING EXAMS

In reports, remember …
Use a formal style. Include a title and information in sections.

➤ EXAM SUCCESS page 147

9 Look at the task and decide what headings and how many paragraphs you will have. Write your report.

A news website wants to know how interested people are in the news. You have been asked to write a report about:
- how young people follow the news (TV, the Internet, etc.)
- what sections (sport, entertainment, world news, etc.) young people are most interested in

(adj) = adjective
(adv) = adverb
(conj) = conjunction
(det) = determiner
(n/n pl) = noun/noun plural
(phr) = phrase
(prep) = preposition
(pron) = pronoun
(v) = verb

The most common and useful words in English are marked according to the Macmillan Dictionary 'star rating'. This is so you can easily recognise the vocabulary you need to know especially well.

★★★ = very common words ★★ = common words ★ = fairly common words

If there is no star next to the word, this means that it is not very common.

In the Macmillan Dictionary, (r) is used to indicate where the sound /r/ is pronounced in American English and some other regional varieties of English. In a standard British accent, (r) is only pronounced if it occurs at the end of a word which is followed by another word starting with a vowel sound, for example *far away* /fɑːr ə'weɪ/.

Unit 1

Studying at university

assignment (n) ★★ /ə'saɪnmənt/
cheat (v) ★ /tʃiːt/
continuous assessment (n) /kənˌtɪnjʊəs ə'sesmənt/
course (n) ★★★ /kɔː(r)s/
coursework (n) /'kɔː(r)sˌwɜː(r)k/
degree (n) ★★★ /dɪ'griː/
fail (v) ★★★ /feɪl/
grade (n) ★★ /greɪd/
graduate (v) ★ /'grædʒueɪt/
lecture (n) ★★ /'lektʃə(r)/
mark (n) ★★★ /mɑː(r)k/
master's (n) /'mɑːstə(r)z/
notes (n pl) ★★★ /nəʊts/
pass (v) ★★★ /pɑːs/
resit (v) /ˌriː'sɪt/
revise (v) ★ /rɪ'vaɪz/
term (n) ★★★ /tɜː(r)m/
tutor (n) ★★ /'tjuːtə(r)/
tutorial (n) /tjuː'tɔːriəl/
undergraduate (n) /ˌʌndə(r)'grædʒʊət/

Life at university

become independent (phr) /bɪˌkʌm ɪndɪ'pendənt/
extracurricular activities (phr) /ˌekstrəkəˌrɪkjʊlər æk'tɪvətiz/
hall of residence (n) /ˌhɔːl əv 'rezɪd(ə)ns/
make new friends (phr) /ˌmeɪk njuː 'frendz/
student facilities (n pl) /ˌstjuːd(ə)nt fə'sɪlətiz/
student loan (n) /ˌstjuːd(ə)nt 'ləʊn/
study abroad (phr) /ˌstʌdi ə'brɔːd/

Do and *make*

make a cake (phr) /ˌmeɪk ə 'keɪk/
make a decision (phr) /ˌmeɪk ə dɪ'sɪʒ(ə)n/
make a noise (phr) /ˌmeɪk ə 'nɔɪz/
make friends (phr) /ˌmeɪk 'frendz/
make the dinner (phr) /ˌmeɪk ðə 'dɪnə(r)/
do a course (phr) /ˌduː ə 'kɔː(r)s/
do an assignment (phr) /ˌduː ən ə'saɪnmənt/
do an exam (phr) /ˌduː ən ɪg'zæm/
do chores (phr) /ˌduː 'tʃɔː(r)z/
do homework (phr) /ˌduː 'həʊmˌwɜː(r)k/
do the shopping (phr) /ˌduː ðə 'ʃɒpɪŋ/
do the washing (phr) /ˌduː ðə 'wɒʃɪŋ/
do well (phr) /ˌduː 'wel/

Other words and phrases

academic (adj) ★★★ /ˌækə'demɪk/
ages (n) /'eɪdʒɪz/
already (adv) ★★★ /ɔːl'redi/
annoy (v) ★★ /ə'nɔɪ/
anyway (adv) ★★★ /'eniˌweɪ/
arrange (v) ★★★ /ə'reɪndʒ/
avoid (v) ★★★ /ə'vɔɪd/
balance (n) ★★★ /'bæləns/
base (v) ★★★ /beɪs/
be like (somebody) (phr) /biː 'laɪk/
blame (v) ★★★ /bleɪm/
brave (adj) ★★ /breɪv/
break (n) ★★★ /breɪk/
by the way (phr) /ˌbaɪ ðə 'weɪ/
can't stand (phr) /ˌkɑːnt 'stænd/
career (n) ★★★ /kə'rɪə(r)/
choice (n) ★★★ /tʃɔɪs/
chore (n) /tʃɔː(r)/
come up (v phr) /ˌkʌm 'ʌp/
complain (v) ★★★ /kəm'pleɪn/
details (n pl) /'diːteɪlz/
discuss (v) ★★★ /dɪ'skʌs/
don't mind (phr) /ˌdəʊnt 'maɪnd/
duration (n) ★★ /djʊ'reɪʃ(ə)n/
encourage (v) ★★★ /ɪn'kʌrɪdʒ/
ever (adv) ★★★ /'evə(r)/
expect (v) ★★★ /ɪk'spekt/
experience (v) ★★★ /ɪk'spɪəriəns/
find out about (v phr) /ˌfaɪnd 'aʊt əˌbaʊt/
folder (n) ★ /'fəʊldə(r)/
forum (n) ★★ /'fɔːrəm/
hand in (v phr) /ˌhænd 'ɪn/
helpline (n) /'helpˌlaɪn/
improve (v) ★★★ /ɪm'pruːv/
instead of (adv) /ɪn'sted ɒv/
irritate (v) ★ /'ɪrɪteɪt/
just (adv) ★★★ /dʒʌst/
look forward to (v phr) /ˌlʊk 'fɔː(r)wə(r)d tuː/
manage (v) ★★★ /'mænɪdʒ/
nerves (n pl) ★★ /nɜː(r)vz/
never (adv) ★★★ /'nevə(r)/
noise (n) ★★★ /nɔɪz/
practical (adj) ★★★ /'præktɪk(ə)l/
realise (v) ★★★ /'rɪəlaɪz/
relatively (adv) ★★★ /'relətɪvli/
research (n & v) ★★★ /rɪ'sɜː(r)tʃ/
risk (v) ★★ /rɪsk/
since (adv) ★★★ /sɪns/
specific (adj) ★★★ /spə'sɪfɪk/
take your mind off something (phr) /ˌteɪk jɔː(r) 'maɪnd ɒf ˌsʌmθɪŋ/
theoretical (adj) ★★ /ˌθɪə'retɪk(ə)l/
topic (n) ★★★ /'tɒpɪk/
uni (n) /'juːni/
unspecified (adj) /ʌn'spesɪfaɪd/
valid (adj) ★★ /'vælɪd/
wallet (n) /'wɒlɪt/
wet (adj) ★★★ /wet/

Unit 2

Work conditions and responsibilities

bad conditions (phr) /ˌbæd kən'dɪʃ(ə)nz/
be on flexitime (phr) /biː ɒn 'fleksitaɪm/
be responsible for (v) /biː rɪ'spɒnsəb(ə)l fɔː(r)/
dangerous conditions (phr) /ˌdeɪndʒərəs kən'dɪʃ(ə)nz/
deal with (v) /'diːl wɪð/
do shift work (phr) /ˌduː 'ʃɪft ˌwɜː(r)k/
earn (v) ★★★ /ɜː(r)n/
employee (n) ★★★ /ɪm'plɔɪiː/
experience (n) ★★★ /ɪk'spɪəriəns/
from nine to five (phr) /frɒm ˌnaɪn tə 'faɪv/
full-time (adj) ★★ /'fʊl ˌtaɪm/
good conditions (phr) /ˌgʊd kən'dɪʃ(ə)nz/
indoors (adv) ★ /ɪn'dɔː(r)z/

long hours (n pl) /ˌlɒŋ ˈaʊə(r)z/
manual (adj) ★ /ˈmænjʊəl/
outdoors (adv) /ˌaʊtˈdɔː(r)z/
overtime (adv) /ˈəʊvə(r)ˌtaɪm/
paperwork (n) ★ /ˈpeɪpə(r)ˌwɜː(r)k/
part-time (adj) ★★ /ˈpɑː(r)t ˌtaɪm/
qualification (n) ★★★ /ˌkwɒlɪfɪˈkeɪʃ(ə)n/
salary (n) ★★ /ˈsæləri/
self-employed (adj) /ˌself ɪmˈplɔɪd/
skilled (adj) ★★ /skɪld/
stressful (adj) /ˈstresf(ə)l/
training (n) ★★★ /ˈtreɪnɪŋ/
well-paid (adj) /ˌwel ˈpeɪd/

Working life

apply for a job (phr) /əˌplaɪ fə(r) ə ˈdʒɒb/
become unemployed (phr) /bɪˌkʌm ˌʌnɪmˈplɔɪd/
be dismissed /biː dɪsˈmɪst/
be fired /biː ˈfaɪə(r)d/
be made redundant /biː ˌmeɪd rɪˈdʌndənt/
be offered a job /biː ˌɒfə(r)d ə ˈdʒɒb/
be sacked /biː ˈsækt/
get promotion (phr) /ˌget prəˈməʊʃ(ə)n/
look for a job (phr) /ˌlʊk fə(r) ə ˈdʒɒb/
resign (v) ★★★ /rɪˈzaɪn/
retire (v) ★★ /rɪˈtaɪə(r)/
sign a contract (phr) /ˌsaɪn ə ˈkɒntrækt/

Phrasal verbs: work

fill in (v phr) /ˌfɪl ˈɪn/
get ahead (v phr) /ˌget əˈhed/
keep at (v phr) /ˌkiːp ˈæt/
keep up with (v phr) /ˌkiːp ˈʌp wɪð/
set up (v phr) /ˌset ˈʌp/
take over (v phr) /ˌteɪk ˈəʊvə(r)/
turn down (v phr) /ˌtɜː(r)n ˈdaʊn/
work on (v phr) /ˈwɜː(r)k ɒn/

Other words and phrases

all things considered (phr) /ˌɔːl θɪŋz kənˈsɪdə(r)d/
apply to (v phr) /əˈplaɪ tuː/
attach (v) ★★ /əˈtætʃ/
beg (v) ★★ /beg/
bus fare (n) /ˈbʌs ˌfeə(r)/
candidate (n) ★★★ /ˈkændɪdeɪt/
caretaker (n) /ˈkeə(r)ˌteɪkə(r)/
challenging (adj) /ˈtʃælɪndʒɪŋ/
crowd (n) ★★★ /kraʊd/
distraction (n) ★ /dɪˈstrækʃ(ə)n/
driving licence (n) /ˈdraɪvɪŋ ˌlaɪs(ə)ns/
firefighter (n) /ˈfaɪə(r)ˌfaɪtə(r)/
flexibility (n) ★★ /ˌfleksəˈbɪləti/
flexible (adj) ★★ /ˈfleksəb(ə)l/
for instance (phr) /fər ˈɪnstəns/
furthermore (adv) ★★ /ˈfɜː(r)ðə(r)ˌmɔː(r)/
gap year (n) /ˈgæp ˌjɪə(r)/
gravity (n) ★ /ˈgrævəti/
ground (n) ★★★ /graʊnd/
however (conj) ★★★ /haʊˈevə(r)/
hurry (n) ★ /ˈhʌri/
in addition (phr) /ɪn əˈdɪʃ(ə)n/
interrupt (v) ★★ /ˌɪntəˈrʌpt/
jellyfish (n) /ˈdʒeliˌfɪʃ/
location (n) ★★★ /ləʊˈkeɪʃ(ə)n/
luxurious (adj) /lʌgˈzjʊəriəs/
motivate (v) ★★ /ˈməʊtɪveɪt/
nevertheless (adv) ★★★ /ˌnevə(r)ðəˈles/
particle (n) ★★ /ˈpɑː(r)tɪk(ə)l/
passenger (n) ★★★ /ˈpæsɪndʒə(r)/
personal assistant (n) /ˌpɜː(r)s(ə)nəl əˈsɪst(ə)nt/
press conference (n) ★ /ˈpres ˌkɒnf(ə)rəns/
promote (v) ★★★ /prəˈməʊt/
promotional (adj) /prəˈməʊʃ(ə)nəl/
properly (adv) ★★★ /ˈprɒpə(r)li/
share (v) ★★★ /ʃeə(r)/
single (adj) ★★★ /ˈsɪŋg(ə)l/
software engineer (n) /ˈsɒf(t)weə(r) ˌendʒɪˌnɪə(r)/
sting (n & v) /stɪŋ/
straight away (adv) /ˌstreɪt əˈweɪ/
sum up (v phr) /ˌsʌm ˈʌp/
unlock (v) ★ /ʌnˈlɒk/
volunteer (n) ★★ /ˌvɒlənˈtɪə(r)/
what is more (phr) /ˌwɒt ɪz ˈmɔː(r)/

Gateway to exams: Units 1–2

atmosphere (n) ★★ /ˈætməsˌfɪə(r)/
behave (v) ★★ /bɪˈheɪv/
campus (n) ★ /ˈkæmpəs/
constructively (adv) /kənˈstrʌktɪvli/
Erasmus programme (n) /ɪrˈæzməs ˌprəʊgræm/
exchange (n) ★★★ /ɪksˈtʃeɪndʒ/
frustrating (adj) ★ /frʌsˈtreɪtɪŋ/
fulfil (v) ★★ /fʊlˈfɪl/
linguistic (adj) ★ /lɪŋˈgwɪstɪk/
memorable (adj) /ˈmem(ə)rəb(ə)l/
passionate (adj) ★ /ˈpæʃ(ə)nət/
politics (n) ★★★ /ˈpɒlətɪks/
professor (n) ★★ /prəˈfesə(r)/
remove (v) ★★★ /rɪˈmuːv/
solve (v) ★★★ /sɒlv/
stimulating (adj) /ˈstɪmjʊˌleɪtɪŋ/

Unit 3

Transport and travel

astronaut (n) ★ /ˈæstrəˌnɔːt/
board (v) ★ /bɔː(r)d/
crew (n) ★★★ /kruː/
flight (n) ★★★ /flaɪt/
gate (n) /geɪt/
get in (v phr) /ˌget ˈɪn/
get off (v phr) /ˌget ˈɒf/
get on (v phr) /ˌget ˈɒn/
get out (v phr) /ˌget ˈaʊt/
high-speed train (n) /ˌhaɪ spiːd ˈtreɪn/
land (v) ★★★ /lænd/
landing (n) ★★ /ˈlændɪŋ/
launch (n & v) ★★ /lɔːntʃ/
motorway (n) ★★ /ˈməʊtə(r)ˌweɪ/
orbit (n & v) ★ /ˈɔː(r)bɪt/
passenger (n) ★★★ /ˈpæsɪndʒə(r)/
platform (n) ★★ /ˈplætˌfɔː(r)m/
rocket (n) ★ /ˈrɒkɪt/
spacecraft (n) /ˈspeɪsˌkrɑːft/
space station (n) /ˈspeɪs ˌsteɪʃ(ə)n/
take off (v phr) /ˌteɪk ˈɒf/
the Underground (n) /ðiː ˈʌndə(r)ˌgraʊnd/
the subway (n) /ðə ˈsʌbˌweɪ/
the tube (n) /ðə ˈtjuːb/
traffic jam (n) /ˈtræfɪk ˌdʒæm/

Prefixes

cooperate (v) ★ /kəʊˈɒpəreɪt/
disadvantage (n) ★★ /ˌdɪsədˈvɑːntɪdʒ/
disagree (v) ★★ /ˌdɪsəˈgriː/
disappear (v) ★★★ /ˌdɪsəˈpɪə(r)/
discomfort (n) /dɪsˈkʌmfə(r)t/
disobey (v) /ˌdɪsəˈbeɪ/
illogical (adj) /ɪˈlɒdʒɪk(ə)l/
impatient (adj) ★ /ɪmˈpeɪʃ(ə)nt/
impossible (adj) ★★★ /ɪmˈpɒsəb(ə)l/
incapable (adj) /ɪnˈkeɪpəb(ə)l/
incomplete (adj) /ˌɪnkəmˈpliːt/
interactive (adj) ★ /ˌɪntərˈæktɪv/
irregular (adj) ★ /ɪˈregjʊlə(r)/
irresponsible (adj) /ˌɪrɪˈspɒnsəb(ə)l/
miscalculate (v) /mɪsˈkælkjʊleɪt/
misunderstand (v) /ˌmɪsʌndə(r)ˈstænd/
overbook (v) /ˌəʊvə(r)ˈbʊk/
overpopulated (adj) /ˌəʊvə(r)ˈpɒpjʊˌleɪtɪd/
postgraduate (adj) /ˌpəʊs(t)ˈgrædʒʊət/
reinvent (v) /ˌriːɪnˈvent/
rewrite (v) ★ /ˌriːˈraɪt/
subway (n) /ˈsʌbˌweɪ/
sub-zero (adj) /ˌsʌbˈzɪərəʊ/
superhuman (adj) /ˌsuːpə(r)ˈhjuːmən/
supersonic (adj) /ˌsuːpə(r)ˈsɒnɪk/

unbelievable (adj) /ˌʌnbɪˈliːvəb(ə)l/
underestimate (v) ★ /ˌʌndərˈestɪˌmeɪt/
underpaid (adj) /ˌʌndə(r)ˈpeɪd/
unexpected (adj) ★★ /ˌʌnɪkˈspektɪd/
unlikely (adj) ★★★ /ʌnˈlaɪkli/
unnecessary (adj) ★★ /ʌnˈnesəs(ə)ri/
unsuccessful (adj) ★ /ˌʌnsəkˈsesf(ə)l/
unusual (adj) ★★★ /ʌnˈjuːʒʊəl/

Other words and phrases

appointment (n) ★★★ /əˈpɔɪntmənt/
be on board (v) /biː ɒn ˈbɔː(r)d/
bold (adj) ★★ /bəʊld/
collision (n) ★ /kəˈlɪʒ(ə)n/
environmental (adj) ★★★ /ɪnˌvaɪrənˈment(ə)l/
grow (v) ★★★ /grəʊ/
ice age (n) /ˈaɪs ˌeɪdʒ/
impact (n) ★★★ /ˈɪmpækt/
last (v) ★★★ /lɑːst/
look up (v phr) /ˌlʊk ˈʌp/
manned (adj) /mænd/
model (n) ★ /ˈmɒd(ə)l/
myth (n) ★★ /mɪθ/
nervous (adj) ★★ /ˈnɜː(r)vəs/
occasion (n) ★★★ /əˈkeɪʒ(ə)n/
organic (adj) ★ /ɔː(r)ˈgænɪk/
parcel (n) ★ /ˈpɑː(r)s(ə)l/
positive (adj) ★★★ /ˈpɒzətɪv/
pregnant (adj) ★★ /ˈpregnənt/
rocket (v) /ˈrɒkɪt/
roughly (adv) ★★ /ˈrʌfli/
save up (v phr) /ˌseɪv ˈʌp/
telescope (n) ★ /ˈtelɪˌskəʊp/

Unit 4

Personality adjectives

ambitious (adj) ★★ /æmˈbɪʃəs/
arrogant (adj) ★ /ˈærəgənt/
assertive (adj) /əˈsɜː(r)tɪv/
bad-tempered (adj) ★ /ˌbæd ˈtempə(r)d/
big-headed (adj) /ˌbɪg ˈhedɪd/
bossy (adj) /ˈbɒsi/
broad-minded (adj) /ˌbrɔːd ˈmaɪndɪd/
brusque (adj) /bruːsk/
determined (adj) ★★ /dɪˈtɜː(r)mɪnd/
down-to-earth (adj) /ˌdaʊn tuː ˈɜː(r)θ/
easygoing (adj) /ˌiːziˈgəʊɪŋ/
frank (adj) ★ /fræŋk/
gifted (adj) /ˈgɪftɪd/
good-natured (adj) /ˌgʊd ˈneɪtʃə(r)d/
immature (adj) /ˌɪməˈtjʊə(r)/
insecure (adj) /ˌɪnsɪˈkjʊə(r)/
mature (adj) ★★ /məˈtʃʊə(r)/
modest (adj) ★★ /ˈmɒdɪst/
narrow-minded (adj) /ˌnærəʊ ˈmaɪndɪd/
outgoing (adj) /ˈaʊtgəʊɪŋ/
pushy (adj) /ˈpʊʃi/
reserved (adj) /rɪˈzɜː(r)vd/
self-confident (adj) /ˌself ˈkɒnfɪd(ə)nt/
sensitive (adj) ★★★ /ˈsensətɪv/
shy (adj) ★ /ʃaɪ/
slow (adj) ★★★ /sləʊ/
stubborn (adj) ★ /ˈstʌbə(r)n/
tactful (adj) /ˈtæk(t)f(ə)l/
tactless (adj) /ˈtæk(t)ləs/
talented (adj) ★ /ˈtæləntɪd/

Noun suffixes

ability (n) ★★★ /əˈbɪləti/
action (n) ★★★ /ˈækʃ(ə)n/
activity (n) ★★★ /ækˈtɪvəti/
actor (n) ★★★ /ˈæktə(r)/
appearance (n) ★★★ /əˈpɪərəns/
artist (n) ★★★ /ˈɑː(r)tɪst/
confidence (n) ★★★ /ˈkɒnfɪd(ə)ns/
creation (n) ★★★ /kriˈeɪʃ(ə)n/
creativity (n) ★ /ˌkriːeɪˈtɪvəti/
creator (n) ★ /kriˈeɪtə(r)/
darkness (n) ★★ /ˈdɑː(r)knəs/
difference (n) ★★★ /ˈdɪfrəns/
direction (n) ★★★ /daɪˈrekʃ(ə)n/
education (n) ★★★ /ˌedjʊˈkeɪʃ(ə)n/
educator (n) /ˈedjʊˌkeɪtə(r)/
electrician (n) /ɪˌlekˈtrɪʃ(ə)n/
electricity (n) ★★★ /ɪˌlekˈtrɪsəti/
employer (n) ★★★ /ɪmˈplɔɪə(r)/
employment (n) ★★★ /ɪmˈplɔɪmənt/
enjoyment (n) ★ /ɪnˈdʒɔɪmənt/
happiness (n) ★★ /ˈhæpinəs/
illness (n) ★★★ /ˈɪlnəs/
importance (n) ★★★ /ɪmˈpɔː(r)t(ə)ns/
improvement (n) ★★★ /ɪmˈpruːvmənt/
invention (n) ★★ /ɪnˈvenʃ(ə)n/
inventor (n) ★ /ɪnˈventə(r)/
investigation (n) ★★★ /ɪnˌvestɪˈgeɪʃ(ə)n/
investigator (n) ★ /ɪnˈvestɪˌgeɪtə(r)/
madness (n) ★ /ˈmædnəs/
musician (n) ★★ /mjʊˈzɪʃ(ə)n/
performance (n) ★★★ /pə(r)ˈfɔː(r)məns/
politician (n) ★★★ /ˌpɒləˈtɪʃ(ə)n/
relevance (n) ★★ /ˈreləv(ə)ns/
scientist (n) ★★★ /ˈsaɪəntɪst/
writer (n) ★★★ /ˈraɪtə(r)/

Other words and phrases

bottom (adj) ★★ /ˈbɒtəm/
bully (v) ★ /ˈbʊli/
calm (adj) ★★ /kɑːm/
demonstrate (v) ★★★ /ˈdemənˌstreɪt/
equal (adj) ★★★ /ˈiːkwəl/
get on somebody's nerves (phr) /ˌget ɒn ˌsʌmbədiz ˈnɜː(r)vz/
hardly (adv) ★★★ /ˈhɑː(r)dli/
intelligence (n) /ɪnˈtelɪdʒ(ə)ns/
kinaesthetic (adj) /ˌkɪniːsˈθetɪk/
make a point (phr) /ˌmeɪk ə ˈpɔɪnt/
measure (v) ★★★ /ˈmeʒə(r)/
mission (n) ★★ /ˈmɪʃ(ə)n/
navigate (v) /ˈnævɪgeɪt/
opportunity (n) ★★★ /ˌɒpə(r)ˈtjuːnəti/
pack (n) ★★ /pæk/
painful (adj) ★★ /ˈpeɪnf(ə)l/
quiet (adj) ★★★ /ˈkwaɪət/
rise (n) ★★★ /raɪz/
shock (v) ★★ /ʃɒk/
spatial (adj) /ˈspeɪʃ(ə)l/
surface (n) ★★★ /ˈsɜː(r)fɪs/
talented (adj) ★ /ˈtæləntɪd/
turn into (v phr) /ˌtɜː(r)n ˈɪntuː/

Gateway to exams: Units 3–4

authority (n) ★★★ /ɔːˈθɒrəti/
colleague (n) ★★★ /ˈkɒliːg/
distinguish (v) ★★★ /dɪˈstɪŋgwɪʃ/
elite (adj) /ɪˈliːt/
encouraging (adj) ★★ /ɪnˈkʌrɪdʒɪŋ/
mathematician (n) /ˌmæθ(ə)məˈtɪʃ(ə)n/
neurologist (n) /njʊərˈɒlədʒɪst/
outstanding (adj) ★★ /aʊtˈstændɪŋ/
potential (n) ★★★ /pəˈtenʃ(ə)l/
prestigious (adj) /preˈstɪdʒəs/
rebellious (adj) /rɪˈbeljəs/
researcher (n) /rɪˈsɜː(r)tʃə(r)/
run up (v phr) /ˈrʌn ʌp/
soloist (n) /ˈsəʊləʊɪst/
supportive (adj) /səˈpɔː(r)tɪv/
violinist (n) /ˌvaɪəˈlɪnɪst/

Unit 5

Buying and selling

afford (v) ★★★ /əˈfɔː(r)d/
bargain (n) ★★ /ˈbɑː(r)gɪn/
cash (n) ★★★ /kæʃ/
change (n) ★★★ /tʃeɪndʒ/
discount (n) ★★ /ˈdɪsˌkaʊnt/
receipt (n) ★★ /rɪˈsiːt/
refund (n) /ˈriːfʌnd/
sale (n) ★★★ /seɪl/
value for money (phr) /ˌvæljuː fə(r) ˈmʌni/
waste (v) ★★ /weɪst/

Money and banking

ATM (n) /ˌeɪ tiː ˈem/
bank charges (n pl) /ˈbæŋk ˌtʃɑː(r)dʒɪz/

bank fees (n) /ˈbæŋk ˌfiːz/
bill (n) ★★★ /bɪl/
cashpoint (n) /ˈkæʃˌpɔɪnt/
current account (n) /ˈkʌrənt əˌkaʊnt/
get into debt (phr) /ˌget ɪntuː ˈdet/
give somebody a loan (phr) /ˌɡɪv sʌmbədi ə ˈləʊn/
interest (n) ★★★ /ˈɪntrəst/
lend money (v phr) /ˌlend ˈmʌni/
overdraft (n) /ˈəʊvə(r)ˌdrɑːft/
savings account (n) /ˈseɪvɪŋz əˌkaʊnt/
withdraw money (v phr) /ˌwɪðdrɔː ˈmʌni/

Phrasal verbs: money and shopping

come to (v phr) /ˈkʌm tuː/
cut back (v phr) /ˌkʌt ˈbæk/
get by (v phr) /ˌget ˈbaɪ/
give away (v phr) /ˌɡɪv əˈweɪ/
pay back (v phr) /ˌpeɪ ˈbæk/
pick up (v phr) /ˌpɪk ˈʌp/
sell out (v phr) /ˌsel ˈaʊt/
set aside (v phr) /ˌset əˈsaɪd/
splash out (v phr) /ˌsplæʃ ˈaʊt/

Other words and phrases

abbreviation (n) ★ /əˌbriːviˈeɪʃ(ə)n/
afford (v) ★★★ /əˈfɔː(r)d/
a great deal of (phr) /ə ˌɡreɪt ˈdiːl ɒv/
apology (n) ★ /əˈpɒlədʒi/
assurance (n) ★★ /əˈʃɔːrəns/
as well as (conj) /æz ˈwel æz/
be worth (v) /biː ˈwɜː(r)θ/
bleep (v) /bliːp/
civil servant (n) /ˌsɪv(ə)l ˈsɜː(r)v(ə)nt/
coin (n) ★★ /kɔɪn/
demand (v) ★★★ /dɪˈmɑːnd/
designer (n) ★★ /dɪˈzaɪnə(r)/
destroy (v) ★★★ /dɪˈstrɔɪ/
doubt (n) ★★★ /daʊt/
force (v) ★★★ /fɔː(r)s/
fortune (n) ★★ /ˈfɔː(r)tʃən/
handwriting (n) ★ /ˈhændˌraɪtɪŋ/
incident (n) ★★★ /ˈɪnsɪd(ə)nt/
insert (v) ★★★ /ɪnˈsɜː(r)t/
issue (v) ★★★ /ˈɪʃuː/
luxury (adj) ★ /ˈlʌkʃəri/
majority (n) ★★★ /məˈdʒɒrəti/
massive (adj) ★★★ /ˈmæsɪv/
note (n) ★★★ /nəʊt/
optional (adj) ★ /ˈɒpʃ(ə)nəl/
owe (v) ★★★ /əʊ/
print (v) ★★★ /prɪnt/
proof (n) ★★ /pruːf/
reach (v) ★★★ /riːtʃ/
reduce (v) ★★★ /rɪˈdjuːs/
retain (v) ★★ /rɪˈteɪn/
reveal (v) ★★★ /rɪˈviːl/
sensible (adj) ★★ /ˈsensəb(ə)l/
sign (v) ★★★ /saɪn/
swallow (v) ★★ /ˈswɒləʊ/
terminal illness (n) /ˌtɜː(r)mɪn(ə)l ˈɪlnəs/
transaction (n) ★★ /trænˈzækʃ(ə)n/
unattended (adj) /ˌʌnəˈtendɪd/
vending machine (n) /ˈvendɪŋ məˌʃiːn/
whereas (conj) ★★★ /weərˈæz/

Unit 6

Parts of the body

ankle (n) ★★ /ˈæŋk(ə)l/
artery (n) /ˈɑː(r)təri/
bone (n) ★★★ /bəʊn/
brain (n) ★★★ /breɪn/
chest (n) ★★★ /tʃest/
chin (n) ★★ /tʃɪn/
forehead (n) ★★ /ˈfɒrɪd/ , /ˈfɔː(r)ˌhed/
heart (n) ★★★ /hɑː(r)t/
heel (n) ★★ /hiːl/
hip (n) ★★ /hɪp/
kidney (n) ★ /ˈkɪdni/
liver (n) ★★ /ˈlɪvə(r)/
lung (n) ★★ /lʌŋ/
skin (n) ★★★ /skɪn/
thigh (n) ★★ /θaɪ/
throat (n) ★★★ /θrəʊt/
toe (n) ★★ /təʊ/
tongue (n) ★★ /tʌŋ/
vein (n) ★★ /veɪn/
wrist (n) ★★ /rɪst/

Words connected with health

be allergic to (phr) /biː əˈlɜː(r)dʒɪk tuː/
be addicted to (phr) /biː əˈdɪktɪd tuː/
be in danger of (phr) /biː ɪn ˈdeɪndʒə(r) ɒv/
be obese (phr) /biː əʊˈbiːs/
be painful (phr) /biː ˈpeɪnf(ə)l/
become addicted to (phr) /bɪˌkʌm əˈdɪktɪd tuː/
become obese (phr) /bɪˌkʌm əʊˈbiːs/
break (v) ★★★ /breɪk/
catch an infection (phr) /ˌkætʃ ən ɪnˈfekʃ(ə)n/
dislocate (v) /ˈdɪsləkeɪt/
eat fatty food (phr) /ˌiːt ˌfæti ˈfuːd/
eat food high in salt (phr) /ˌiːt fuːd ˌhaɪ ɪn ˈsɔːlt/
feel dizzy (phr) /ˌfiːl ˈdɪzi/
fracture (v) /ˈfræktʃə(r)/
get an infection (phr) /ˌget ən ɪnˈfekʃ(ə)n/
get a prescription (phr) /ˌget ə prɪˈskrɪpʃ(ə)n/
get over an illness (phr) /get ˌəʊvə(r) ən ˈɪlnəs/
give an injection (phr) /ˌɡɪv ən ɪnˈdʒekʃ(ə)n/
give a prescription (phr) /ˌɡɪv ə prɪˈskrɪpʃ(ə)n/
go for a check-up (phr) /ˌɡəʊ fər ə ˈtʃek ʌp/
have a balanced diet (phr) /ˌhæv ə ˌbælənst ˈdaɪət/
have an injection (phr) /ˌhæv ən ɪnˈdʒekʃ(ə)n/
have an operation (phr) /ˌhæv ən ˌɒpəˈreɪʃ(ə)n/
have a temperature (phr) /ˌhæv ə ˈtemprɪtʃə(r)/
increase the risk of (phr) /ɪnˌkriːs ðə ˈrɪsk ɒv/
injure yourself (phr) /ˈɪndʒə(r) jə(r)ˌself/
lose weight (phr) /ˌluːz ˈweɪt/
processed food (n) /ˌprəʊsest ˈfuːd/
put on weight (phr) /ˌpʊt ɒn ˈweɪt/
relieve symptoms (phr) /rɪˌliːv ˈsɪmptəmz/
shiver (v) ★ /ˈʃɪvə(r)/
sprain (v) /spreɪn/
suffer from heart disease (phr) /ˌsʌfə(r) frɒm ˈhɑː(r)t dɪˌziːz/
take your blood pressure (phr) /ˌteɪk jɔː(r) ˈblʌd ˌpreʃə(r)/
treat somebody (for) (phr) /ˈtriːt ˌsʌmbədi/
twist (v) ★★ /twɪst/
work out (phr) /ˌwɜː(r)k ˈaʊt/

Idioms: health and illness

be back on your feet (phr) /biː ˌbæk ɒn jɔː(r) ˈfiːt/
be on top of the world (phr) /biː ɒn ˌtɒp əv ðə ˈwɜː(r)ld/
be under the weather (phr) /biː ˌʌndə(r) ðə ˈweðə(r)/
black out (v phr) /ˌblæk ˈaʊt/
come down with (v phr) /ˌkʌm ˈdaʊn wɪð/
feel on top of the world (phr) /fiːl ɒn ˌtɒp əv ðə ˈwɜː(r)ld/
feel under the weather (phr) /fiːl ˌʌndə(r) ðə ˈweðə(r)/
keep in shape (phr) /ˌkiːp ɪn ˈʃeɪp/
pull through (v phr) /ˌpʊl ˈθruː/

Other words and phrases

as long as (phr) /æz ˈlɒŋ æz/
available (adj) ★★★ /əˈveɪləb(ə)l/
ban (v) ★★ /bæn/
beat (v) ★★★ /biːt/
bend (v) ★★★ /bend/
calcium (n) ★ /ˈkælsiəm/

campaign (n) ★★★ /kæm'peɪn/
chronic (adj) ★ /'krɒnɪk/
computer file (n) /kəm'pjuːtə(r) ˌfaɪl/
despite (prep) ★★★ /dɪ'spaɪt/
dessert (n) ★ /dɪ'zɜː(r)t/
dietary (adj) /'daɪət(ə)ri/
dive (v) ★★ /daɪv/
encourage (v) ★★★ /ɪn'kʌrɪdʒ/
fibre (n) ★★ /'faɪbə(r)/
follow-up (adj) /'fɒləʊ ʌp/
gluten (n) /'gluːt(ə)n/
highlight (v) ★★ /'haɪˌlaɪt/
in case (adv) /ɪn 'keɪs/
in spite of (phr) /ɪn 'spaɪt ɒv/
intake (n) ★ /'ɪnteɪk/
iron (n) ★★ /'aɪə(r)n/
lack (n) ★★★ /læk/
multiply (v) ★ /'mʌltɪplaɪ/
nutrient (n) /'njuːtriənt/
operation (n) ★★★ /ˌɒpə'reɪʃ(ə)n/
option (n) ★★★ /'ɒpʃ(ə)n/
overall (adv) ★★ /ˌəʊvər'ɔːl/
pollen (n) /'pɒlən/
portion (n) ★★ /'pɔː(r)ʃ(ə)n/
prescription (n) ★ /prɪ'skrɪpʃ(ə)n/
provided (conj) ★★★ /prə'vaɪdɪd/
purpose (n) ★★★ /'pɜː(r)pəs/
reduce (v) ★★★ /rɪ'djuːs/
regret (v) ★★ /rɪ'gret/
saturated (adj) /'sætʃəˌreɪtɪd/
semi-skimmed (adj) /ˌsemi 'skɪmd/
sensation (n) ★★ /sen'seɪʃ(ə)n/
standard (n) ★★★ /'stændə(r)d/
strength (n) ★★★ /streŋθ/
therefore (adv) ★★★ /'ðeə(r)fɔː(r)/
unless (conj) ★★★ /ən'les/
varied (adj) ★ /'veərɪd/

Gateway to exams: Units 5–6

amino acid (n) /əˌmiːnəʊ 'æsɪd/
caffeine (n) /'kæfiːn/
energy drink (n) /'enə(r)dʒi ˌdrɪŋk/
teaspoon (n) /'tiːˌspuːn/
use up (v phr) /ˌjuːz 'ʌp/

Unit 7

Music and film

acting (n) ★ /'æktɪŋ/
crowd (n) ★★★ /kraʊd/
gig (n) ★ /gɪg/
lighting (n) ★★ /'laɪtɪŋ/
live (adv) ★ /'laɪv/
lyric (n) /'lɪrɪk/
performance (n) /pə(r)'fɔː(r)məns/
plot (n) ★★ /plɒt/
record (v) ★★★ /rɪ'kɔː(r)d/
role (n) ★★★ /rəʊl/
scene (n) ★★★ /siːn/
soundtrack (n) /'saʊn(d)ˌtræk/
stage (n) ★★★ /steɪdʒ/
star (v) ★★★ /stɑː(r)/
track (n) ★★★ /træk/

Media habits

download films (phr) /daʊnˌləʊd 'fɪlmz/
file-sharing site (n) /'faɪl ʃeə(r)ɪŋ ˌsaɪt/
live stream (n) /'laɪv ˌstriːm/
make purchases on the Net (phr) /meɪk ˌpɜː(r)tʃəsɪz ɒn ðə 'net/
mobile device (n) /'məʊbaɪl dɪˌvaɪs/
peer-to-peer (adj) /ˌpɪə(r) tə 'pɪə(r)/
purchase (v) ★★ /'pɜː(r)tʃəs/
stream (v) ★ /striːm/
transfer music (phr) /ˌtrænsfɜː(r) 'mjuːzɪk/

Compound nouns

blockbuster (n) /'blɒkˌbʌstə(r)/
box office (n) /'bɒks ˌɒfɪs/
download (n) /'daʊnləʊd/
drawback (n) /'drɔːˌbæk/
feedback (n) ★★ /'fiːdbæk/
file-sharing (n) /'faɪl ˌʃeə(r)ɪŋ/
marketplace (n) ★ /'mɑː(r)kɪtˌpleɪs/
outcome (n) ★★★ /'aʊtˌkʌm/
page-turner (n) /'peɪdʒ ˌtɜː(r)nə(r)/
screenplay (n) /'skriːnˌpleɪ/
songwriter (n) /'sɒŋˌraɪtə(r)/
soundtrack (n) /'saʊn(d)ˌtræk/
turnout (n) /'tɜː(r)naʊt/

Compound adjectives

brand new (adj) ★ /ˌbrænd 'njuː/
fast-moving (adj) /ˌfɑːst 'muːvɪŋ/
thought-provoking (adj) /'θɔːt prəˌvəʊkɪŋ/

Other words and phrases

accuse (v) ★★★ /ə'kjuːz/
admit (v) ★★★ /əd'mɪt/
advise (v) ★★★ /əd'vaɪz/
agree (v) ★★★ /ə'griː/
amazing (adj) ★★ /ə'meɪzɪŋ/
amusing (adj) ★ /ə'mjuːzɪŋ/
announce (v) ★★★ /ə'naʊns/
apologise for (v) /ə'pɒlədʒaɪz fɔː(r)/
appealing (adj) ★ /ə'piːlɪŋ/
awful (adj) ★★ /'ɔːf(ə)l/
brilliant (adj) ★★★ /'brɪljənt/
channel (n) ★★★ /'tʃæn(ə)l/
character (n) ★★★ /'kærɪktə(r)/
claim (v) ★★★ /kleɪm/
clever (adj) ★★ /'klevə(r)/
clichéd (adj) /'kliːʃeɪd/
congratulate (v) ★ /kən'grætʃʊleɪt/
convincing (adj) ★★ /kən'vɪnsɪŋ/
core (n) ★★ /kɔː(r)/
credible (adj) ★ /'kredəb(ə)l/
critic (n) ★★★ /'krɪtɪk/
criticise (v) ★★ /'krɪtɪsaɪz/
criticism (n) ★★★ /'krɪtɪˌsɪz(ə)m/
deep (adj) ★★★ /diːp/
deny (v) ★★★ /dɪ'naɪ/
disturb (v) ★★ /dɪ'stɜː(r)b/
emotional (adj) ★★★ /ɪ'məʊʃ(ə)nəl/
fascinating (adj) ★★ /'fæsɪneɪtɪŋ/
gripping (adj) /'grɪpɪŋ/
hilarious (adj) /hɪ'leəriəs/
incredible (adj) ★ /ɪn'kredəb(ə)l/
indie (adj) /'ɪndi/
inspiring (adj) /ɪn'spaɪərɪŋ/
instruct (v) ★★ /ɪn'strʌkt/
intricate (adj) /'ɪntrɪkət/
intriguing (adj) /ɪn'triːgɪŋ/
invest (v) ★★★ /ɪn'vest/
lively (adj) ★★ /'laɪvli/
loyalty (n) ★★ /'lɔɪəlti/
moving (adj) ★★ /'muːvɪŋ/
mysterious (adj) ★★ /mɪ'stɪəriəs/
object to (v phr) /əb'dʒekt tuː/
order (v) ★★★ /'ɔː(r)də(r)/
perceptive (adj) /pə(r)'septɪv/
perform (v) ★★★ /pə(r)'fɔː(r)m/
plot (n) ★★ /plɒt/
predictable (adj) ★ /prɪ'dɪktəb(ə)l/
principle (n) ★★★ /'prɪnsəp(ə)l/
profit (n) ★★★ /'prɒfɪt/
promise (v) ★★★ /'prɒmɪs/
raise (v) ★★★ /reɪz/
realistic (adj) ★★ /ˌrɪə'lɪstɪk/
regret (v) ★★ /rɪ'gret/
relationship (n) ★★★ /rɪ'leɪʃ(ə)nʃɪp/
relaxing (adj) /rɪ'læksɪŋ/
release (n) ★★★ /rɪ'liːs/
remind (v) ★★★ /rɪ'maɪnd/
scary (adj) ★ /'skeəri/
screen (n) ★★★ /skriːn/
spectacular (adj) ★★ /spek'tækjʊlə(r)/
store (v) ★★ /stɔː(r)/
stunning (adj) ★ /'stʌnɪŋ/
stupid (adj) ★★ /'stjuːpɪd/
terrible (adj) ★★★ /'terəb(ə)l/
thrilling (adj) /'θrɪlɪŋ/
unconvincing (adj) /ˌʌnkən'vɪnsɪŋ/
uninspiring (adj) /ˌʌnɪn'spaɪərɪŋ/
vivid (adj) ★ /'vɪvɪd/
warn (v) ★★★ /wɔː(r)n/
well-produced (adj) /ˌwel prə'djuːst/
wild (adj) ★★★ /waɪld/

Unit 8

Natural disasters

avalanche (n) /'ævəˌlɑːntʃ/
drought (n) /draʊt/
earthquake (n) ★ /'ɜː(r)θˌkweɪk/
epidemic (n) /ˌepɪ'demɪk/
flood (n) ★★ /flʌd/
forest fire (n) /ˌfɒrɪst 'faɪə(r)/
hurricane (n) /'hʌrɪkən/
landslide (n) /'læn(d)ˌslaɪd/
tsunami (n) /tsuː'nɑːmi/
volcanic eruption (n) /vɒlˌkænɪk ɪ'rʌpʃ(ə)n/

Words connected with natural disasters

Nouns

aftershock (n) /'ɑːftə(r)ˌʃɒk/
ash (n) ★★ /æʃ/
bank (of a river) (n) ★★★ /bæŋk/
casualty (n) /'kæʒuəlti/
damage (n) ★★★ /'dæmɪdʒ/
destruction (n) ★★ /dɪ'strʌkʃ(ə)n/
injury (n) ★★★ /'ɪndʒəri/
molten lava (phr) /ˌməʊltən 'lɑːvə/
mud (n) ★★ /mʌd/
panic (n) ★★ /'pænɪk/
refugee (n) ★★ /ˌrefjʊ'dʒiː/
survivor (n) ★ /sə(r)'vaɪvə(r)/
torrential rain (phr) /təˌrenʃ(ə)l 'reɪn/
tremor (n) /'tremə(r)/
victim (n) ★★★ /'vɪktɪm/

Verbs

burst (v) ★★ /bɜː(r)st/
collapse (v) ★★ /kə'læps/
damage (v) ★★★ /'dæmɪdʒ/
evacuate (v) ★ /ɪ'vækjueɪt/
head towards (v phr) /'hed təˌwɔː(r)dz/
panic (v) ★ /'pænɪk/
put out (v phr) /ˌpʊt 'aʊt/
spread (v) ★★★ /spred/
sweep across (v phr) /'swiːp əˌkrɒs/

Prepositional phrases with verbs

agree with (v phr) /ə'griː wɪð/
apologise for (v phr) /ə'pɒlədʒaɪz fɔː(r)/
believe in (v phr) /bɪ'liːv ɪn/
belong to (v phr) /bɪ'lɒŋ tuː/
complain about (v phr) /kəm'pleɪn əˌbaʊt/
depend on (v phr) /dɪ'pend ɒn/
dream of (v phr) /'driːm ɒv/
listen to (v phr) /'lɪs(ə)n tuː/
protect (somebody) from (v) /prə'tekt (ˌsʌmbədi) frɒm/
rely on (v phr) /rɪ'laɪ ɒn/
spend on (v phr) /'spend ɒn/
wait for (v phr) /'weɪt fɔː(r)/

Other words and phrases

a sixth (n) /ə 'sɪksθ/
asteroid (n) /'æstəˌrɔɪd/
bee (n) ★★ /biː/
border (n) ★★★ /'bɔː(r)də(r)/
burn (v) ★★★ /bɜː(r)n/
burst (n) /bɜː(r)st/
catastrophic (adj) /ˌkætə'strɒfɪk/
collapsed (adj) /kə'læpst/
debris (n) /'debriː/
decrease (n) ★ /'diːkriːs/
decrease (v) ★ /diː'kriːs/
destruction (n) /dɪ'strʌkʃ(ə)n/
double (n & v) ★ /'dʌb(ə)l/
dramatic (adj) ★★★ /drə'mætɪk/
elderly (adj) ★★★ /'eldə(r)li/
equipment (n) ★★★ /ɪ'kwɪpmənt/
fall (n & v) ★★★ /fɔːl/
first aid (n) /ˌfɜː(r)st 'eɪd/
fumes (n pl) ★ /fjuːmz/
go missing (phr) /ˌgəʊ 'mɪsɪŋ/
gradual (adj) ★ /'grædʒuəl/
grateful (adj) ★★ /'greɪtf(ə)l/
headquarters (n pl) ★★ /hed'kwɔː(r)tə(r)z/
humanitarian (adj) /hjuːˌmænɪ'teəriən/
impact (n) ★★★ /'ɪmpækt/
increase (n) ★★★ /'ɪŋkriːs/
increase (v) ★★★ /ɪn'kriːs/
low (adj) ★★★ /ləʊ/
meteorite (n) /'miːtiəraɪt/
oxygen (n) ★★ /'ɒksɪdʒ(ə)n/
pie chart (n) /'paɪ ˌtʃɑː(r)t/
powder (n) ★★ /'paʊdə(r)/
proportion (n) ★★★ /prə'pɔː(r)ʃ(ə)n/
rise (n & v) ★★★ /raɪz/
route (n) ★★★ /ruːt/
sharp (adj) ★★★ /ʃɑː(r)p/
significant (adj) ★★★ /sɪg'nɪfɪkənt/
slight (adj) ★★★ /slaɪt/
slightly (adv) ★★★ /'slaɪtli/
spot (v) ★★ /spɒt/
steadily (adv) /'stedili/
steady (adj) ★★ /'stedi/
storm (n) ★★ /stɔː(r)m/
triple (n & v) /'trɪp(ə)l/
unsinkable (adj) /ʌn'sɪŋkəb(ə)l/
vibration (n) ★ /vaɪ'breɪʃ(ə)n/
wave (n) ★★★ /weɪv/

Gateway to exams: Units 7–8

base (n) ★★★ /beɪs/
be in awe of (phr) /biː ɪn 'ɔː ɒv/
belch out (v phr) /ˌbeltʃ 'aʊt/
bite (v) ★★ /baɪt/
bitten by the bug (phr) /ˌbɪt(ə)n baɪ ðə 'bʌg/
brief (v) ★ /briːf/
chilly (adj) /'tʃɪli/
civilisation (n) ★ /ˌsɪvəlaɪ'zeɪʃ(ə)n/
compass (n) ★ /'kʌmpəs/
cope with (v phr) /'kəʊp wɪð/
curiosity (n) ★ /ˌkjʊəri'ɒsəti/
disrupt (v) ★ /dɪs'rʌpt/
establish (v) ★★★ /ɪ'stæblɪʃ/
evacuation (n) /ɪˌvækju'eɪʃ(ə)n/
extent (n) ★★★ /ɪk'stent/
fair share of (phr) /ˌfeə(r) 'ʃeər ɒv/
fissure (n) /'fɪʃə(r)/
glacier (n) /'glæsiə(r)/
hire (v) ★★ /'haɪə(r)/
impressive (adj) ★★ /ɪm'presɪv/
occur (v) ★★★ /ə'kɜː(r)/
pass (n) ★★ /pɑːs/
privilege (n) ★★ /'prɪvəlɪdʒ/
ranch style (adj) /'rɑːntʃ ˌstaɪl/
seldom (adv) ★★ /'seldəm/
site (n) ★★ /saɪt/
skilled (adj) ★★ /skɪld/
vent (n) /vent/

Unit 9

Everyday technology

broadband (n) /'brɔːdˌbænd/
charger (n) /'tʃɑː(r)dʒə(r)/
coverage (n) ★★ /'kʌv(ə)rɪdʒ/
device (n) ★★★ /dɪ'vaɪs/
digital camera (n) /ˌdɪdʒɪt(ə)l 'kæm(ə)rə/
dishwasher (n) /'dɪʃˌwɒʃə(r)/
drop-down menu (n) /ˌdrɒp daʊn 'menjuː/
flash drive (n) /'flæʃ ˌdraɪv/
food processor (n) /'fuːd ˌprəʊsesə(r)/
glitch (n) /glɪtʃ/
headphones (n pl) /'hedˌfəʊnz/
keyboard (n) ★ /'kiːˌbɔː(r)d/
microwave (n) ★ /'maɪkrəˌweɪv/
network (n) ★★★ /'netˌwɜː(r)k/
plug (n) ★ /plʌg/
remote control (n) ★ /rɪˌməʊt kən'trəʊl/
satnav (n) /'sætˌnæv/
touch screen (n) /'tʌtʃ ˌskriːn/
vacuum cleaner (n) /'vækjʊəm ˌkliːnə(r)/
washing machine (n) ★ /'wɒʃɪŋ məˌʃiːn/
webcam (n) /'webˌkæm/
wireless (adj) ★ /'waɪə(r)ləs/

Verbs connected with technology

adjust (v) ★★ /ə'dʒʌst/
connect (v) ★★★ /kə'nekt/
crash (v) ★★ /kræʃ/
delete (v) ★★ /dɪ'liːt/
disconnect (v) /ˌdɪskə'nekt/
freeze (v) ★★ /friːz/
go dead (phr) /ˌɡəʊ 'ded/
hold (v) ★★★ /həʊld/
insert (v) ★★★ /ɪn'sɜː(r)t/
install (v) ★★ /ɪn'stɔːl/
pinch (v) /pɪntʃ/
plug in (v phr) /ˌplʌɡ 'ɪn/
press (v) ★★★ /pres/
push (v) ★★★ /pʊʃ/
recharge (v) /riː'tʃɑː(r)dʒ/
select (v) ★★★ /sɪ'lekt/
set (v) ★★★ /set/
swipe (v) /swaɪp/
tap (v) ★★ /tæp/
upgrade (v) ★ /ʌp'ɡreɪd/

Phrasal verbs: technology and computers

back up (v phr) /ˌbæk 'ʌp/
go off (v phr) /ˌɡəʊ 'ɒf/
pick up a signal (phr) /ˌpɪk ʌp ə 'sɪɡn(ə)l/
pop up (v phr) /ˌpɒp 'ʌp/
print out (v phr) /ˌprɪnt 'aʊt/
run out (v phr) /ˌrʌn 'aʊt/
scroll across (v phr) /'skrəʊl əˌkrɒs/
scroll down (v phr) /ˌskrəʊl 'daʊn/
scroll up (v phr) /ˌskrəʊl 'ʌp/
set up (v phr) /ˌset 'ʌp/
zoom in (v phr) /ˌzuːm 'ɪn/

Other words and phrases

access (v) /'ækses/
acquire (v) ★★ /ə'kwaɪə(r)/
backpack (n) /'bækˌpæk/
battery (n) ★★ /'bæt(ə)ri/
bury (v) ★★ /'beri/
cable (n) ★★ /'keɪb(ə)l/
concentration (n) ★★★ /ˌkɒns(ə)n'treɪʃ(ə)n/
conduct (v) ★★★ /kən'dʌkt/
controversial (adj) ★★ /ˌkɒntrə'vɜː(r)ʃ(ə)l/
experiment (n) ★★★ /ɪk'sperɪmənt/
foil (n) /fɔɪl/
freeze (v) ★★ /friːz/
key (n) ★★★ /kiː/
old-fashioned (adj) ★★ /ˌəʊld 'fæʃ(ə)nd/
outline (v) ★★ /'aʊtlaɪn/
overall (adj) ★★★ /ˌəʊvər'ɔːl/
physicist (n) /'fɪzɪsɪst/
proud (adj) ★★ /praʊd/
replace (v) ★★★ /rɪ'pleɪs/
router (n) /'ruːtə(r)/
short circuit (n) /ˌʃɔː(r)t 'sɜː(r)kɪt/
source (n) ★★★ /sɔː(r)s/
spare (adj) ★★ /speə(r)/
striker (n) ★ /'straɪkə(r)/
supply (n) ★★★ /sə'plaɪ/
tie (n) ★★ /taɪ/
upside down (adv) ★ /ˌʌpsaɪd 'daʊn/
wire (n) ★★ /'waɪə(r)/
youngster (n) ★★ /'jʌŋstə(r)/

Unit 10

News sections

arts (n pl) /ɑː(r)ts/
business (n) ★★★ /'bɪznəs/
comment (n & v) ★★★ /'kɒment/
editor's blog (n) /ˌedɪtə(r)z 'blɒɡ/
entertainment (n) ★★ /ˌentə(r)'teɪnmənt/
features (n pl) /'fiːtʃə(r)z/
finance (n) ★★★ /'faɪnæns/
gossip (n) /'ɡɒsɪp/
have your say (phr) /ˌhæv jɔː(r) 'seɪ/
health (n) ★★★ /helθ/
life and style (n) /ˌlaɪf ən(d) 'staɪl/
obituaries (n pl) /ə'bɪtʃuəriz/
opinion (n) ★★★ /ə'pɪnjən/
showbiz (n) /'ʃəʊbɪz/
sport (n) ★★★ /spɔː(r)t/
weather forecast (n) ★ /'weðə(r) ˌfɔː(r)kɑːst/
world news (n) /ˌwɜː(r)ld 'njuːz/

News headlines

aid (v) ★★ /eɪd/
axe (v) /æks/
back (v) ★★★ /bæk/
ban (v) ★★ /bæn/
blast (v) ★ /blɑːst/
blaze (n) ★ /bleɪz/
boost (v) ★★ /buːst/
boss (n) ★★★ /bɒs/
clash (v) ★ /klæʃ/
cut (v) ★★★ /kʌt/
drama (n) ★★★ /'drɑːmə/
head (n) ★★★ /hed/
hit (v) ★★★ /hɪt/
key (adj) ★★★ /kiː/
link (n) ★★★ /lɪŋk/
move (v) ★★★ /muːv/
plea (n) ★★ /pliː/
pledge (n) /pledʒ/
PM (n) /ˌpiː 'em/
probe (v) /prəʊb/
quit (v) ★ /kwɪt/
riddle (n) /'rɪd(ə)l/
spark (v) ★ /spɑː(r)k/
wed (v) /wed/

Collocations: the news

breaking news (phr) /ˌbreɪkɪŋ 'njuːz/
front page news (phr) /ˌfrʌnt peɪdʒ 'njuːz/
hold a press conference (phr) /ˌhəʊld ə 'pres ˌkɒnf(ə)rəns/
keep somebody informed (phr) /ˌkiːp sʌmbədi ɪn'fɔː(r)md/
make the headlines (phr) /ˌmeɪk ðə 'hedlaɪnz/
newsflash (n) /'njuːzˌflæʃ/
news item (n) /'njuːz ˌaɪtəm/
news updates (n pl) /'njuːz ˌʌpdeɪts/
turn of events (phr) /ˌtɜː(r)n əv ɪ'vents/

Other words and phrases

alter (v) ★★ /'ɔːltə(r)/
argue (v) ★★★ /'ɑː(r)ɡju/
as (conj) ★★★ /æz/
blast (n) ★ /blɑːst/
broadcast (n) ★ /'brɔːdˌkɑːst/
empty-handed (adj) /ˌempti 'hændɪd /
headline (n) ★★ /'hedˌlaɪn/
moreover (adv) ★★★ /mɔːr'əʊvə(r)/
nevertheless (adv) ★★★ /ˌnevə(r)ðə'les/
paparazzi (n) /ˌpæpə'rætsi/
privacy (n) ★ /'prɪvəsi/
publish (v) ★★★ /'pʌblɪʃ/
quotation (n) ★ /kwəʊ'teɪʃ(ə)n/
season (n) ★★★ /'siːz(ə)n/
since (conj) ★★★ /sɪns/
spokesperson (n) /'spəʊksˌpɜː(r)s(ə)n/

Gateway to exams: Units 9–10

branch (n) ★★★ /brɑːntʃ/
claim (v) ★★★ /kleɪm/
clip (n) ★ /klɪp/
costume (n) ★ /'kɒstjuːm/
deaf (adj) ★★ /def/
donation (n) ★★ /dəʊ'neɪʃ(ə)n/
fancy dress (n) /ˌfænsi 'dres/
feature (n) ★★★ /'fiːtʃə(r)/
hysterical (adj) ★ /hɪ'sterɪk(ə)l/
integrity (n) ★★ /ɪn'teɡrəti/
ironic (adj) /aɪ'rɒnɪk/
policy (n) ★★★ /'pɒləsi/
prove (v) ★★★ /pruːv/
publicity stunt (n) /pʌb'lɪsəti ˌstʌnt/
resigned (adj) /rɪ'zaɪnd/
settle (v) ★★★ /'set(ə)l/
settle in (v phr) /ˌset(ə)l 'ɪn/
shoplifter (n) /'ʃɒpˌlɪftə(r)/
smartphone (n) /'smɑː(r)tˌfəʊn/
suspicious (adj) ★★ /sə'spɪʃəs/
track (v) ★ /træk/
unpleasant (adj) ★★ /ʌn'plez(ə)nt/
villain (n) ★ /'vɪlən/

Irregular verbs

Infinitive	Past simple	Past participle
be	was/were	been
beat	beat	beaten
become	became	become
begin	began	begun
break	broke	broken
bring	brought	brought
build	built	built
burn	burnt	burnt
buy	bought	bought
catch	caught	caught
choose	chose	chosen
come	came	come
cost	cost	cost
cut	cut	cut
do	did	done
draw	drew	drawn
drink	drank	drunk
drive	drove	driven
eat	ate	eaten
fall	fell	fallen
feel	felt	felt
find	found	found
fly	flew	flown
forget	forgot	forgotten
forgive	forgave	forgiven
get	got	got
give	gave	given
go	went	gone
grow	grew	grown
hang out	hung out	hung out
have	had	had
hear	heard	heard
hide	hid	hidden
hit	hit	hit
hurt	hurt	hurt
keep	kept	kept
know	knew	known
lay	laid	laid
leave	left	left
learn	learned/learnt	learned/learnt

Infinitive	Past simple	Past participle
let	let	let
lie	lay	lain
lose	lost	lost
make	made	made
mean	meant	meant
meet	met	met
pay	paid	paid
put	put	put
read	read	read
ride	rode	ridden
ring	rang	rung
run	ran	run
say	said	said
see	saw	seen
sell	sold	sold
send	sent	sent
set up	set up	set up
shine	shone	shone
shoot	shot	shot
show	showed	shown
sing	sang	sung
sit	sat	sat
sleep	slept	slept
speak	spoke	spoken
speed	sped	sped
spell	spelt	spelt
spend	spent	spent
split up	split up	split up
stand up	stood up	stood up
steal	stole	stolen
swim	swam	swum
take	took	taken
teach	taught	taught
tell	told	told
think	thought	thought
understand	understood	understood
wake up	woke up	woken up
wear	wore	worn
win	won	won
write	wrote	written

Unit 1

READING: MATCHING ACTIVITIES

In this type of activity, you have to say which text or part of a text contains a piece of information or answers a question.

Step 1: Read all the texts or parts of the text quickly to get a general understanding.

Step 2: Read the piece(s) of information that you need to find. Look for any special words that help you to find the text or part of the text which contains the information. Remember that in the text the same information will probably be expressed in different words.

Step 3: Read that specific text or part of the text again in more detail.

Step 4: If you are not sure that you have found the correct answer, read other sections again in more detail.

Step 5: When you finish, check that you have an answer for each question. Never leave answers blank in an exam.

WRITING: TRANSACTIONAL TASKS

- Transactional writing tasks are ones where the instructions tell you who you are writing to and what information to include.
- When a question asks you to put specific information in your text, you lose marks if you do not include the information.
- Sometimes the information you need to include is indicated in the form of notes written on the letter or email. In this case, remember to expand the notes and give extra information. For example, if the note is 'Say when you can come', do not just say 'I can come in the summer.' Explain why the summer is the best/only option. You can ask questions too in your reply.
- When you write letters, invitations, messages and notes it is essential to write in the correct style. When you write to a friend, use contractions and informal expressions. When you write a formal or semi-formal letter, invitation, message or note, do not use contractions or informal language. If your letter is grammatically correct but not in the correct style, you will lose marks.

Unit 2

LISTENING: MATCHING PEOPLE AND STATEMENTS

In this type of activity you match different speakers with the ideas that they express.

Before you listen:

- Think about the topic of what you are going to listen to. Think of words that could appear in the listening text.
- Read the questions and underline important information. This can help you to know what the people may say and helps you to concentrate more while you listen.

While you listen:

- The speakers may say the same things as in the questions, but using different words; other speakers may use the actual words that come in the questions, but there is only one correct answer for each speaker.
- Don't worry if you don't understand everything the first time you listen. Usually you listen twice. Use the second listening to find the answers you didn't hear the first time and to check the answers you already have.

After you listen:

- Check that you have an answer for each question. Never leave answers blank in an exam.

SPEAKING: NEGOTIATING AND COLLABORATING

In negotiating activities, you usually work with another person. The examiner explains a situation where you and the other speaker need to come to a decision.

- In this type of activity, remember that there isn't usually a right or wrong answer. However, you should make sure that you come to some type of conclusion or decision by the end of the activity. A useful strategy is to agree with your partner, but then suggest alternative ideas. It is better not to agree completely straight away because the conversation will end too quickly. Disagreeing completely could seem aggressive. Just remember that, above all, the examiner wants to hear you speaking English.
- It is important that neither of you dominates the conversation or is silent. The examiner will usually help you to do this. But remember to take turns and help your partner to speak if you think you are speaking too much or if your partner is not speaking enough.
- If you can't think of something to say, ask your partner a question like 'What do you think?' This gives you time to think of what you can say next. You can also use fillers like 'Well', 'Hmm' or 'Let me think'.
- Don't be afraid to say something that you think is obvious.
- Give full explanations for your opinions and ideas.
- Listen to what your partner or the examiner is saying. In a conversation we speak *and* listen.
- If you don't understand what the examiner or your partner is saying, ask them in English to repeat or to speak more slowly. Use expressions like: 'Sorry, can you say that again?' or 'Sorry, could you speak more slowly?'

Unit 3

READING: MISSING SENTENCES ACTIVITIES

In this type of activity, you have to fill gaps in a text with sentences taken out of the text. There are usually more sentences than spaces.

Step 1: Read the text to get a general idea of the overall meaning.

Step 2: Read the missing sentences and identify the key information. What is the sentence about? Do you remember anything connected with this topic when you read the text for the first time? Look again at this part of the text in more detail.

Step 3: Look for words and phrases in the sentence which connect with the information that comes in the text just before or after each gap.

Step 4: Try out each sentence in the most probable space and continue reading. Is the meaning logical? Do pronouns like *this* or *it* make sense, or linking words like *and, but* or *although*?

Step 5: If there are gaps which you cannot complete, continue with other, easier gaps first and then go back later to the difficult ones.

Step 6: When you finish, read the completed text again to check that it makes sense. Check also that you have an answer for each question. Never leave answers blank in an exam.

Unit 3 (continued)

WRITING: STORIES

- Before you write a story, make a plan. Make sure that you have a beginning, a middle and an end. Sometimes you can change the order of these three sections in a story, but always make sure the sequence of events and the chronology are clear. We can use linkers of time and sequence to do this.
- Make the main events of the story clear. What happened? Why? What happened later? How did the story end? We usually use the past simple for this.
- Give background information so that we know about the characters and the situation. We usually use the past perfect simple and continuous for this.
- Make the story interesting by describing scenes in detail. We often use the past continuous for this.
- For more information on writing stories, see page 152 of the Writing bank.

Unit 4

USE OF ENGLISH: WORD FORMATION CLOZE ACTIVITIES

In this type of activity you must use the word given to form a word that fits in the gap. The words can be any type – noun, adjective, adverb or verb.

Step 1: Read the text once quickly to know the general meaning.

Step 2: Look at the words just before and after the gap. They can help you to decide what type of word you need. Usually to change the type of word you will need a suffix (e.g. *-ion* to make a noun, *-ly* to make an adverb).

Step 3: Make sure you understand the whole sentence. This will help you to decide if you need to change the meaning of the word, e.g. making it negative. Usually to change the meaning of the word you will need a prefix (e.g. *im-, re-*).

Step 4: Remember that you may need to change the spelling of the word they give you. For example, from the word *strong* you may need to make the noun, *strength*. Also, look carefully to decide if your word needs to be in the plural form.

Step 5: Read the completed sentence and check your answer. Check that you have an answer for each question. Never leave answers blank in an exam.

SPEAKING: GIVING PRESENTATIONS

In this type of activity, you have to talk about a topic. This could be in the form of a question, title, text or photo. You usually have a fixed amount of time to prepare the presentation and give it.

- Make notes with the information you want to give in your presentation and use them when you are giving it. However, don't just read your notes aloud.
- Look at your audience. See if they understand you and are interested.
- Don't speak too fast. If you speak too quickly, people will not be able to follow you.
- Try to speak for exactly the right amount of time. The more you practise, the easier it will become.
- Use intonation to show that you are interested and to make others interested.
- Don't worry excessively about vocabulary. When you don't know a word, explain it or use a simpler word.
- Don't let mistakes stop you from speaking. Correct your own mistakes if possible, or start the sentence again, but don't stop completely.

Unit 5

LISTENING: COMPLETING NOTES

In this type of activity, you have incomplete notes. You listen to a text and complete the notes with the correct information.

- Always read the incomplete notes *before* you listen. This helps you to know what to listen for. Look carefully at the words that come just before or after each gap and think about what *type* of word is missing (noun, verb, adjective, adverb, etc.). But be careful. If you know that you need a number, for example, do not simply write the first number that you hear.
- It is not usually necessary to understand every word that you hear. Listen out for the sections which correspond to the information in the notes. Pay special attention to these sections. Remember that you may not hear the exact words that appear in the incomplete notes.
- You usually need to write between one and three words in each gap. Write the words you actually hear. Be careful with spelling and your handwriting.
- Don't worry if you don't understand everything the first time you listen. Usually you listen twice. Use the second listening to find the answers you didn't hear the first time and to check the answers you already have.

SPEAKING: TALKING ABOUT PHOTOS

In this type of activity, you have one or two photos to discuss and answer a question or questions about.

- Listen very carefully to the examiner's instructions. Your marks will depend on completing the whole task, so if you only complete one part, you will lose marks. If you aren't sure that you have understood what the examiner says, ask them to repeat.
- If you have two photos, it is not usually a good idea to describe each photo in great detail. The important thing is to compare and contrast the two photos.
- Try to speak for exactly the right amount of time. The more you practise the easier it will become.
- Give your own opinion if the examiner asks for it and give reasons to justify your opinions. There is not usually a right or wrong answer. The examiner wants to hear you speak English.
- Do not worry too much about vocabulary for things that appear in the photos. When you don't know a word, explain it or use a simpler word. You can also use language of speculation when you are not sure what you can see (e.g. *It might/may be …, It must be …, I think it's probably …*).
- Speak loudly and clearly so that the examiner can hear you.
- Don't let mistakes stop you from speaking. Correct your own mistakes if possible, or start the sentence again, but don't stop completely.
- Use *Well, Hmm* or *Let me think* to give you time to think of what you want to say next.

Unit 6

USE OF ENGLISH: SENTENCE TRANSFORMATION ACTIVITIES

In this type of activity you have a sentence and you must complete a second sentence so that it means the same as the original sentence. Usually you must use a word that they give. In this case, you cannot change the form of this word. Generally, you can only use between two and five words, including the word they give you.

Step 1: Read the original sentence carefully. Think about the meaning of the sentence, the type of structure(s) used, the tense(s) used, etc.

Step 2: If they give you a word, think about its meaning. Think also about the grammatical function of the word. Does it always or usually go with another word or tense?

Step 3: Write your sentence.

Step 4: When you finish, check that you have:

- not changed the meaning from the original sentence.
- not changed the form of the word they gave you.
- not written more than the maximum number of words permitted. Contractions count as two words, apart from *can't* which is written as one word. (*cannot*).

WRITING: FOR-AND-AGAINST AND OPINION ESSAYS

- In for-and-against essays you must present both sides of the argument. In opinion essays you can just give your own side of the argument.
- In for-and-against essays and opinion essays, you should have a number of relevant points to make. Think about how to organise these points in a logical way.
- The style in for-and-against and opinion essays should be formal.
- Remember that there are no right or wrong answers. The examiner wants to see that you can write and express yourself clearly and effectively.
- For more information on writing for-and-against essays and opinion essays, see pages 151 and 155 of the Writing bank.

Unit 7

SPEAKING: DISCUSSIONS

In speaking exams, you sometimes have to talk to one or more students about a topic. You must be ready to express and justify your opinions, especially if somebody disagrees with you.

- Make sure you understand the topic that you are to discuss. If you aren't sure, ask for clarification before you begin.
- Make sure you listen carefully to what other people say. In a discussion we speak, but we also listen and react to what others say. You can agree, disagree, make suggestions or ask questions.
- If you are working with other students, be sensitive. Don't talk for too long without giving others a chance to speak.
- In some discussions, you must come to an agreement, but in others it is not necessary. Make sure you know before you begin.
- Remember that there are not usually any right or wrong answers. The important thing is to have an opinion, to explain it clearly, to justify it and to give examples to support it.

WRITING: REVIEWS

- The important thing in a review is to give a detailed picture of the thing that you are reviewing (e.g. book, film, TV programme), and to make your own opinion clear. To do this, use a wide variety of adjectives and adverbs and use expressions of opinion.
- The style in a review should not be particularly formal or informal.
- For more information on writing reviews, see page 156 of the Writing bank.

Unit 8

READING: MULTIPLE-CHOICE ACTIVITIES

In this type of activity, you read a text and answer questions about it by choosing the best answer from three or four different options.

Step 1: Read the text quickly to get a general understanding.

Step 2: Read all the answers carefully. Sometimes the difference between two options is just one word.

Step 3: Find the section of the text where you think each answer comes from and read it again slowly, in more detail. You may find the same words in the text and in one of the options, but this does not mean it is the correct answer. The correct option will probably express the information in the text using different words. The answers usually come in order in the text.

Step 4: If you aren't 100% sure which answer is best, take away any answers which you know are not correct.

Step 5: When you finish, check that you have an answer for each question. Never leave answers blank in an exam.

LISTENING: TRUE/FALSE ACTIVITIES

In this type of activity, you have to listen and decide if answers are true or false. In some True/False activities there are three possibilities: *True/False/Not Mentioned*. Choose *Not Mentioned* if you cannot hear the information when you listen to the recording.

Step 1: Read the questions *before* you listen. They can give you ideas about the topic of the text and the vocabulary you are going to hear.

Step 2: You can usually hear the recording twice. Do not panic if you do not understand information the first time. If you don't hear the answer to one question, start listening immediately for the answer to the next question. The questions are usually in the order that you hear them in the recording.

Step 3: Use the second listening to find the answers you didn't hear the first time and to check the answers you already have.

Step 4: When you finish, check that you have an answer for each question. Never leave answers blank in an exam.

Unit 9

USE OF ENGLISH: CLOZE ACTIVITIES

In cloze activities, you have a text with gaps. Sometimes there are different options and you must choose the best one for each space (multiple-choice cloze activities). Sometimes there are no options (open cloze activities). You must fill in each gap by thinking of a word which is grammatically correct and is logical.

Multiple-choice cloze activities

Step 1: Read the text or sentence to get a general idea of the overall meaning. Do not worry about the gaps at first. This is to get a general understanding.

Step 2: Read more carefully and try to predict which word comes in each gap. Look especially at the words which come just before and after the gap. Do those words need a special preposition? Is an article or auxiliary verb missing? Think about the type of word you need (noun, verb, pronoun, article, etc.) and the general meaning.

Step 3: Look at the alternatives. Is one of them the same as the word you thought of in Step 2? Be careful because often the meaning of the different options can be very similar, but the difference may be that each word goes with a different preposition, for example.

Step 4: If you aren't sure which answer is correct, think about why other answers are definitely wrong and eliminate them.

Step 5: When you finish, check that you have an answer for each question. Never leave answers blank in an exam.

Open cloze activities

Step 1: Read the complete text or sentences without thinking about the gaps.

Step 2: Look again at the gaps and especially the words which come just before and after the gap. Do those words need a special preposition? Is an article or auxiliary verb missing? Think about the type of word you need (noun, verb, pronoun, article, etc.) and the general meaning. The spaces in cloze activities will often be for prepositions, articles, pronouns, auxiliary verbs, modal verbs and conjunctions (*and*, *but*, *although*, etc.).

Step 3: Fill in the gap with the word that you think is best. Read again with your answer in the gap. Sometimes there is more than one possible answer, but you only need to put one.

Step 4: When you finish, check that you have one answer for each question. Never leave answers blank in an exam.

WRITING: REPORTS

- Reports should have a title.
- Separate reports into sections and give each one a suitable heading.
- In reports you should be ready to make recommendations or suggestions if they ask you to.
- Make sure you include all the information that they ask for.
- The style in a report should usually be formal since you usually write a report for an organisation or people that you do not know personally.
- For more information on writing reports, see page 157 of the Writing bank.

Unit 10

READING: TRUE/FALSE ACTIVITIES

In this type of activity, you decide if statements are True or False depending on the information in the text. In some True/False activities there are three possibilities: *True/False/ Not Mentioned*. Choose *Not Mentioned* if you can't find any information in the text to prove or disprove the statements.

Step 1: Read the text quickly to get a general understanding.

Step 2: Read the sentences that you need to prove true or false.

Step 3: Find the parts of the text where you think the information comes. Read them again in more detail.

Step 4: When you finish, check that you have an answer for each question. Never leave answers blank in an exam.

LISTENING: MULTIPLE-CHOICE ACTIVITIES

In this type of activity, you choose the best answer from three or four different answers.

You usually hear the text twice. The questions are usually in the order that you hear them in the recording.

Step 1: Read the different answers before you listen. They can give you ideas about the topic of the text and the vocabulary you are going to hear in it. Remember that sometimes the difference between two answers is just one word.

Step 2: When you listen, remember that you may hear the correct answer but expressed in different words. You may also hear a word or words that come in one of the possible answers, but this does not mean it is the answer. The word(s) may be there just to distract you.

Step 3: You usually hear the recording twice. Do not panic if you do not understand information the first time. If you don't hear the answer to one question, start listening immediately for the answer to the next question.

Step 4: Use the second listening to find the answers you didn't hear the first time and to check the answers you already have.

Step 5: When you finish, check that you have an answer for each question. Never leave answers blank in an exam.

Units 1–2

1 How well can you do these things in English now? Give yourself a mark from 1 to 4.

1 = I can do it very well.
2 = I can do it quite well.
3 = I have some problems.
4 = I can't do it.

a I can talk about present situations, routines and actions using the present simple and present continuous. ☐
b I can use *do* and *make* appropriately. ☐
c I can understand written and spoken texts about studying and university. ☐
d I can express preferences using a variety of structures. ☐
e I can reply to informal emails and include relevant information. ☐
f I can talk about past events, situations and habits using a wide variety of tenses and structures. ☐
g I can use gerunds and infinitives correctly. ☐
h I can understand written and spoken texts related to the world of work. ☐
i I can negotiate and collaborate in conversations. ☐
j I can write texts expressing my opinion on topics related to school and work. ☐

2 Now decide what you need to do to improve.

1 Look again at my book/notes.
2 Do more practice exercises.
➤ WORKBOOK Units 1 and 2
3 Ask for help.
4 Other: ....

Units 3–4

1 How well can you do these things in English now? Give yourself a mark from 1 to 4.

1 = I can do it very well.
2 = I can do it quite well.
3 = I have some problems.
4 = I can't do it.

a I can talk about the future using different tenses including the future continuous, future perfect simple and future perfect continuous. ☐
b I can talk about transport and travel. ☐
c I can use prefixes to change the meaning of words. ☐
d I can compare and contrast photos. ☐
e I can write stories using a variety of tenses, structures and linkers. ☐
f I can compare different people, things and actions using a variety of structures, including comparative and superlative adverbs. ☐
g I can form nouns by using suffixes. ☐
h I can understand written and spoken texts about people with special talents. ☐
i I can give structured presentations on different topics. ☐
j I can write articles giving detailed personal descriptions. ☐

2 Now decide what you need to do to improve.

1 Look again at my book/notes.
2 Do more practice exercises.
➤ WORKBOOK Units 3 and 4
3 Ask for help.
4 Other: ....

Units 5–6

1 How well can you do these things in English now? Give yourself a mark from 1 to 4.

1 = I can do it very well.
2 = I can do it quite well.
3 = I have some problems.
4 = I can't do it.

a I can talk about obligation, prohibition and advice in the present and past. ☐
b I can make speculations and deductions about the present, past and future. ☐
c I can understand written and spoken texts on topics related to money. ☐
d I can make present and past speculations about photos. ☐
e I can write a formal letter/email of complaint. ☐
f I can talk about possible, imaginary and impossible situations and their consequences using different types of conditional structures. ☐
g I can talk about wishes for the present, past and future. ☐
h I can talk about the body and health using a range of vocabulary and idioms. ☐
i I can collaborate with a partner using different expressions to agree, disagree and make choices. ☐
j I can express opinions, contrasts and consequences in for-and-against essays. ☐

2 Now decide what you need to do to improve.

1 Look again at my book/notes.
2 Do more practice exercises.
➤ WORKBOOK Units 5 and 6
3 Ask for help.
4 Other: ....

Units 7–8

1 How well can you do these things in English now? Give yourself a mark from 1 to 4.

1 = I can do it very well.
2 = I can do it quite well.
3 = I have some problems.
4 = I can't do it.

a I can report what other people have said or asked using different reporting verbs and structures. ☐
b I can talk about music, film and media habits. ☐
c I can join words to make compound nouns and adjectives. ☐
d I can present solid arguments in discussions. ☐
e I can write reviews using a wide variety of adjectives. ☐
f I can use different passive structures to talk about processes and procedures and to say what people say, know or believe. ☐
g I can understand written and spoken texts about natural disasters. ☐
h I can use a variety of verbs with the appropriate preposition. ☐
i I can use different words and expressions to talk about statistics. ☐
j I can use a variety of linkers in opinion essays. ☐

2 Now decide what you need to do to improve.

1 Look again at my book/notes.
2 Do more practice exercises.
➤ WORKBOOK Units 7 and 8
3 Ask for help.
4 Other: ....

Units 9–10

1 How well can you do these things in English now? Give yourself a mark from 1 to 4.

1 = I can do it very well.
2 = I can do it quite well.
3 = I have some problems.
4 = I can't do it.

a I can describe or give extra information about people, things or places using defining or non-defining relative clauses. ☐
b I can talk about everyday technology using a wide variety of words, expressions and phrasal verbs. ☐
c I can understand written and spoken texts about pros and cons of everyday technology. ☐
d I can clarify and check understanding when discussing topics. ☐
e I can write reports using determiners and quantifiers. ☐
f I can talk about the future in the past using a variety of tenses and expressions. ☐
g I can use indirect questions to be polite. ☐
h I can understand written and spoken news stories. ☐
i I can present and respond to opposing views when giving oral presentations. ☐
j I can write structured magazine articles. ☐

2 Now decide what you need to do to improve.

1 Look again at my book/notes.
2 Do more practice exercises.
➤ WORKBOOK Units 9 and 10
3 Ask for help.
4 Other: ....

Unit 1

INFORMAL EMAILS AND LETTERS

p15

EXAMPLE QUESTION **Write an email to a friend. Tell them some recent news, talk about your plans and ask them for some advice.**

Start with *Hi* or *Dear* and the name (not surname) of the person you are writing to.

Use contractions and the short form of words (e.g. *I'm*, not *I am*.).

Use *By the way* or *Anyway* to change the subject.

Use interjections like *Oh* and *Well*.

MODEL TEXT

Hi Sandra,

Thanks for your last email. Sorry it's taken me a while to reply, but I was ill all last week with flu. Luckily, I'm feeling better now.

My big piece of news is that I'm going to the US at the end of August! Our school is doing an exchange programme, so we're going to a high school in Michigan for three weeks and then, at Easter, the American students come here and stay with us. I'm really looking forward to going.

When we go, we're staying in Chicago for two or three days. You've been to Chicago, haven't you? Can you give me some tips about where to go and what to see?

Anyway, what about you? What are your plans for August? Are you going to work in that supermarket, like last year?

Write back soon. Oh, and don't forget to tell me about Chicago!

Best wishes,

Ed

Begin with introductory phrases like *Thanks for your last letter, It was great to hear from you, Sorry I haven't written for a long time* or *I'm writing to tell you about …*

Use exclamation marks.

Ask questions like *How are you? How are things? Are you doing exams/ on holiday at the moment? What about you?*

End with phrases like *Write back soon, That's all for now, All the best, Bye for now, Best wishes.*

Suggested paragraph plan:
Paragraph 1: Introductory phrases and salutations.
Paragraph 2: Saying why you are writing the email. Giving news.
Paragraph 3: Any additional information. Questions, etc.
Paragraph 4: Concluding phrases.

OPINION ESSAYS

p27 (Unit 2) and p105 (Unit 8)

EXAMPLE QUESTION **'Teenage years are the best years of your life.' Do you agree?**

The style is formal. Do not use contractions.

To put opinions and ideas in order, use *Firstly, To begin with, Secondly, Next, Finally, Lastly.*

Explain and justify your opinions with *This is because, The reason is …, For instance, For example.*

To give a conclusion, use *To sum up, In conclusion, All things considered.*

MODEL TEXT

In my opinion, each different stage of life has good and bad moments and so it is difficult to say which is the 'best' period in life. Personally, I think that being a teenager is a good time of life as I will explain.

The first point to make is that when you are a teenager you have more time to enjoy life. Although you have to study a lot, you also have a lot of time to be with your friends and you don't need to take care of basic chores like cooking, shopping or doing all the housework.

Another thing to bear in mind is that, despite the fact that life for teenagers can be stressful, I think it is less stressful than life for adults. This is because when you are an adult you have more duties and responsibilities such as paying bills and being on top of financial matters. Furthermore, if you are a parent, you have the responsibility of looking after your children.

To sum up, I believe that being a teenager isn't perfect because teenagers often lose sleep over things like school, friends, family and the future. However, it is an exciting time when you start preparing for new challenges, experiences and opportunities.

Use linkers to join two halves of a sentence.

To contrast ideas and opinions, use *However, Nevertheless, On the one hand, On the other hand, although, despite, whereas.*

To add opinions and ideas, use *Furthermore, What's more, In addition.*

Give your opinion with expressions like *Personally, I think, As far as I'm concerned, In my opinion, I agree/disagree with …, I believe that …*

Suggested paragraph plan:

Paragraph 1: Introduction. General statement on the topic and state your opinion.

Paragraph 2: First and most important reason for your opinion.

Paragraph 3: One or two other reasons for your opinion OR other people's arguments against your opinion and why you don't agree with them.

Paragraph 4: Summary and conclusion. Restate your opinion.

Unit 3

STORIES

p41

EXAMPLE QUESTION **You have decided to enter a short story competition in an international magazine. The story must begin with the following words:**
It was not going to be easy, but I knew I had to do it.

Your story must include:

- **a difficult or scary situation**
- **a happy ending**

MODEL TEXT

It was not going to be easy, but I knew I had to do it. I had never liked heights, but here I was, standing on a platform in the middle of a forest, looking down at the ground 20 metres below. How had I got myself into this situation?

My little brother had been bored. That's how it had all started. Two weeks ago, Neil and I were in the middle of our summer holidays and we were both getting tired of watching TV and playing computer games all day long.

At first, we'd been enjoying doing nothing, but after a while we got tired of it, and so we started to look for something different to do. That was when we saw an advert for a place called Gorilla Park. It was an amazing adventure centre where you could climb up trees and do a series of cool activities getting past obstacles. There were two courses, one easy and the other 20 metres high. Being afraid of heights, I agreed to take Neil as long as he let me do the easy course.

However, having got there, we discovered Neil was too young to do the big course on his own. Someone had to accompany him, and, of course, that someone was me. That was why I was now in the middle of the course, about to swing from one terrifyingly high tree platform to another.

I shouted to the monitor to tell him that I couldn't do it. But the monitor told me that there was no other way down. Finally, I held onto the rope with all my strength, I closed my eyes and jumped off the platform. The next thing I remember were strong arms pulling me safely onto the next platform. I'd done it! But I promised myself that I would never get into that situation again.

Explain the sequence of events, use *At first, First of all, Next, Then, After that, Later, Suddenly, Finally, In the end.*

Use a variety of tenses.

Use participle clauses to describe actions happening at the same time or in sequence.

Say when things happened, use: *Last weekend, Two weeks ago, On Friday, On Saturday night.*

Use adjectives and adverbs to make the story more descriptive.

Useful grammar: Narrative tenses and participle clauses

1 Past simple. We use it to tell the main events and actions in the story.

2 Past continuous. We use it to describe scenes, to say what activity was in progress when another interrupted it.

3 Past perfect. We use it for the background of the story, to talk about actions that happened before other actions in the past.

4 Past perfect continuous. We use it for the background of a story, particularly when the duration of an activity is important.

5 *used to*. We use it to talk about past habits.

6 *must/may/might/can't have*. We use these to make speculations or deductions about what happened.

7 *was going to, was doing, would*. We use these to talk about future activities in the past.

8 Participle clauses. These describe two actions happening at the same time, or in sequence.

Suggested paragraph plan:

First paragraph: Explain where and when the story began. Introduce the characters.

Middle paragraphs: Explain the main events in the story, and the background to these events.

Final paragraph: Explain how the story ended and what the consequences were.

ARTICLES

p53 (Unit 4) and p131 (Unit 10)

EXAMPLE QUESTION You see this announcement in an international magazine.

Articles wanted

NO TV FOR A WEEK!

Could you live without television for a week? Would living without TV change your life? Write an article telling us how difficult life would be with no TV. Send us your article today!

MODEL TEXT

A week without TV – is it mission impossible?

When you got home yesterday after school, did you switch the TV on, or was it already on? Did you have dinner watching TV? Let's imagine for a second that there was no TV. Could you survive?

Whether we like it or not, we would all probably have to admit that television is part of our daily lives. Personally, I don't have time to watch much TV. Nevertheless, there are certain programmes that I enjoy watching each day, and they help me to relax, especially when I have just arrived home after school. If I couldn't watch those programmes, I would do something else to help me relax, for example read a book or listen to music. Maybe those activities would be better for me than watching TV.

However, TV is not just about relaxing. At dinnertime in my house we often watch the news. If I had to live without TV for a week, I'm sure I would know less about what is happening in my country and in the world. Television is a window that allows us to see what is going on anywhere at any time.

All in all, I am sure that I could live without TV for a week, but some of the consequences of this would be positive and some negative. What's more, as far as I'm concerned, it would be much more difficult today to live without a computer and the Internet than to live without TV.

> You can give your article a title.

> It can be very effective to begin with questions to involve the reader.

> State opinions with phrases like *As far as I'm concerned, Personally, In my opinion.*

> Magazine articles should not be very formal or informal.

> Make contrasts with phrases like *However, Nevertheless, Although, Despite, Whereas, On the other hand.*

> Add arguments with phrases like *What's more, Furthermore, Moreover, In addition, Not only … but also.*

> Conclude with phrases like *In conclusion, To sum up, All in all.*

Suggested paragraph plan:

Paragraph 1: Introduction saying what your article is about.
Paragraph 2: Main point.
Paragraph 3: Additional points.
Paragraph 4: Conclusion – restate the most important points and your opinion(s).

Unit 5

A FORMAL LETTER/EMAIL OF COMPLAINT

p67

EXAMPLE QUESTION **You ordered a DVD from an online store, but there were problems with your order. Write a letter to complain and demand a solution.**

MODEL TEXT

Dear Sir or Madam,

I am writing to complain about a DVD that I ordered from your online shop two months ago (order number 844XC01). When I ordered the DVD, your store guaranteed that you would send the DVD within three days. This was a key factor in deciding to purchase the DVD from your store since other stores made it clear that the DVD would take two to three weeks to dispatch.

However, despite your guarantee, the DVD was not sent until one month after making the order. When I tried to contact you before this date in order to cancel my order, all my emails were ignored.

To make matters worse, the DVD arrived in a terrible state. The box was completely crushed and when I inserted the DVD into my player, it made a highly unusual noise and would not work.

I am very disappointed with the treatment I have received from your store. I demand that you send me a replacement copy of the DVD as soon as possible. If this is not possible, I expect you to refund me the full cost of the DVD immediately. If I do not hear from you promptly, I shall take my complaint to a Consumer Advice Centre.

Yours faithfully,

Joanne Howe

Write *Dear Mr (Smith)* (for a man), *Dear Mrs (Smith)* (for a married woman), or *Dear Ms (Smith)* (when we make no distinction if a woman is married or not). When you do not know the name of the person you are writing to, write *Dear Sir or Madam.*

Use linkers.

Do not use contractions.

When you know the name of the person you are writing to, end with *Yours sincerely.* When you don't know the name of the person you are writing to, end with *Yours faithfully.*

Use formal expressions.

Useful expressions in letters of complaint:

I am writing to complain about …

I demand (a refund/replacement/ apology)

If I do not hear from you (in the next two weeks), I will take my complaint to a Consumer Advice Centre.

I believe (instead of *I think*)

I would be very grateful (instead of *I'd like*)

I look forward to receiving your reply.

I look forward to hearing from you.

Useful linkers:

Consequence: *Therefore, and so, As a result*

Time and sequence: *Firstly, Next, Then, In the end*

Contrast: *but, although, However, Nevertheless*

Reason: *because, as, since*

Addition: *In addition, What is more, Furthermore*

Suggested paragraph plan:

First paragraph: Explain why you are writing.

Middle paragraphs: Give details of the complaint. Say where and when the problem began.

Final paragraph: Demand a solution. Say what action you will take if there is no solution.

FOR-AND-AGAINST ESSAYS

p79

EXAMPLE QUESTION **'The best way to learn a language is to go and live in a country where they speak it.' Write arguments for and against this statement.**

For-and-against essays are normally formal. Do not use contractions.

Make contrasts with phrases like *On the one hand …, On the other hand …, In contrast, However, But, Although, Despite/In spite of* (+ noun/gerund/ *the fact that …*), *Nevertheless.*

Conclude with phrases like *In conclusion, To sum up, All in all.*

MODEL TEXT

Nowadays, more and more people are learning languages, perhaps as a result of the growth of global communication and business. The problem is that there are different ways to learn a language, and not everybody agrees on the best way.

On one hand, by going to live in a new country and speaking the language 24 hours a day every day, you can learn the real language and you can learn it very fast and intensively. Every time you speak to somebody, watch TV, or even just read signs in the street, you are picking up new vocabulary and expressions and you can become more fluent.

On the other hand, if you are a shy person you might find it very difficult to speak to people at first. What is more, if you have a very low level of language when you arrive, even basic communication is difficult and you may find that you understand so little that you make very slow progress.

All in all, I think that going abroad is a great way to learn a language, but it is certainly not the only way. In your own country, you can learn lots by taking classes and by reading and listening to the language, especially on the Internet. In my opinion, this is the best way for a beginner to learn. At a later date you can travel to the country to perfect your knowledge of the language.

Use linkers of consequence such as *Therefore, and so, As a result.*

Add arguments with phrases like *Furthermore, What is more, In addition, Not only … but also.*

Give your own opinion with phrases like *Personally, I think …, As far as I'm concerned.*

Useful vocabulary:

advantage, disadvantage

Useful linkers:

Introducing and sequencing arguments: *Firstly, Secondly, Finally*

Reason: *because, as, since*

Suggested paragraph plan:

Paragraph 1: State the topic of the composition using general statements.

Paragraph 2: Make points for (or against).

Paragraph 3: Make points against (or for).

Paragraph 4: Conclusion – restate the most important arguments and give your own opinion.

Unit 7

REVIEWS

p93

EXAMPLE QUESTION **You recently saw this notice in an international magazine.**

> **Reviews needed!**
> We'd like you to send us a review of the latest book that you've read. In your review, tell us what happens in the book, your opinion of it, and who you would recommend it to.

Write your review.

MODEL TEXT

Across the Nightingale Floor is the title of the latest book that I've read. It is written by an Australian author called Lian Hearn. It's a gripping historical novel set in Japan, but there are also elements of fantasy and romance in the story.

The plot of the story is fascinating because you're never really sure what is going to happen next. The main character is a teenage boy called Tomasu, who lives in a quiet farming village with his mother and stepfather. One night there is a terrible attack on the village and everybody is killed, except Tomasu. An important nobleman called Lord Otori rescues him and takes him to his palace. He gives him a new name, Takeo, and a new life. There is an extremely good scene where we find that Takeo has amazing skills such as invisibility and the ability to be in two places at the same time. The plot takes another intriguing turn when Takeo falls in love with a kind girl called Kaede.

In my opinion, this book is very thought-provoking because it makes you wonder about different themes like loyalty, revenge and the fight between good and evil. Lian Hearn is very perceptive when she describes her characters, making them imperfect and therefore real. Among the things that I liked the most were the vivid descriptions. They really helped me to feel what it was like to live in Japan in this period.

All things considered, if you're a fan of stories that combine fast-moving action, inspiring characters and lively descriptions, you'll love this book. And the great news is that there are more books in the series!

Use modifying adverbs to make adjectives stronger or softer in order to give more accurate descriptions. For example, use *very, extremely* and *really* to make 'normal' adjectives (e.g. *good, bad*) stronger. Use *totally, absolutely, really* and *completely* to make 'extreme' adjectives (e.g. *fantastic, awful*) stronger. Use *quite* and *rather* to make 'normal' adjectives a little softer.

Use a variety of adjectives and adverbs.

Explain and justify your opinions with phrases like *This is because, For example, For instance, That is why …*

Explain what you like/dislike with phrases like *The best/worst part, The … was amazing/ terrible, What I like most about …*

Make a recommendation with phrases like *I would/wouldn't recommend you to see/buy/ play this because …*

Useful expressions:

To give your opinions: *Personally, I think, As far as I'm concerned, In my opinion, I agree/disagree with …*

To give a conclusion: *To sum up, In conclusion*

Useful vocabulary:

amazing • amusing • appealing
awful • brilliant • clever • clichéd
convincing • credible • deep
fascinating • fast-moving • gripping
hilarious • incredible • inspiring
intricate • intriguing • lively
moving • mysterious • perceptive
predictable • realistic • relaxing
scary • sensitive • spectacular
stunning • stupid • terrible
thought-provoking • thrilling
unconvincing • uninspiring • vivid
well-produced

Suggested paragraph plan:

Paragraph 1: Basic information about what you are reviewing.

Paragraph 2: More detailed information.

Paragraph 3: Your opinion and justification(s) for it.

Paragraph 4: Your recommendation.

REPORTS

p119

EXAMPLE QUESTION **The local council wants to know what teenagers think about sports and recreational facilities for teenagers where you live. You have been asked to write a report saying:**

- **what the present facilities are**
- **your opinion of them**
- **your recommendations about how they can be improved**

Write your report.

MODEL TEXT

Report on sports and recreational facilities for teenagers in this area

Introduction

The aim of this report is to explain what sports and recreational facilities exist at the moment in our area and to outline our opinion of them and our recommendations for the future.

Current facilities

At the moment, the main centre for sports activities is the sports pavilion in Franklin Park. Local teams are based in this pavilion, and there are courses in different indoor sports such as badminton and volleyball. For outdoor sports, the only local facility is the park itself, but there are no organised sports activities there.

Our opinion of the current facilities

The sports pavilion in Franklin Park is now in poor condition. It was built in 1960 and has had no work done to it since that date. Moreover, there are very few places on the courses that are given there, probably due to the fact that there are so few instructors employed. The park has no special areas prepared for sports, apart from one football pitch.

Recommendations

In conclusion, we believe that the sports pavilion in Franklin Park could be greatly improved if the floor was repaired and if more instructors were employed to give lessons in sports such as gymnastics, judo and taekwondo. We suggest that the park itself needs special tracks and other areas prepared for training in different athletics events for both boys and girls. These changes are needed urgently since in the area where we live there are no alternative activities on offer for teenagers.

Give your report a title.

Separate the report into sections and give each one a suitable heading.

Style: Reports are formal when you write them for an organisation or people that you do not know personally.

Explain and justify your opinion with phrases like *This is because*, *For example*, *Due to the fact*, *For instance*.

To give a conclusion, use *To sum up*, *In conclusion*, *All in all*.

To give your opinion, use *Personally, I think*, *As far as I'm concerned*, *In my opinion*, *I believe*, *I agree/disagree with …*

Make recommendations with phrases like *I recommend that X should …*, *I would/wouldn't …*, *It would be a good idea (for X) to* (+ infinitive), *I suggest that X should …*

Suggested paragraph plan:

Paragraph 1: Introduction stating the aim of the report.

Paragraph 2: Main point.

Paragraph 3: Additional points.

Paragraph 4: Conclusion restating your opinion(s) and making a recommendation if asked for.

EDITING YOUR WRITING

Check for and take away:

- unnecessary repetition of words or ideas in the text
- irrelevant information
- confusing examples or details

CHECKING YOUR WRITING

Check for mistakes with:

- punctuation
- capital letters
- word order
- spelling
- tenses
- vocabulary
- missing words
- agreement between the subject and verb (e.g. ~~He go~~. He goes)
- style
- content

Gateway to exams: Units 1–2

SPEAKING

Exercise 11, p31

1. Look at the different things that people sometimes have to do in a job. Talk to each other about what you think the advantages and disadvantages are of each.
2. Then you have a minute to talk about the things that would be important for you when choosing a job.

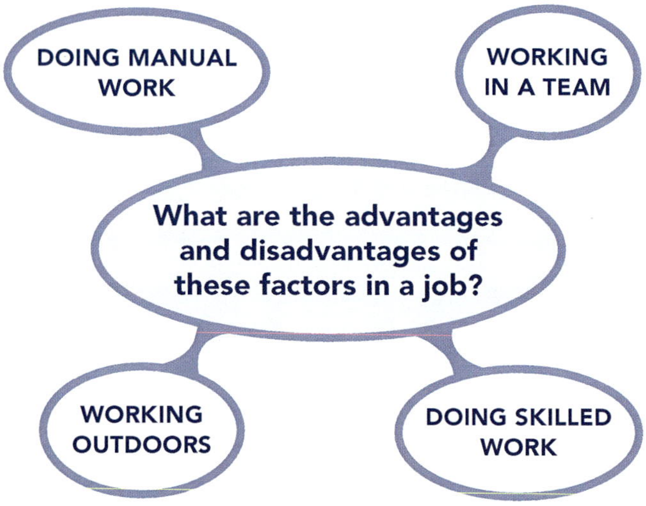

Unit 3

DEVELOPING SPEAKING

Exercises 5a–c, p40

Student B:

Compare the photos and say why people travel in these different ways.

Unit 5

DEVELOPING SPEAKING

Exercise 6b, p66

Student B:

Compare the photos and say why you think people like receiving these different things.

Unit 4

GATEWAY TO LIFE SKILLS

Academic task, p49

Tick (✓) the coloured box next to the statements that are true for you.

I find it easy to remember telephone numbers.		□					
I play a sport or dance.					□		
I often see clear images when I close my eyes.			□				
I really enjoy reading.	□						
I enjoy individual sports best.							□
Singing makes me feel happy.				□			
I find graphs, charts and diagrams easy to understand.			□				
I find it easy to make up stories.	□						
I have always been physically well co-ordinated.					□		
I keep a diary.							□
I prefer team sports.						□	
I like to think through problems carefully.		□					
I can play a musical instrument.				□			
My friends always come to me for emotional support.						□	
I find mental arithmetic (sums in my head) easy.		□					
I can tell easily whether someone likes or dislikes me.						□	
I often have a song or piece of music in my head.				□			
I love adrenaline sports and scary rides.					□		
I find it easy to remember poems or song lyrics.	□						
When I am concentrating I tend to doodle.			□				
I am happy spending time alone.							□
Total score:							
Intelligence type:	1	2	3	4	5	6	7

Count the number of ticks in each column (1–7). The columns with the highest total score show your strongest types of intelligence. Turn to page 49 to find out which these are. Do you agree?

Unit 5

GATEWAY TO LIFE SKILLS

Life task, p63

Samara is 18 years old. She is about to start university. She will receive €150 a month from her parents and €575 as part of a grant. She needs to spend her money to live comfortably and be happy, too. Choose her expenses from the different sections below.

1 Select one of the following to decide where Samara is going to live.
- with her parents, paying a small amount to them each month for food and accommodation (€120)
- share a house with three of her friends (€350)
- share a flat with her best friend (€400)
- live on her own in a rented room (€380)
- live in self-catering student accommodation (€320)

2 Select the different things that you think Samara would like to do in her leisure time during one month.
- go clubbing with her friends (€120)
- go to the cinema (€50)
- work out at the university gym (€0)
- climb at a local club (€30)
- go to drama and dance classes (€25)

3 Decide what else Samara would spend her money on each month. Unless she lives with her parents, she will have to pay for food and bills.
- utility bills (water/electricity/gas) (€30)
- food, drink and housekeeping (€130)
- books and stationery (€50)
- computer games (€20)
- mobile phone (€25)
- clothes (€30)
- music (€25)
- laundry (€20)
- toiletries (€15)
- hair (€30)
- transport and travel (€40)
- personal insurance (€4)
- savings account (€20)

Macmillan Education Limited
4 Crinan Street
London N1 9XW

Companies and representatives throughout the world

ISBN 978-0-230-47096-5

This edition published 2016
First edition published in 2011

Designed by emc design ltd
Illustrated by A Corazón Abierto (Sylvie Poggio Artists Agency) pp73, 116; Laura Martinez (Sylvie Poggio Artists Agency) pp9, 13; Mark Ruffle p113.
Cover design by emc design ltd and Macmillan Publishers Ltd
Cover potography by Getty/Helena Schaeder Söderberg and Shutterstock/Cultura Limited
Picture research by Emily Taylor

Author's acknowledgements:
I would like to give a big thank you to the whole Macmillan team in the UK for their dedication, hard work, and enthusiasm throughout the writing of this course. Thanks also to all the other Macmillan teams around the world for their help, encouragement and always making me feel welcome. Very special thanks to Colegio Europeo Aristos in Getafe, Spain. The daily contact with my students there continues to be a main source of inspiration and I am sincerely grateful to every one of my students, past and present. Massive thanks, as always, to Gemma, Jamie and Becky for their unending love and support.

This book is dedicated to Emily Rosser.

The publishers would like to thank staff and pupils at the following schools in Mexico and Spain for helping us so enthusiastically with our research for the course:
Concha Campos, IES Burgo de Las Rozas, Las Rozas, Madrid; Félix Gaspar, IES Las Encinas; Villanueva de la Cañada, Madrid; Cristina Moisen, IES Joaquín Turina, Madrid; Colegio Montessori Cuautitlán; Colegio Conrad Gessner; Colegio Erasmo de Rotterdam; Colegio Kanic, Centro Educativo Erich Fromm; Universidad Franco Mexicana; Centro Pedagógico María Montessori de Ecatepec; Instituto Cultural; Escuela Maestro Manuel Acosta; Liceo Sakbé De México.

The publishers would also like to thank all those who reviewed or piloted the first edition of Gateway:
Benjamin Affolter, Evelyn Andorfer, Anna Ciereszynska, Regina Culver, Anna Dabrowska, Justyna Deja, Ondrej Dosedel, Lisa Durham, Dagmar Eder, Eva Ellederovan, H Fouad, Sabrina Funes, Luiza Gervescu, Isabel Gonzalez Bueno, Jutta Habringer, Stela Halmageanu, Marta Hilgier, Andrea Hutterer, Nicole Ioakimidis, Mag. Annemarie Kammerhofer, Irina Kondrasheva, Sonja Lengauer, Gabriela Liptakova, Andrea Littlewood, Maria Cristina Maggi, Silvia Miranda Barbara Nowak, Agnieska Orlińska, Anna Orlowska, Maria Paula Palou, Marta Piotrowska, N Reda, Katharina Schatz, Roswitha Schwarz, Barbara Ścibor, Katarzyna Sochacka, Joanna Spoz, Monica Srtygner, Marisol Suppan, Stephanie Sutter, Halina Tyliba, Prilipko, Maria Vizgina, Vladyko, Pia Wimmer, Katarzyna Zadrożna-Attia and Katarzyna Zaremba-Jaworska.

The author and publishers would like to thank the following for permission to reproduce their images:

Alamy/Mile Atanasov p83(cr), Alamy/Bon Appetit p7(3), Alamy/EPA european pressphoto agency b.v p99, Alamy/Craig Joiner Photography p41(bl), Alamy/Darkened Studio p112, Alamy/GL Archive p57, Alamy/Nick Hanna p76(a), Alamy/incamerastock p7(5), Alamy/JGI/Jamie Grill/Blend Images p158(br), Alamy/OJO Images Ltd p130(tr), Alamy/Tony Taylor p47, Alamy/Pete Titmuss p64(e), Alamy/V&A Images p7(1), Alamy/Gregg Vignal p70(header), Alamy/Wig Worland p40(tm); **Corbis** p101(desert), Corbis/68/Ocean p51, Corbis/Mike Blake/Reuters p64(tl), Corbis/CelebrityVibe/Splash News p102, Corbis/Jim Craigmyle p66(tcl), Corbis/Digital Focus/Splash News p131(cm), Corbis/Hoberman Collection p59(coin), Corbis/Dennis Galante p64(a), Corbis/Hulton-Deutsch Collection p52(b), Corbis/Billy Hustace p158(tl), Corbis/Simon Jarratt p70(1), Corbis/JGI/Jamie Grill/Blend Images p111(tr), Corbis/Moxie Productions/Blend Images p14, Corbis/Plush Studios/Bill Reitzel/Blend Images p79, Corbis/Steve Prezant p66(tl), Corbis/XploreAir/Splash News p35(tl, inset), Corbis/The Star-Ledger p52(a), Corbis/Roberto Westbrook p70(2), Corbis/Westend61 p75(eating watermelon), Corbis/Rick Wilking/Reuters p98; **Comstock Images** pp37(tomato), 89(bm); **Digital Vision** pp7(b), 30(a), Digital Vision/Punchstock p110(header); **Eyevine**/Nigel Howard/Evening Standard p129(inset); **Getty Images** pp44(stars), 53(bl), 56(cl), 62(scissors), 64(b), 74(strawberries, kiwis), 75(egg), Getty Images/Andresr p91, Getty Images/antfoto p84(tr), Getty Images/Thomas Barwick p124, Getty Images/Torsten Blackwood/AFP p21, Getty Images/Blend Images pp77(cr), 127(bl), Getty Images/Bloom Productions p15(tr), Getty Images/Brand X p110(tr), Getty Images/Brand X/Thinkstock p7(d), Getty Images/Buena Vista Images p38(tl), Getty Images/Caiaimage pp6(cr), 26(construction worker), Getty Images/ChinaFotoPress p25, Getty Images/CR7 p52(c), Getty Images/Creatas RF p118(tl), Getty Images/Cultura Exclusive p78(cl), Getty Images/Cultura RF p82(1b), Getty Images/Peter Dazeley p26(police), Getty Images/DreamPictures p125, Getty Images/EyeEm p19(bl), Getty Images/Flickr RM p78(br), Getty Images/Fuse p26(f1 driver), Getty Images/Christopher Gould p36(tr), Getty Images/Hemera/Thinkstock p96(e), Getty Images/Hero Images pp24(tl), 40(br), Getty Images/Red Huber/Orlando Sentinel/TNS p32(tcl), Getty Images/Image Source pp27, 61(bl), 65, Getty Images/iStockphoto p49(tr), Getty Images/iStockphoto/Thinkstock pp10(wood texture, tr), 30(d), 41(tl), 53(tl), 59(chocolate), 62(wooden background), 71(a,b), 74(header), 75(milk), 83(cl), 93(tm), 97(tr), 111(icons), 114-115(background), 117, 127(cr), Getty Images/Jupiter Images p61(br), Getty Images/Bernhard Lang p114(tr), Getty Images/Chelsea Lauren/Clear Channel p85(tl), Getty Images/Butch Martin p72, Getty Images/Maskot p30(b), Getty Images/Mediaphotos p12(tl), Getty Images/Jason Merritt p87(tl), Getty Images/Ethan Miller p84(cl), Getty Images/Moment Open p96(header), Getty Images/Emre Ogan p158(bl), Getty Images/Joe Polillio p76(b), Getty Images/Monique Rodriguez p123, Getty Images/Daniel Sambraus p62(bl), Getty Images/Oli Scarff p40(tl), Getty Images/Alex Slobodkin p23(tr), Getty Images/Philip and Karen Smith p24(br), Getty Images/Tetra images RF p88(tr), Getty Images/Thinkstock p33, Getty Images/UIG p56(cr), Getty Images/Klaus Vedfelt p82(1a), Getty Images/Vetta p31, Getty Images/Dougal Waters p7(e), ImageSource pp7(c), 32(tcml), 36(br), 64(c); **ImageSource**/Bill Miles p100(tr); **Macmillan Publishers Ltd** p15(tl), Macmillan Publishers Ltd Australia pp50, 74(forks); **Newsteam.co.uk**/SWNS Group p113(tl,inset); **Penguin Books Ltd** p93(cm); **Photoalto** p88-89(background); **PhotoDisc**/Getty Images pp36(apple), 39, 40(bcr), 74(orange), 75(bread); **Photoshot**/Face to Face p85(br); **PlainPicture**/Caiaimages p12(br), PlainPicture/Cultura p70(3), PlainPicture/Maskot p87(br), PlainPicture/Christian Plochacki p44(br), PlainPicture/Kniel Synnatzschke p158(tr), PlainPicture/R. Wolf p67; **Rex Features**/David Bagnall/REX Shutterstock p19(cr), Rex Features/Business Images p7(a), Rex Features/Cultura/REX Shutterstock p66(bcr), Rex Features/Everett/REX_Shutterstock pp84(bm), 92(cm), 92(bl), Rex Features/Image Broker/REX_Shutterstock p59(cow), Rex Features/OJO Images/REX Shutterstock pp90, 130(tl), Rex Features/REX_Shutterstock p45(cm), Rex Features/UN Photo/SIPA/REX_Shutterstock p52(d), Rex Features/Simon Webster/REX_Shutterstock p129(taxi); **Shutterstock**/Hugo Felix p88(br), Shutterstock/Gts p126(cr), Shutterstock/Michael Jung p101(br), Shutterstock/MaraZe p75(fish), **ShutterStock**/Sarunyu_foto p61(tr); **Stirling Elmendorf**/Used with permission of juliansharpe@survival-capsule.com p97(cr); **Stockbyte** p37(cm); **StockDisc** p71(d); **Thinkstock** pp18(header), 36(magnifying glass), 48(tr), 48-49(background), 49(tl), 59(money background), 62(euros), 63(euros), 88-89(people illustration), 88(cl), 126(magnifying glass), Thinkstock/Getty Images/Creatas p76(c), Thinkstock/Getty Images/Fuse p44(footballer), Thinkstock/Getty Images/Ian Gavan p45(tr), Thinkstock/Getty Images/Hemera p75(cr), Thinkstock/Getty Images/iStockphoto pp7(2,4), 10(cl, br), 10-11(background), 11, 18(people-tr), 22-23(background), 22(tr, 1, 2, 3, 4, 5, 6), 23(7, 8, 9), 26(pilot, firefighter), 30(c), 32(header-tr, header background), 36(background map, foil bag, potatoes, asparagus), 36-37(background), 37(food miles background), 38(br), 44(guitarist), 58(header, cl), 62(credit cards), 63(br), 64(d), 66(br), 70(tr), 70(4), 74-75(background, bm), 77(tl), 82(2b), 84(header background), p89(cr), 96(a, c, d), 100-101(background), 103, 108(cm), 110(br), 114(br), 118(cl), 122, 126-127(background), p127(cl), 131(bl), Thinkstock/Getty Images/Lightwavemedia p44(ballerina), Thinkstock/Getty Images/Minden Pictures RM p96(b), Thinkstock/Getty Images/moodboard pp6(tr), 62-63(background), Thinkstock/Getty Images/Purestock p82(2a), Thinkstock/Getty Images/Wavebreak Media p44(singer), Thinkstock/iStockphoto/scanrail p84(cr), Thinkstock/Jupiterimages pp36(pizza), 108(tr), Thinkstock/Jupiterimages/Brand X Pictures p48(bl), Thinkstock/Siri Stafford p44(cl), Thinkstock/Erwin Wodicka p32(cml).

The author and publisher are grateful for permission to reprint the following copyright material:
Extract adapted from 'University's petting zoo helps students manage stress' originally published on Storify.com.
Material adapted from 'You can be a tsunami hero or heroine!' by Lori Dengler originally published by Times Standard on 27 March 2013.
Graphs from PreventionWeb.net © United Nations. Reprinted with the permission of the United Nations.
Material from article 'What is Money?' by Irena Asmundson and Ceyda Oner in Finance and Development, September 2012. Published by the International Monetary Fund. Reprinted with permission.
Extract from 'Helpful schoolboy handed print by train passenger claiming to be Banksy who told him 'this will be worth about £20,000' – but artist denies it was him' by Hannah Parry and Jo Davies (freelance writers). Originally published in the MailOnline on 8 January 2015. Reprinted with permission.
Extract from 'Teenager catches gang that stole iPhone after mobile-tracking app locates thief's address'. Originally published in the MailOnline on 29 July 2009. Reprinted with permission.
Extract from 'Hell of being a living statue' by Jane Fryer. Originally published in the Daily Mail on 11 December 2014. Reprinted with permission.
Extract from 'Prepare to be amazed' by Jon Wilde. Originally published in the Mail on Sunday on 1 July 2012. Reprinted with permission.
Extract from 'Diet, nutrition and schoolchildren' January 2014. Published by The British Nutrition Foundation. Reprinted with permission.
Material adapted from 'Gizmag checks out Survival Capsules' tsunami survival pods' by David Szondy, originally published on Gizmag.com, 22 May 2014. Reprinted with permission.
Material adapted from 'Why do I have pain?' originally published on KidsHealth.org. © The Nemours Foundation/KidsHealth. Reprinted with permission.
Dahlstrom, Eden, and Jacqueline Bichsel. ECAR Study of Undergraduate Students and Information Technology, 2014. Louisville, CO: EDUCAUSE Center for Analysis and Research, October 2014.
Available from http://www.educause.edu/library/resources/2014-student-and-faculty-technology-research-studies.
Extract from 'Runaway debt: It's the new norm for university students now' by Iona Bain. Originally published in The Independent on 26 September 2015 © The Independent, 2015. Reprinted with permission. www.theindependent.co.uk
Extract from 'A-level results: are exams getting easier?' by Katharine Birbalsingh, and Chris Keates. Originally published in the Daily Telegraph on 18 August 2011 © Telegraph Group Limited, 2011. Reprinted with permission. www.telegraph.co.uk
Extract from 'Teenager floats £30 camera into space to capture curvature of Earth'. Originally published in the Daily Telegraph on 09 September 2012 © Telegraph Group Limited, 2012. Reprinted with permission. www.telegraph.co.uk
'How We Treat Ebola' poster created by Natasha Lewer & Lou Lewer for Médecins Sans Frontières. Used with permission. www.msf.org.uk

Printed and bound in Argentina
2020
40